MORYA *and* YOU

LOVE

MORYA *and* YOU

LOVE

MARK L. PROPHET
ELIZABETH CLARE PROPHET

SUMMIT UNIVERSITY PRESS®
Gardiner, Montana

MARK L. PROPHET

ELIZABETH CLARE PROPHET

MORYA AND YOU: Love
by Mark L. Prophet and Elizabeth Clare Prophet

For information, contact
The Summit Lighthouse, 63 Summit Way, Gardiner, MT 59030 USA
Tel: 1-800-245-5445 or +1 406-848-9500
TSLinfo@TSL.org
SummitLighthouse.org
www.SummitLighthouse.org/El-Morya/
www.ElMorya.org

Library of Congress Control Number: 2018940128
ISBN: 978-1-60988-292-1 (softbound)
ISBN: 978-1-60988-293-8 (eBook)

SUMMIT UNIVERSITY PRESS®

Cover portrait by John Paul, by agreement with Inner Artz LLC

21 20 19 18 1 2 3 4

CONTENTS

PROLOGUE

Imagine you are an ascended master. You've spent countless eons perfecting yourself for that glorious moment of your release from the wheel of birth and rebirth that we call the ascension in the light. Now you're a blazing being of pure light, free to roam the universe and experience its infinite splendor. Free to enter into the indescribable bliss of oneness with the divine consciousness.

What would you do with your time if you were privileged to enjoy such an extraordinary existence? Well, if you're an ascended master worth your salt, you wouldn't just sit back, relax and enjoy the fruits of your labor. No, you would feel a burning desire to share your newfound freedom with all those you've left behind: people with whom you've spent many lifetimes—husbands, wives, parents, children, teachers, students, colleagues, friends and foes from bygone ages. You love them all with a deep, abiding love that yearns to set them free from the ignorance and illusion that is human life.

It should be easy to free all life when the all-power of heaven and earth is at your fingertips. But there's a hitch: free will. The law of free will is one of the most fundamental spiritual principles that govern human life. The Creator gave us free will to decide whether or not to return to our spiritual source at the end of our allotted time span. By free will we decide what we do daily and hourly with our energy, our thoughts, our feelings. By free will we decide whether we will take the helping hand of those who have gone before us—the ascended hosts—or whether we're going to ignore the call to soul liberation and continue in our merry ways.

Such would be your challenge if you were Morya.

Who Is Morya?

Of all the ascended hosts working with the evolutions on this planet, El Morya is one of the best known. His name came to us in the second half of the nineteenth century—but in a moment you'll see we've been familiar with Morya in many other garbs and guises throughout recorded history.

So let's begin with that precious moment when humanity first learned about the existence of this great master. It was around 1875. A capricious Russian noblewoman named Helena P. Blavatsky, together with some friends, founded the Theosophical Society in New York City.

The adventurous Blavatsky claimed that while traveling in the Himalayas she met mysterious adepts or mahatmas—"great souls"—whose knowledge and powers far exceeded those of anyone in the West. She apprenticed herself to them and at their instruction wrote voluminous spiritual works *(Isis Unveiled, The Secret Doctrine)* and founded her organization. Theosophy was intended to promote universal brotherhood as well as the scientific study of realms of life just beyond the reach of our physical senses.

Blavatsky attracted many followers whom she instructed in what she had learned from the adepts. She claimed that even half a world away, she was able to remain in constant communication with them by means of their spiritual powers. As fate would have it, one of her students, Englishman Alfred P. Sinnett, editor of the

Pioneer in Simla, India, was not satisfied with this roundabout way of learning from the adepts. If they were real people, he insisted, he should be able to communicate with them directly. Sinnett sent a letter to the Himalayan adepts, via Blavatsky, to request a direct line of correspondence. And quite unexpectedly, one of these elusive beings—"K.H.," or Kuthumi Lal Singh—stepped forward to engage in this unprecedented experiment of communicating one-on-one with a student born in the West.

It was the beginning of a most interesting revelation about these mysterious adepts: the extent of their knowledge about the universe, how they trained their students, and what motivated them to work tirelessly behind the scenes to improve life on this planet.

With great patience Kuthumi tried to explain the adepts' way of life to the skeptical Western mind. But at times, for various pressing reasons, he was unable to keep up with the correspondence. That's when he asked his close friend and spiritual brother to step in and cover for him. And this is how the adept "M.," or El Morya Khan, was introduced to the Western world.

Though both were highly advanced on the spiritual path, Kuthumi and Morya couldn't be more different. Their letters, often precipitated out of thin air, showed that Kuthumi was contemplative, patient, philosophical, a vast being with a vast mind who seemed to know everything about everything. Morya, though just as knowledgeable as his brother, was characteristically brisk, energetic, forceful and impatient with the slow progress of the Western pupils who could barely grasp the profound Eastern concepts the adepts tried to convey to them.

By and by, more of the adepts made their presence known. Theosophy opened a door to the existence of these highly spiritualized beings who revealed themselves as the unseen guardians of the human race. Though their correspondence with Mr. Sinnett[1] came to an end after just a few prolific years, Morya and Kuthumi remained active sponsoring Theosophy as unascended adepts.

El Morya attained his final liberation in 1898; his friend Kuthumi also made his ascension in the late nineteenth century. Both are now known as ascended masters, and both continue to guide and teach us from the ascended state.

In 1958 El Morya directed his student Mark L. Prophet to found a new spiritual organization—The Summit Lighthouse—to bring his teachings to a world that didn't know how desperately it was waiting to hear back from an old friend.

Past Lives

How old a friend? Well, in the course of time, as Morya gingerly lifted the veil, we discovered who this great being really was. Little by little we learned that we have known him forever as a teacher and friend on the path. Chances are, whether we've lived in the East or the West, whether we've been Hindu or Buddhist, Muslim or Christian or Jew, we've crossed paths with Morya.

Take, for instance, one of the earliest-known of Morya's embodiments. He was Abraham, the fierce Middle-Eastern chieftain who left hearth and home to found a new religion that recognized the existence of the One Divine Source. More than 4.2 billion people in three different religions—Judaism, Christianity and Islam—look to him as their divinely inspired patriarch who followed the inner voice and pulled mankind away from the idolatrous consciousness that kept them tied to gods of wood and stone and bone.

In the uncertain days of post-Roman Britain, Morya emerged as the legendary King Arthur who united the fledgling nation and inspired the dream of the quest for the Holy Grail. Though Camelot's success was short lived, Arthur's ideals of noble knighthood and self-sacrificing love were planted firmly in the subconscious of the Western world.

Morya's soul later returned to England as Thomas Becket, chancellor to King Henry II and Archbishop of Canterbury (twelfth century), and Sir Thomas More, chancellor to King Henry VIII (fifteenth-sixteenth century). In both cases, his fearless stance for principle and truth cost him his life—but left indelible impressions of courage and fortitude on the pages of history.

Returning to the East, as the Mogul emperor Akbar the Great (sixteenth century), El Morya brought peace to a vast region in central Asia. He inspired scholars from different religions to cherish the beliefs they had in common and conceived of a new eclectic religion—*Din-i-Ilahi,* or "Divine Faith"—that he hoped would bring an end to religions strife.

After all these incarnations as a leader, life granted Morya a reprieve. He came back as the nineteenth-century Irish poet, songwriter and singer Thomas Moore. Now, Morya's soft side could flourish. When his wife, Elizabeth, the love of his life, was disfigured by smallpox and refused to leave her room, he composed and sang to her these immortal lines:

Believe me, if all those endearing young charms,
Which I gaze on so fondly to-day,
Were to change by to-morrow, and fleet in my arms,
Like fairy-gifts fading away,
Thou wouldst still be adored, as this moment thou art,
Let thy loveliness fade as it will,
And around the dear ruin each wish of my heart
Would entwine itself verdantly still. . . .

This gifted artistic life set the stage for Morya's final round in physical embodiment: the Master M., the illustrious Mahatma of the Himavat. This brief summary of his soul's journey, weaving back and forth from East to West, shows unswerving devotion to honor, righteousness and the Will of God.

The Appendix (p. 303) presents a more detailed overview of Morya's known embodiments. May it help you trace his remarkable influence on your own life through the ages. For after all,

Morya is no stranger to you. He's been watching over you as you explored the science of being and experimented with the laws of life. He's been cheering you on from afar as you intensify your desire to push beyond your current limitations. Wherever you've come from, whatever your striving has been, Morya honors your journey. And now, as your soul wakes up to this wise teacher and friend of old, he stands ready to guide you to the next step on your spiritual path.

Lord of the First Ray

When we think of El Morya's many accomplishments, one particular quality stands out: he is a leader. A strategist *and* a doer. A no-nonsense master who takes us by the fastest route from point A to point B. So how does this work? How do we learn from an ascended being?

Following the early days of Theosophy when the adepts first revealed their existence, they have since explained much about the inner workings of the invisible dimensions. That which many simply call "heaven" is a multilayered, multifaceted place of great purpose and splendor. It's the biding place of the ascended masters who work with this planet and are collectively known as the Great White Brotherhood. The word "white" does not refer to race but to the white light in the aura of those who have made their ascension, whatever the race or religion or ethnic group they have originally come from.

The Great White Brotherhood is a highly organized body. One of its most prominent organizing principles is that of the seven rays—pure emanations of the divine consciousness that manifest as seven light rays resembling the colors of the rainbow.

The masters teach that all of us pursue our spiritual self-mastery on one of the seven rays. To accomplish this we need highly qualified teachers, and we are therefore invited by the Great White Brotherhood to apprentice ourselves to one of the Lords, or Chohans, of the seven rays. In other words, we can become a student or *chela*[2] of one of these seven revered masters. But at the same time, we must gain a certain basic level of mastery of each of the other six rays to accelerate spiritually and ultimately make our own ascension in the light, meaning we must do foundational work with each of the seven chohans.

The first of the seven rays is the blue ray. Its electric-blue energy represents power, perfection and direction.[3] El Morya serves as Chohan of the First Ray. He teaches aspiring souls the mastery of that ray, which is a ray of leaders and pioneers in every field. With his extensive experience at the head of kingdoms and governments, Morya is the perfect master to help us assimilate the necessary qualities of this ray so that we, too, can become leaders in our own fields.

Among his students El Morya is known as the blue-ray master. He's the Lord of the ray of the Will of God. When you look into his eyes—whether with the eyes of the soul or with your physical eyes, gazing at his portrait—you cannot help but sense the unflinching majesty of his being. You know instantly that his blue-flame thrust will never bend to the winds of human whimsicality.

Morya's gaze can be intimidating. And he knows it. In the first book he dictated to his messenger Elizabeth Clare Prophet, he wrote, right on page one:

> The strong gaze of the true master is upon the stalwart. The weak-willed, unable to look upon their own image, can scarcely receive our eye. I write for those who have a will to change; for transmutation is the requirement of the hour.[4]

In just these few lines you can feel the strength and directness of this master. No-nonsense. Either you're with me or you're not. You decide. Right now.

Yet, this bluntness doesn't stem from authoritarianism or a

superiority complex. Rather, it originates from his deep love for your soul. Enough is enough, says this fiery master. Enough dilly-dallying, enough time wasting and self-indulgence. If you want to transform yourself, if you want to become the fullness of who you really are, come, take my hand and I'll get you there. The ultimate prize is waiting for you. But there's a price to pay in exchange for this prize: you must surrender that part of yourself that isn't real, that's held you back for way too long.

Morya summarizes it like this:

> We demand the all of those to whom we would give our all. The question is, Are you ready to exchange your lesser self for our Greater Self?[5]

Are you ready to grasp Morya's hand? Only you can answer that question. And answering with a resounding "yes" can be daunting, given the intensity of this mighty master. Which reminds me of a story I once heard that's good to reflect on in moments like this.

This story dates back to about 1983. At that time The Summit Lighthouse had just opened an ashram in New Delhi, India. The call went forth for students of the masters to take a turn serving at the ashram. India was a sought-after place because of its association with the Eastern adepts and also because it brought aspiring Western students closer to El Morya's etheric retreat, the Temple of Good Will. This magnificent retreat is located above the city of Darjeeling, high in the Himalayan foothills.

A friend—let's call her Becky—felt drawn to serve at the ashram. However, once there, she realized that El Morya's strong, tangible presence made her feel uneasy and uncertain about being able to live up to his expectations. Morya's very blueness became a barrier to her joy of serving there.

One day, a housemate at the ashram who had noticed her trepidation towards Morya took her by the arm to a large portrait of the master. "I want to show you something," he said. "Look closely." She squirmed as she tried to meet the master's stern gaze. "What do you mean? What should I be looking at?" "Look here," he said, pointing to the bottom of the frame. She studied it closely but didn't see anything unusual. "Down there," he said, now pointing to the wall below the frame. "Way down there. Look at his feet. He's got pink socks!"

Morya's pink socks. The soft spot in his heart. Back in 1882 his friend K.H. made a similar observation. In one of the Mahatma letters Kuthumi explained to a Western pupil that Morya was

> . . . a man as stern for himself, as severe for his own shortcomings, as he is indulgent for the defects of others, not *in words* but in the innermost feelings of heart; for, while ever ready to tell you to your face anything he may think of you, he yet was ever a stauncher friend to you than myself, who may often hesitate to hurt anyone's feelings, even in speaking the strictest truth.[6]

Morya and You

In the course of forty years of working with his messengers Mark L. Prophet and Elizabeth Clare Prophet, El Morya gave an astounding 450 dictations. Dictations are spoken messages, usually released before a live audience that is in a meditative state. But more than just conveying information, these dictations envelop you in the light-radiation of the master that floods your soul senses and lifts you up to an exalted state of consciousness.

Morya's dictations cover a broad spectrum, from commentary on the global political and economic scene to profound pleas to the soul to come up higher. But more than that, they wrap you in his powerful vibration and allow you to experience the very essence of his being.

The editors of this book combed through the abundance of Morya's dictations to bring you a special selection of 26 messages:

Morya's sweetest, gentlest teachings that show his pink side and reveal the depth of his love for you, the student whom his heart is longing and looking for.

This book is the first in a three-part series. Book 2 will bring you Morya's emanations of wisdom, and in Book 3 you'll receive the full intensity of Morya's power. But begin with this book. Get to know him deeply by this flame of tender love. Drink in his kindness and care for your soul, his fondest hopes for your spiritual path. Feel his longing for you to come home to his heart. And then, yes, take his hand and let this dear master lead you to the summit of who you really are.

Carla Groenewegen
Director, Summit University

CHAPTER 1

*March on, children of the heavenly hosts—
march on! Hold high your shield of faith
before you. Yes, hold it high and realize
that your hand is indeed in our hand. . . .
Forget that which is past,
for the past is indeed prologue.*

CHAPTER 1

WITH A SMILE OF HOPE

"Thy Will, O God, Is Good!"

March on, children of the heavenly hosts—march on! Hold high your shield of faith before you. Yes, hold it high and realize that your hand is indeed in our hand.

It is much better that you smile, dear hearts, than that you frown. For after all, the angelic host do externalize the smile of God wherever they go, for they spread abroad the quality of comfort. And I am sure that as the Maha Chohan spoke to you, you also felt the radiation of his comfort and his love.[1]

And now I want you to feel the radiation of my power and my will. Do you know, dear hearts, that the energy that I have charged forth in the threefold activities is tremendous?[2] Do you know that I do not believe, if you were to add it up, that this planet could contain all at once the tremendous energy and the attendant knowledge that I have charged forth over the years?

Nevertheless, here I am again at work. And I am somewhat reminded of the work of one of your cartoonists, when he created the pattern that has amused the children, of Snow White and the seven dwarfs. And he had the dwarfs singing, "Heigh-ho, heigh-ho, it's off to work we go!"[3] Once again I say to you, "To work we go!"

And so you must roll up your sleeves. You must forget that which is past, for the past is indeed prologue. But you must recognize that the expanse of the future is before you—a future that can be as beautiful as you will to make it.

Now, if you take a crystal cube of pure light that has no engravings and you make mud pies on it, I am sure that no one will admire your crystal cube. But if you take this crystal cube and with the energies of your lifestream you engrave upon it the beautiful faces of the ascended beings by doing their will, what you accomplish shall indeed be made manifest for the eyes of all mankind, who should give glory to God for your works in him.

You have heard it said of old, "A city that is set on an hill cannot be hid."[4] And I tell you that there are, among the various student bodies whom you will contact, any number of students in other occult groups, guardians of the sacred mysteries, who are able to know what sort of manifestation you are bringing forth.

Therefore I urge you, dear hearts—not merely because I take pride (without blushing) in presenting you to the world, but because the souls of the lifestreams whom you will reach will be given great help through you if they accept you in faith—to do those things in your life that will give no discredit to me or to the ascended hosts.

In the past activities we have sponsored, unfortunately (and I shall not dwell upon it), there have been lifestreams who have thought because they had free will that they could do as they pleased. And so we have said to them, "Do as you will."

Now, in this new activity of The Summit Lighthouse of Freedom, I shall not take you by the coattails and compel you to do this or compel you to do that. But I am reaching out my love to you and telling you that I do expect you to give your wills freely to God. I do not compel you, but I expect you to do it because you have signified to me at inner levels that you are willing to do it.

And I have believed you, and on that basis I have secured from Helios and Vesta at great cost a grant for this new activity.

I assure you that because of certain actions that took place in previous activities sponsored by the ascended masters, it was not as easy to secure the grant for this one. Nevertheless, in the hope of heaven, I have laid down (as collateral on behalf of my chelas*) spiritual treasures of which I shall not speak.

And I stand today before you, wearing my turban and my sash, with a smile of hope that is not dimmed by the failures of my chelas in any past actions. I am crystallizing before you the light of the diamond heart in a tremendous power.

Each one of these little diamond crystals is triangular in shape and the blue flame is blazing within it and it is singing a song to the Creator of all life, saying: "Thy will, O God, is Good! Thy will, O God, is Good! Thy will, O God, is Good!"

And these blue flames are singing a paean of praise to the Father of life. And the crystal around them is made up of the radiant hopes of the children of the light as they are assembled. I have taken the spiritual hopes of many from among the unascended as well as the ascended hosts, and with my own hands I have formed in the air before you the crystal symbol of the diamond heart. This heart is actually made up of their hopes, even as it carries the radiation of my own heart.

I surround this beautiful diamond heart, which was externalized by Mary, the Mother of Jesus, with a larger pattern of my own heart. And I charge into that diamond heart the qualities from my heart of flesh, not the physical flesh but the flesh of new birth—the flesh of the living Spirit of God!

O my chelas, it is not fitting that Morya should weep, but I should weep if I thought that it would help to give you greater efficiency in bringing Home a harvest with dignity.

**chela:* [Sanskrit], a student or disciple of a master.

There are so many who believe that our energies are unlimited, and of course it is so. But I wish to emphasize that while we feel no pangs of unpleasantness as we extend ourselves to our chelas, it is hardly fitting that we should constantly pour out our energies with no hope of a return. Furthermore, the Great Law will not allow it.

I call to your attention the parable of the man who buried his lord's talent in the earth and upon his return said to him, "Here, lord, is that which thou gavest me. Receive it back." His master said, "Thou oughtest to have put my money to the exchangers, and then at my coming I should have received my own with usury. . . . Cast ye the unprofitable servant into outer darkness."[5]

When I shall stand before the Karmic Lords in years to come, having delivered to The Summit Lighthouse so great an investment of energy as they have granted me, and I am asked, "What has been the harvest?" if I can offer in return only that which they gave me as the original grant, without it having been multiplied in the works of my chelas, in your human level you will hang your heads in shame. But in my level I will bear the responsibility. I will be accountable and I will stand to lose more than the collateral I have put up this day.

And so it is not pleasing to those of the ascended hosts that they should receive no return on their investment. For we know that when we knock again on behalf of our chelas here below, the door may not be opened to us.

Therefore, I urge you to safeguard our investment in this activity with your very life and be partners with us. I know what you have already invested, and I know what you will invest because you love me and because I love you.

Rejoice in the mutuality of our faith. We are partners with God. And as his partners, it is true that we cannot fail. Nevertheless remember, dear hearts, that it is the outer flesh that is weak. It is only the flesh that is weak. The spirit is indeed willing.[6]

O God, give us more spirits—give us more spirits who are willing and likewise strengthen them in the flesh!

And so, we of the ascended hosts have assembled this day in your midst, touching you with a special radiation of the will of God at the same place on your heads that the fingers of the Maha Chohan touched.

Wherever you go, around your lifestreams within a circle of a diameter of one thousand feet, there shall pour, as little shining diamonds, the light of God's will. Realize that as lighthouses for God you will carry this radiation, and try to hold your being calm and to control the tremendous drives of energy that pour through you at times.

Remember, of course, that I am a "first-ray man" and I am well aware of just how powerful the energies of the first ray are. I smile because there are so many people who in their blissful ignorance presume that all of this activity is merely a figment of the human imagination.

It is hard for us of the ascended hosts, as we look backward even to our own past embodiments, to realize exactly what the limitations are that humankind have. For when you reach our realm and you look backward in time and space, you see nothing but the limitless glory of God! The limitations of the past are forgotten.

You see the beautiful power of God, you see the will of God, you see its radiant beams and you say, "Oh, this is easy." And then, as you charge them forth into the recalcitrant substance of humanity, you feel the sword of life itself bend and give because mankind has solidified their will in the wrong direction.

Remember, dear hearts, that human will when misused is still possessed with the qualities of God's will and therefore it can cause form to be molded in miscreations even as it can cause form to be molded in just creations. And so, there is blunted spiritual force upon spiritual force—one a creation of shadow and the other a creation of light and life.

I could speak to you for many hours and tell you many wonderful experiences that we have in the ascended realms, but I realize that your ears might grow weary. But this afternoon I do not think that any of you feel in the slightest bit weary! I think that you would rejoice to have me speak to you at greater length.

I promise you that there will be other times when the sun of life shall shine forth and we shall be together. In the meantime, you will rejoice every day to gather the pearls as they come forth fresh from God's hand. String the messages of these pearls upon the cord of life in such a manner as to present them beautifully to mankind.

O Frances, lift up your hands![7] O dear heart, our friendship is so old and there are times that I long to reach out and once again, as in the flesh, clasp your hand in friendship. The time will come when that will be possible. In the meantime, hold fast to my hand in Spirit.

Beloved Chrystel,[8] the chalice of life is always of the quality of the crystal. Even as Frances externalizes the quality of faith, so you shall externalize the quality of love. You shall radiate the quality of love because of the tremendous love you bear for Jesus and the ascended hosts.

And the contact through whom I am speaking shall externalize the quality of hope in your activity because he has been very hopeful and has not always seen the harvest manifest in exactly the manner in which he would. But I assure him also that the future shall hold brighter days.

And all of you shall see brighter days as you lift up your cup of consciousness to the mighty Presence of God, which I AM, and behold the light (the Christ) of God, which cannot fail. It cannot fail because it *is* the life of God and because it *will* externalize the will of God regardless of the recalcitrant substance or any phantasm of the human consciousness or imagination.

And it is the will of God that the blazing Son of God go forth victorious in each one of you and in all who are to come into this activity who are of the light. And the blazing Son of God is going forth victorious in full glory now!

I hope that the unascended of God's people will put their hand in ours and will climb up this glorious mountain of faith and illumination. I hope that this will come to pass. And I shall do all that is in my power that this may be so, together with the ascended hosts of light and the children of the Great White Brotherhood. And the Sons of the morning in the flame, the archangels, the archeiai, the Lords of the holy mountains Meru and Himalaya will do their part.

I have spoken! I have spoken! I have spoken!
I adore the light! I adore the light!
I adore the light!
Lift up your heads to the light!
Lift up your heads to the light and praise it!
I AM Son of the Most High, El Morya Khan.

Vondir!

August 7, 1958
Philadelphia, Pennsylvania
Upon the founding of The Summit Lighthouse
through the messenger Mark L. Prophet (MLP)

N.B. *Khan* is a title used in India. It means "ruler" or "lord." The beloved Master El Morya, also known as the Master M., often uses *Vondir* (pronounced von-deer) after his signature or at the close of a message or instruction. It means "God bless and keep and speed you on your way!"

CHAPTER 2

This new Lighthouse activity shall bring the greatest release of freedom to life since the days of the former golden ages. No longer shall ascensions be solitary releases from earth.

CHAPTER 2

CHELAS MINE!

To so possess you is for me but to do God's will!

The highest offering of my heart is ever to reveal to you the opportunities known to us of the ascended host. For these will afford your lifestreams the necessary experiences and avenues of service to make possible the release of the greatest good to all, individually and collectively, according to divine wisdom. Such service, lovingly and willingly given, will also expand the service and light of that great hierarchy of light, so well named the Great White Brotherhood.

How often have you felt my vibrations! How often have you responded to the magnetic power of my love as I sent forth the Call! Now once again, born of necessity and cosmic law, I have found it necessary to direct my energies along a new line of activity through certain of my unascended chelas.

When the first waves of my endeavors faintly began to stir in the heart of the beloved Daddy Ballard,[1] few of mankind dreamed in the outer consciousness just what a magnificent activity was being born or how tremendous would be the result of the applications made therein.

Many—most of you—were fortunate enough to have been included among those who experienced the powerful drive of my radiance as it charged forth the first impetus of fulfilling God's divine will in the I AM Activity.[2] You all saw the tiny beginning truly expand and expand into a magnificent blue plume of faith, whose radiance has covered this planet round with the blessings of goodwill.

In the midst of apparent victory, however, many were startled to find that I had begun the work of formulating yet another plan of action, starting the movement of the Bridge to Freedom.[3] Once again you responded to my call and formed the very heart of that most hopeful endeavor, which was intended to bring hope to the hearts of the children of men the world around, whose hearts were yearning for more light. The planned outpicturing of that activity, the wonderful stimulation of hope, was manifest as the golden plume of the threefold flame.

When you remove a chair from behind one who is just being seated, it is not too difficult to know what the result will be. For the law of gravity, as you know, plays no favorites. Just as the law of gravity will draw down dense substance, so do the age-old habits of mankind's thought and feeling cause the outer consciousness to enter into a negative appraisal of most problem situations as it endeavors to find the shadows rather than to instantly call our light into the problem, which would dispel the shadows and make all things right.

Quite naturally, I forgive you for so doing, even before you ask me; but do not be surprised when I tell you that the average person, even our most sincere chelas, will feel that this apparent schism between the Bridge to Freedom and beloved Mrs. Ekey[4] is a personal one. They will quickly look to the personal worlds of all concerned with this matter to behold what manner of fault there be and to determine, if possible, upon whom to fix the blame. Now lift up your heads! Lift up your eyes! Behold the living hand of God in all of this! And as you do, you will see the higher way we are trying to present to you and you will realize that the real reason for this expansion does not stem from the mud of human personality.

The true and real reason for this new cosmic burst, as we march forward into the New Age of beloved Saint Germain's glorious achievements, is progress in the seventh ray's activities. Hence, the potent cause behind it is revealed to you here and now as the necessity to establish the flame of charity, the pink flame of divine love in cosmic action, in the third activity of the threefold flame.

This is the Law, beloved. Do you see? We are marching into greater light, unconditioned by human conduct. In the name of heaven, in the name of Almighty God, your own beloved I AM Presence, do you think that God and the great Karmic Board must develop their plans in the vagaries of human thought? Nay!

Our ideas are born within the flaming heart of Truth itself, and fortunate is every one of you who can share in the glorious karma of producing the perfection that we shall externalize through you if you care willingly and lovingly to serve this cause in the name and by the authority of divine love itself.

This divine love is now flowing and shall continue to flow to you and to all who will lovingly serve with you in this activity of the Lighthouse of Freedom[5]—not only from my heart and that of beloved Nada, Saint Germain, Jesus, beloved Mary and all of the risen host but also from the great Helios and Vesta, with the glorious fiery imprint of Alpha and Omega themselves from the Great Central Sun, in the most buoyant aspects of their holy natures.

This tremendous release of divine love, which is the very light substance of our beings, we are hoping to see personified in you, each one. This, I decree, shall come to pass, freezing, as it were, the thoughtform thereof as a beautiful ascended master prayer for each of you, which decree shall be sustained in our octave until each of you is wholly ascended and free.

O children of my heart, feel my boundless love for you! I am quite aware of the full scope of the service and physical suffering voluntarily assumed by some of you as you lay your energies upon the altar of life. This karma you have selflessly assumed for transmutation through the use of violet fire so that the race may be more quickly set free.

I know, too, that it is not pleasant to the outer self to be constantly undergoing changes. When your roots have scarcely reached down to the water level and have not yet achieved a minimum tenacity, to pull them up and transfer them to the barren desert of uncertainty is not comfortable for you. Yet I ask you to realize, if you can, that this is all in the interest of the forward march of progress.

If you will think upon it for a moment, I am sure that each of you will realize that both Saint Germain and I, as well as every one of the ascended host who has trod earth's way, have passed through similar trials, always loving life enough to cooperate altogether selflessly with life's onward push to its ultimate goal. You know that obedience is but loving cooperation with Good and that it is written, "To obey is better than to sacrifice."[6]

Now, I want you to know something of the positive beauty and magnificence that I am asking you to endeavor to physically externalize at this time in this Lighthouse of Freedom activity in order to complete the threefold flame of my endeavor. For this activity is anchored in the power of the blessed Elohim Hercules and his divine complement, Amazonia, with the full Christ protection of our beloved Lord Michael and the boundless cooperation of my limitless legions of blue flame as well as the full power of myself in action as chohan of the first ray.

The corporate structure of the Lighthouse unquestionably must be of diamond-heart material, and the integrity of the lifestreams that will make up that heart is known to me at inner levels. Strife must be a forgotten record where all are concerned who serve this cause! Loving cooperation with each other, as well as with us, must be a divine fiat of light for you all.

The cells in this heart center here in the eastern area of these United States must make every endeavor to bring forth the crystal clarity of the full-gathered momentums of their own Holy Christ Self. They must blaze this crystal light through their entire beings as the radiant quality of the pink plume, divine love, to all life everywhere, setting that life free by the glorious effulgence of the *light that never, never, never fails.*

The new teachings that we shall release in this forward surge of progress are based on the hope that faith charged by love will transmit to you and to all who will lovingly serve our cause, by the application made to their own I AM Presence, a boundless expansion of the threefold flame that beats the very hearts of all.

As you come into this greater knowledge that we shall release and that shall be your joy to externalize, all of you shall find that peace which passes all understanding[7] of the outer mind. For this new Lighthouse activity shall bring the greatest release of freedom to life since the days of the former golden ages.

No longer shall ascensions be solitary releases from earth; for there shall be mass ascensions when life is loved free and its transmuted energies build such momentums as will cause it to obey the God-command of the children of light: "Beauty, love and truth, be manifest!"

Now, dear hearts, do not think me unaware of the confusions that may have manifested in your minds and feelings in connection with the current appearances of distress. Just see to it that you give this force no more power! Hold fast continually to your own beloved I AM Presence and to me. I shall not fail to pour the light of my very life into all of you who will call it forth with a sincere heart and who will steadfastly hold to it with a high faith in the present and the future, holding steadfast as well to a firm hope and a benign charity. These qualities must be sustained by you on behalf of every child of earth who yearns to find surcease from all distress.

In the future in our Lighthouse activity the decrees must be graded to different levels of consciousness. The instruction must be so simply given forth that all can understand it; and your service must be constant, as the calling of a keeper of the flame implies. As you thus serve, and personally as well as collectively develop these God-qualities within and around you, you will become a spiritually picturesque Lighthouse builded on the rock of truth. This rock of truth will be the solidification of all the living grains of truth which have been embodied in both previous activities.[8]

This Lighthouse shall be an edifice which, strongly builded upon and anchored within the rock of truth, shall raise its great superstructure into the heavens for all to behold. Then with fixed attention will the uplifted eyes of mankind remain constant upon the light and perfection of the ascended host. And the symbol of the Lighthouse will be the most magnificent beacon that has ever flashed its pulsation through the night of human consciousness since Lord Michael took the first root race home in the victory of the ascension.

Such is the need of the moment. Doubt neither your ability nor mine to perform it! God and Good are on your side. You can help us expand the all-powerful light[9] of this Lighthouse until its radiance shall reach and bless the very end of your planetary chain,* filling all space with the pure fragrance of the flowers of freedom.

The love that gave birth to the beauty of God's goodwill in our first I AM Activity is yet eternally sustained by our beloved and gracious Obedience, Daddy Ballard, who is always so near and dear to you.

Now I clasp your hand and heart to mine as together we gaze at the divine pattern of God's eternal perfection, which is embodied

---

*i.e., all the planets in our planetary system till the end of their evolutionary cycle

in every cell of the beings and worlds of the ascended masters. To their love and light I now commend you, hoping to see their qualities outpictured through you, even as I AM—

Faithfully yours,

EL MORYA KHAN—*Vondir!*

August 8, 1958
MLP

CHAPTER 3

If you will hold our hand ever so gently
and yet firmly, if you will daily give us
your attention and tune in with our world,
we so gladly offer you the momentum of
our victory, the tidal wave of pure love.

CHAPTER 3

TO WORK AND TO WIN

Morya salutes all the chelas of the Great White Brotherhood everywhere assembled! Morya salutes the chelas of the light, of freedom, assembled for the glory and the honor of freedom as it expresses in God, as it expresses in nature and as it has been so nobly expressed through the life and the energies of that life of him we lovingly call Freedom himself—I refer to beloved Saint Germain, chohan of the seventh ray.

My words to you today carry a vibrant current of my energy, and as my opening remarks I say to each one of you, "To work and to win!"

Across this broad expanse of earth which you call home, each day countless millions go forth to toil. Be it ever so true that this is not as God intends, in the sense that there ought not to be a sense of struggle, neither ought there to be a sense of labor. But in the midst of all this discussion of the subject itself—to work and to win—I say to you, beloved hearts, that Jesus himself long ago uttered these words, "The Father worketh hitherto and I work."[1] Now, if you will evaluate this thought properly, I am ever so sure each one of you will see that Jesus meant "The Father renders the supreme service to the universe, and I render the supreme service to the universe."

It is not possible, it is true, that each one of you can possibly express the fullness of God. But it is possible that each one of you can admit to its possibility. You see, beloved hearts, when you limit yourself by saying that you are not perfect and by listing, as it were, your imperfections and weaknesses which you presently have expressed or do express, you build a wall between your God Self and life's immortal pattern of perfection for you, which in some small way (and sometimes a larger way) acts to prevent a very real attainment which you seek.

WE GLADLY OFFER YOU THE MOMENTUM OF OUR VICTORY

Inasmuch as this year the Lighthouse of Freedom has been dedicated to the rendering of a service of happiness to all mankind, it is my wish this day, as my service of love, to remove from the hearts of each one of you hearers of my words (and each one who reads my words) any idea of limitation. Truly, the removal of limitation is like taking away a great iron portcullis[2] before an ancient castle. It opens the door wide so that the great hosts of light —even the hosts of light yet unascended, for I salute you as such— can pass through and enter into the victory, the victory which you really are becoming.

In order to do this, to work and to win, above all you must recognize not only the possibility, but you must recognize that God intends that you shall render your service and shall win your victory. To do this in dignity you must take each day as it comes and you must renew your strength each day, as the psalmist of old spoke.

Truly, we of the ascended host did not win our victory in a

day or a year. Sometimes it was the work of centuries. In your case, the Lord on high has heard and has shortened the time required for attainment.

If you will hold our hand ever so gently and yet firmly, if you will daily give us your attention and tune in with our world, we so gladly offer you the momentum of our victory, the tidal wave of pure love. If you have ever listened to the pounding of a surf, no doubt an honest heart would admit to a sense of overwhelming awe, certainly the first time the surf was heard by that individual. The great ocean of infinity, the great ocean of God's love, beats its message upon the hearts of all mankind each day. And it is our purpose in giving you this address to activate your consciousness in such a manner that you will clearly see and perceive this tidal wave of love as a real and tangible substance that comes into your world at our call and at yours.

For you see, beloved hearts, when you call to us, we must answer you. But also, when we call to our own beloved God Presence, I AM, that Presence instantly responds to us. For that is what we have become and that is what you shall become in the victory of your ascension. These are not idle words but these are words to work and to win.

The service of the Holy Spirit, the magnificence of its outpouring the limitless light of freedom itself has begun to shine upon your pathway with a greater brilliance in the Lighthouse. This is not because we desire to bring any discredit upon all the landmarks of the past, for without landmarks of the past, how could there be a present? For "Out of Egypt have I called my son"[3] was spoken long ago of the Christ. And truly, out of bondage God has called you all, called you to enjoy the limitless untrammeled freedom of the ascended host, called you to have and to hold sacred and dear to your hearts the love which we have and gladly share with you.

LET THERE BE A GREAT OUTPOURING OF GOODWILL AND FREEDOM

You are guests at our table this day. And we give you not crumbs, but we give you eternal substance that you may satisfy your souls at the festive board of Almighty God and with thanksgiving may eat of the bread of freedom in the memory of that beloved Saint Germain, whose light I love—and I am so proud and so joyful to call him my brother.

Beloved Saint Germain, stand with me today and blaze into this group—even this first day of the class here in Philadelphia—the magnificence of your heart's light. Let there be a blending of the blue and the violet ray in a great outpouring of goodwill and freedom that shall sweep across this class each day, making strands of pure light which shall weave a tapestry of such beauty as shall enable each one who has attended these meetings to return to their homes with their hearts beating with greater happiness in the externalized freedom that they shall draw from their own beloved I AM Presence and from thee and truly from us all. For the Spirit of the Great White Brotherhood salutes you this day, O blessed chelas of the ascended host!

Truly, this activity is destined to become—as you shall put your shoulder to the wheel to win—a citadel, a tower along the rocky coast of human consciousness. And it will draw from the ocean the magnificent currents to ray the light of God over land and sea, showing to mankind that the light of God never fails and will provide a safe journey home for every heart that loves love, for every heart that loves a lover and every heart that is open to receive the vibrations of purity and freedom in the full confidence and knowledge that God could intend no less as his will. For his virtue and his strength is in the becoming in mankind.

In the Godhead itself, there is a veritable fount of wisdom. And we of the ascended host have entered into that fount to add the droplets of our energies and the mighty torrents of our own beloved I AM Presence and Holy Christ Self. As we receive the sacred energies of your own hearts in this union, this great mounting wave of enthusiasm for the love and goodwill of God will engulf the earth and the universe. And as the sea laps the farther shore, it will come about in your consciousness that peace which passeth all understanding,[4] that peace which comes from knowing true freedom in goodwill—an entering into and an achievement that knows no end but is in itself an eternal beginning.

I BESTOW UPON YOU MY BLESSING

I thank you for the energies of your hearts, students of Philadelphia and through the world. I thank each and every one of you personally and individually. I shake your hand and bestow upon you my blessing—the blessing of the first ray and the chohan thereof.

Godspeed thee through this class with joy, that its now divinely ordained energies may descend on your hearts with the grace of the Holy Spirit and bring you comfort and peace each moment of each sacred day.

Godspeed thee now through the power of his light and love into which I ever seal you, into which all of the ascended host commend you.

Thank you and good afternoon.

June 2, 1959
Washington, D.C.
MLP

CHAPTER 4

Individuals are intended from the
beginning of life to turn to their Source
"as the sunflower turns on her god."
They are intended to turn and drink in
and receive the rays outpoured from the sun.
And the rays are intended to raise them up toward
the light and restore them to their own divinity.

CHAPTER 4

"AS THE SUNFLOWER TURNS ON HER GOD"

Peace be unto you, my beloved heart friends of the ages. Significant indeed is the fact that even before I entered the atmosphere this evening, my opening words to you were intended to contain the statement concerning the song which was just played, the statement, "the same look which she turn'd when he rose."[1]

Beloved ones, if you will stop to ponder upon that song and realize the beauty that there is present within even a humble sunflower, you will realize that as this sunflower follows the sun in its course across the heavens, so it was intended by the Father that all life everywhere should follow the eternal Sun of their own God Presence from their earliest going forth into manifestation until they return at last to the haven of beauty in the heart of that from whence they came—the eternal Source.

You have often heard me speak of the will of God. You have often thought upon the will of God as good. And yet I tell you that many of mankind do not think the will of God is good. There are many individuals who have rebelled against the barbs and the thorns of life, and understandably so inasmuch as they do not always perceive the effects, that is to say, they do not always perceive the causes that lie behind the effects that so distress them.

This is ever understandable, for I, who am now an ascended being, when long ago embodied as you are in physical form at times too did ponder some of the pain and suffering through which I passed. And therefore, we who have escaped from bodies of flesh such as you now wear are able to feel a great sense of compassion for you who are yet, as it were, in bondage to some of the ills inherent to the flesh.

THE TANGIBLE REALITIES OF OUR CONSCIOUSNESS

Precious ones of the light, are you aware that I am aware of every thought that flashes through your consciousness? Beloved ones of the light, are you aware that I as an ascended being am speaking to you through a human instrument? Are you aware of the light and the perfection from whence I am come?

I hope that you are able to perceive that light. For if you are able to perceive it, you will, as a flower, open your consciousness to your own God Presence and to us of the ascended host to receive our radiance, which in itself is a perfect manifestation even if one of our words should not come forth as perfectly or as beautifully as we utter it in the consciousness of the one through whom we speak.

I tell you, beloved ones of the light, it is time for individuals to cease from human nonsense. It is time for them to become aware of the tangible realities of our consciousness. It is true, an ascended being seems somewhat farfetched to those inclined for a period of many years to think only in terms of the visible, tangible things which they may handle with their physical hands and perceive with their physical eyes. Those of us of the ascended host who are able to perceive both the things visible to your sight and all of that which is not visible yet to your sight can also have compassion on you concerning that.

YOUR FREEDOM IS IMMINENT

And therefore I ask, in the name of God, that the beauty of the eternal Presence shall bless you now and shall heal those of you who are out of the way in the sense that you do not know the path that leads to the eternal Father's house. This is the path to the will of God, which is good, to the Spirit of God, which is so lovely, because he would yet receive you regardless of how much error you have walked in or how many times you have doubted the existence even of his Being.

This may come as a shock to some individuals to think that another could doubt the existence of the Being of God. But I tell you that even some of those great, magnificent ascended beings today at some time in a previous earth life found themselves so closed in upon, as it were, by human effluvia that momentarily they doubted some of the existence even of their Creator. And therefore, we are able to understand the weight and oppression of human effluvia. But, precious ones of the light and love of God, do not yield yourselves to a sense of frustration. Do not yield yourselves to a sense that you cannot find your freedom. For your freedom is imminent. Your freedom dwells just above you in your own God Presence, not far from any one of you. Your freedom is in the eternal Presence. When you declare in the name of God, "I AM free!" it is eternally true.

RAISE YOUR CONSCIOUSNESS ABOVE DOUBT AND DESPAIR

Human bondage, human deceit, human conceit in themselves can never produce perfection. Mankind for centuries have studied the intellect. There is nothing wrong in a fine intellect, for the mind was created by God and is a part and portion of the divine intelligence resident within human consciousness. But I tell you that by the intellect alone mankind cannot always perceive God;

although if they would go farther and farther into the realms even of intellect, there comes a point when they must touch upon the garment and hem of the Eternal. But by the feelings, mankind become more easily stirred. It is somewhat easier for individuals to have a feeling of God because when they are in trouble and when they are in pain they cry out and say, "O God, help me!"

Many individuals in battlefields have cried out to the Eternal. These individuals were not aware of the fact that God heard their cry in many cases, but they received often an answer to their call. They did not see their call go up to the throne of the Eternal. They did not perceive the answer in an actual, tangible way in many cases, and yet the answer came. And often afterwards they would say, "Oh, perhaps it would have happened anyway."

This is the human, which is always prone to doubt. I smiled somewhat as the discourse of beloved Mary Myneta[2] was going forth this evening to realize the great truths that were being presented to you concerning the human consciousness and its naturalness to doubt the eternal truths of the cosmos. Beloved ones, I ask you to raise your consciousness. I ask you to raise your consciousness above the realm of human doubt and despair. I ask you to hold to the positive qualities of the light even when you are surrounded by that which does not seem to be in keeping with the will of God.

The will of God is a very precious gift. The will of God is what inspires us here in Darjeeling in our meetings to be able to hold to an immaculate concept for every one of you. We are able, as you have been told in days gone by through the Theosophical movement, to perceive an actual replica of the physical form of every one of our chelas.[3] We are able to perceive therein the subtlest changes which take place. We are able to see the entrance into your consciousness of any quality which is less than the light of God. And being able to perceive these things, we are able to direct our ray consciously to you to protect you, to guide you, to perfect you and to help you in times of need. This is a beautiful manifestation. This is a manifestation of God's will and God's care.

"YE ARE GODS"

So many individuals have often thought of the eternal Father as an old man sitting in some corner of the universe far removed from them and unable to perceive the things they do. It is somewhat difficult for individuals to adjust to the idea of their own divinity. It is somewhat difficult for them to realize that *they* are divine—as Moses declared to the children of Israel in the wilderness, "Ye are gods,"[4] and as the Christ later declared these words saying, "If Moses said to those to whom the Word of God was spoken, 'Ye are gods,' why do ye say that I blaspheme when I declare that I am the Son of God?"[5]

Do you see therefore, beloved ones of the light, that understanding is needed by all? The admonition of God to Solomon, saying, "With all thy getting get understanding,"[6] was a magnificent admonishment. For if mankind would only seek to have understanding in their affairs with one another, so much of karma which is presently forged would not come into manifestation.

Now, it is the will of God that mankind should escape wholly from their negative karma and receive only the benefit of their good karma. Individuals are not intended to walk upon this planet subject to limitation, to despair, to confusion, to any other vibratory action which is less than the light of God. They are intended from the beginning of life to turn to their Source "as the sunflower turns on her god."[7] They are intended to turn and drink in and receive the rays outpoured from the sun, and the rays are intended to raise them up toward the light and restore them to their own divinity. God sent forth the light manifesting as the power of the ray of God. In the ancient Egyptian language the ray was called *ra,* and they called God *Ra.*

Beloved ones, you are all individualized rays from the heart of

God. You are all intended to become one with God. You have heard this spoken of old, and yet the few who have believed it and have lived accordingly have become as we are—ascended beings. We walk in robes of righteousness in cosmic light, but our love has not permitted us to forsake this planet or its people. And therefore we come to you tonight to give you our divine feelings concerning the will of God, our feelings of reverence, and propel you toward the light.

THE REALITY OF MY LOVE

For a long period of time individuals have intimated to mankind that I, Morya El, am extremely stern. This may be true, in a sense, that I am stern because the first ray in itself represents the will of God. And I ask you, beloved hearts, if I, as the chohan of the first ray, am to flinch from the will of God, then where is the foundation and basis for all that is to follow? But I tell you that my love is as real and tangible as any of the other chohans of the rays, and they will be the first to witness to its reality and tangibility. If you contact any other master of light, whether you are sleeping or awake in your finer bodies, they will verify the great love. But I know, my chelas, it is not necessary that you ask. For you know, who know the light, that I love you. You know that I have stood beside you when you needed me. And you know that I will continue to do so as long as you revere in your hearts and minds the will of God, even when sometimes you seem to fall short of it.

However, I do not condone falling short of the will of God. I hope that the day will soon come when every one of you will be so firm that nothing can break you or shake you or change you. I await that day. I await the day when you are ready to give your all to the light as we have done. I await the day when every chela shall have the understanding which beloved Kuthumi has.

LEARN TO EXCHANGE YOUR QUALITIES WITH ONE ANOTHER

I want to say a word concerning beloved Kuthumi. As so many of you know, Kuthumi was the gentle Saint Francis of Assisi in one of his more familiar embodiments. He assisted me so greatly during the Theosophical days, and he stands by my side tonight as I speak to you. Kuthumi's love is a gentle love, it is true. Kuthumi is very kind, it is true, and very wise. But someday you will know that as we meet around our council tables at Darjeeling and the other retreats we share and exchange our qualities, and then you will learn how to share and exchange your qualities with one another.

Some of you are more patient than others. And I tell you that some of you have more staunchness than others. Now, when the day comes that you shall actually enter into the consciousness that we have, those of you who are staunch will exchange your qualities with those who have more patience, and you will suddenly find that, like the loaves and the fishes of old,[8] the multiplication of God-qualities is possible without loss. It is not like money in the bank, because you are dealing with eternal substance. And the more you love eternal substance, the more it expands and the more it multiplies and the more it goes forth to perform its acts of virtue. God's will is so. God's will is so. God's will is good.

Precious ones, how is it possible that mankind, surrounded with all the beauties of nature and the wonders of their physical form and the beauties of the cosmos, can doubt? And yet they do. We forgive that doubt tonight. May every one here be forgiven any doubt they have ever had. I forgive you in the name of the infinite Cosmic Christ. I AM full forgiveness to all.

Go forth, therefore, as Jesus said of old, and sin no more[9] by doubt, but by love and love's power continue to pour your adoration to your God Presence and the ascended host in full faith. And then I think that we can weld a student body together who will possess the qualities of patience and staunchness, who will possess the qualities of devotion and the necessary quality to make an ascended master activity that will draw from out of the great sea of humanity those souls who presently hunger and thirst after righteousness[10] with such hunger and such yearning as to be almost incomprehensible.

TAKE ADVANTAGE OF OPPORTUNITY

Do you realize the opportunity that is given to you? How many of you realize the truth of the series of embodiments that many of you have had? How many of you realize how many opportunities you have had to walk this earth and to receive your perfection? This may surprise you a great deal when I tell you this, but there are some present in this room who actually existed upon the planet before myself and yet they are unascended.

I want you to think about that for a moment, for it shows that opportunity is not always taken full advantage of. And I want you to somberly ponder tonight the fact that life has given all of you an opportunity to do the will of God. I want you to realize that in simplicity and in beauty and in plain talk there is a proximity to the will of God which could not possibly be released if I were to speak to you in the most academic phrases possible.

I want to speak to you as children of God tonight. I want to tell you that the love of God is a priceless love. I have in times past severely lectured individuals. Tonight, I do not plead but I admonish you with the fullness of my love to take a fuller advantage of the opportunity which God has given you. I hope that you will let drop from you, as scales from the eyes of Saint Paul,[11] any feelings that you might have toward any individual upon this planet who is not godlike. I hope you will somberly ponder the necessity of loving one another as God has loved you. I hope you will realize that he who searches the minds and the hearts is able to give you the victory which you have called for when you are ready to receive it and that you have a great deal to do with determining just when that readiness shall be.

I tell you, beloved ones, the Father has been willing from the day you went forth to give you your victory. Like you, we dallied too in the past and we delayed. But the disease of delay, as I have spoken of before, is one which brings pain and suffering to mankind and needlessly so. For the sun is always above the sunflower, and if the flower does not follow the sun from the beginning of the day to the close—from the going forth from the Home to the return to the Home of light—it is not the fault of the sun. The fault would have to be in thee. But because I believe that there is so much goodness in all of you, I am sending forth tonight not my usual message, but I am sending forth a specific admonishment.

THE WAY TO SEEK GOD IS OPEN

Saint Germain spoke to you magnificently last evening. His address, some of you said, was greater than anything you had previously heard. If a magnificent God being like Saint Germain could pour out so much energy and love to you last night, I decided that inasmuch as I could not eclipse Saint Germain, I would at least give you some idea of my love, my simplicity, my humility and my desire to help you too. In other words, I want to propel you toward the same goal of which Saint Germain spoke.[12]

I love you, magnificent souls that are here. I know every one of you who has actually given your all to the light, and those of you who have not, often did not understand. But all of you can understand that the way to seek God is open. You may not fully comprehend the doctrine, the various religions of the world. You may not fully comprehend the meanings of the yearnings within your own heart. But you can understand that there is a light from on high and that this light is calling you to a high destiny and calling.

And like ourselves you can begin anew every time you seem to make the slightest failure, and you can turn defeat into victory.

You can do this because we are on your side. We are not standing in opposition to any child on earth. We are standing wholly behind the will of God, and his will is to give every one of you your victory, your opulence, your supply, your good health, your joy, your happiness and every good thing.

I WANT YOU TO COME HOME

I smile upon you tonight in taking my leave because tomorrow evening the Lord of the World, beloved Gautama, will speak to you from Shamballa, and I think his inspiration will be very great. I did not want you to go home and somehow feel too much of a sense of elation and then be let down at the close of the class into the cold, outer, material world of things. And so I chose to take the more somber role this evening and admonish you to take advantage of the opportunity, because you will see in the forthcoming addresses the beauty which God is going to pour forth upon you, as Saint Germain did last evening. But I want you to come Home. I want you, as they all do, to enter into the fullness of God's desire and will for you.

If this is to be done, I realize that you have got to stop and think many times when indiscretion might seize you and the emotions of the flesh—the flash of anger, fears and other desires—may rise in your consciousness. When that earthly, material fire bursts forth, you must use your extinguisher and you must turn and gravitate, that is to say, lift, your consciousness upward.

I think you will remember my words tonight. And I promise you that the next time many of you hear me speak I will bring you something from Darjeeling that will, perhaps, make you physically a little happier. But I think in time to come, many of you will remember my address this evening as specifically directed to a great cosmic thrust.

Thou infinite cosmic light, thou mighty I AM Presence of all here and all upon the planet Earth, all glory be to thee, all honor be to thee, all thanksgiving, adoration, praise for thy loveliness. Oh, manifest thou now upon earth a spark of the eternal fealty of God-happiness. Let everyone upon this planet sense and feel at this hour a radiant outpouring of God's love for them. And may all rejoice in the knowledge that the end result of God's manifest creation will be for all beautiful, enrichening, strengthening and lovely for all eternity.

Peace be upon you in the unfailing light of God. The brothers at Darjeeling, together with beloved Kuthumi, bless you this night. Be at peace. Be wise. Be chelas of the great ascended beings. Represent your Presence upon earth, and then God will walk and talk with men.

I thank you.

October 14, 1960
New York, New York
MLP

CHAPTER 5

I come with the great enfolding love of the ascended hosts and cosmic beings making a plea for a divine unity which will accomplish the will of God upon this sweet earth and will cut countless individuals free from discord and confusion and unhappiness.

CHAPTER 5

UNITY THROUGH THE SUMMIT LIGHTHOUSE

Heart friends of the ages, I am here this evening with a feeling of intense love and fraternity, for tonight many of you who are present have journeyed some distance—some of you in space and some in time, for there are in this place this evening friends who have known me personally in many embodiments of the past and with whom I am presently happy to be identified in this constructive endeavor. [Audience rises.] I greet you, and I salute you one and all in the name of your own God Presence, I AM. (Won't you please be seated.)

How wonderful, my friends, that the rays of light from your own God Presence are not bedimmed by human tears. How wonderful that the rays of light from your own God Presence do not wane in their effectiveness. I am rejoicing in the fact that your Presence is able today to sustain you in all of the dignity and beauty with which you were brought forth from the heart of God in the beginning. Human consciousness and the human frailties of life may take their toll upon those who accept the negations of life, but those who will keep their gaze unalterably fixed upon their Presence are still sustained by that Presence regardless of the appearances.

Beloved ones, no mere words can alter the power and the perfection of the Presence of God. If mankind declare there is no God, I say to you tonight that this is immediately rendered of no effect, for thousands unknowingly throughout this planet every day when they declare "I am" are affirming the very existence of Being. Likewise, the moment you open your eyes and consciousness floods into your being, you are affirming the existence of God.

LEARN TO MEDITATE UPON THE WILL OF GOD

I say unto every one of you, the will of God, which is good, is flooding into your consciousness in like manner every day. You must learn to listen, you must learn to meditate upon the will of God. Individuals often are taken unawares by a slight bit of quicksand when they allow the mire of human consciousness to seep in upon them, and they accept the imperfections of life. If they would look up to the Presence of God and keep their gaze riveted there regardless of human appearances, they would soon learn how to produce the frequencies of our octave in their own world.

There are some individuals who have smiled within themselves and said that they have tried to do this for a period of many years without the measure of success that they had hoped for. Beloved ones, you have tried a portion of one lifetime. How many lifetimes do you think some of us tried to produce perfection and to call forth perfection before we succeeded? But you are living in an entirely different time. You are living in an era of God-perfection when, with the power of the ascended hosts and with the power of the angelic hosts and the power of the violet flame, you can find your freedom as never before. I know and I am convinced that gratitude should and does flow from the heart of every one of you who are aware of this great gift from the heart of your own Presence.

THE BEAUTY OF FRIENDSHIP

Beloved ones, tonight as you were singing your songs to my humble self I rejoiced, for it took me back in memory to those beautiful isles upon which I spent many a happy year in physical embodiment. I am particularly thinking of the Emerald Isle and of the beauty of Shannon and the countryside in Ireland. There is something especially picturesque and peculiar in the lines of inner beauty to that great and magnificent country to which I would like to pay tribute. Beloved ones, "The Harp That Once through Tara's Halls"[1] rings again in your midst tonight, for I am impelled to speak of all of the beauty of friendship.

Among mankind today in the hustle and bustle of commercial confusion, individuals sometimes fail to take the time to pause and meditate upon the great blessing which friendship brings to all mankind. You are friends, you are neighbors, you are comrades in a spiritual endeavor marching forward toward your victory. And I tell you that the friendship of the ages which endures between my own lifestream and beloved Kuthumi and Djwal Kul is in itself a living, eternal memorial to the power of friendship. Recently mankind have caroled out "We Three Kings of Orient Are," and both Djwal Kul and beloved Kuthumi themselves always rejoice with me on this occasion and bring a sweet blessing to the youthful and aged carolers who are thus honoring that mission which we made across the desert sands, guided by the star that holy night.

Blessed ones, the beauty of all eternal endeavors is in the permanence of those endeavors. To this present day, mankind are honoring that trek across the sands, yet many of mankind who were great war heroes and so-called warlords have gone down into the ranks of infamy and are scarcely mentioned by history.

How precious it is that lifestreams can be devoted to a principle. I am constantly rejoicing in the thought that there are men who are willing to stand for a principle, men who are willing to stand for beauty, men who are willing to stand for the perfection of their own

Presence. I have tried, beloved Kuthumi has tried, the entire Great White Brotherhood has tried through the ages to bring to the mankind of this blessed planet all of the power, all of the beauty of God. Some men do not feel that we have manifested that perfection.

AN ASCENDED MASTER'S EYE VIEW OF LIFE'S PERFECTION

Blessed ones, if there be any lack, the lack is in the human octave. It is because individuals have kept their attention riveted to the imperfections of life. When mankind shall turn their whole hearts toward God with the same intensity with which they turn it toward the imperfections of life, they will swiftly bring about a change in their dimensions of consciousness—an expansion will occur. And for this purpose this night I am here. I am here to give you not just a bird's-eye view, blessed ones, but an ascended master's eye view of life's perfection.

In this place tonight there are a large number of you who particularly yearn to visit me at Darjeeling in my lovely retreat. I have opened my doors constantly to different lifestreams who have desired to come closer to the will of God, and when they have warmed themselves by my fires, some of them were not aware that the fires were the burning, flaming beauty of God's will, which is always in existence and manifestation in our library. Blessed ones, I stand with open arms and open heart to everyone who is willing to come here that they may learn more about the beauty, more about the plan of eternal perfection.

Mankind's attention today is frequently turned to so much of the outer world that it is difficult for them to envision the perfection of the ascended masters' octave. I would that you would gain a greater sense of the perfection of the Presence. The Presence has arms of light which reach out to enfold every lifestream upon this earth at every moment, and this is a tangible manifestation. And individuals turn their backs upon the Presence and the light thereof and choose to look at shadowed creation. Then whom do they have to blame when they outpicture shadows? I do not think they can blame the ascended hosts. I do not think they ought to blame their Presence. I think that mankind should be honest in heart and fix the blame upon their misplaced attention.

We have been extremely patient and we continue to be patient. But the Great Law, blessed ones, knows no partiality. The blessed Law acts in accordance with your thoughts. If your thoughts choose to go in the direction of error, the Law follows; and the Law does not err, neither does it make a mistake. Some men have thought that they might be able to cheat the Great Law, but the Law always functions with perfection. Where the will of God, therefore, is brought into manifestation by obedience to the presence of life within the beating heart, then the Great Law brings its own reward of love, and love never fails.

FOLLOW THE LIGHT WHEREVER THE LIGHT MAY LEAD

Blessed ones, long ago during the days of the Theosophical movement I worked exceedingly hard to bring forth and externalize through Madame Helena Blavatsky the teachings of the Theosophical movement.[2] And there were many individuals who at that particular time hearkened to the knowledge, the inspiration and the wisdom which came forth through us and were illumined. Then the call went forth at a later date to beloved Godfre,[3] and there were any number of individuals who responded with alacrity throughout the country and nation. There was a galvanization, and the knowledge of the I AM Presence was made manifest. Some individuals who followed us in the days of the Theosophical movement did not choose to leave the comfort and safety of that movement but chose to remain there and would not march into the greater light which came forth through the mighty I AM Presence.

Down through the centuries, mankind have often failed to stir themselves to accept a greater light as it bursts into manifestation. But, beloved ones, those of us of the ascended hosts, as you know, are not conditioned by man's responses. We are of ourselves a part of the Great Law; and therefore, as a part of the Great Law in God-manifestation, we bring forth a plan of divine perfection from our level whose purpose is the enlightenment of all mankind. And it is up to individuals to find a spark of response in their own heart and consciousness so that they may follow that light wherever the light may lead.

THE PURPOSE OF THE SUMMIT LIGHTHOUSE

The purpose, the reason in this day and age that we have brought forth The Summit Lighthouse activity has been entirely that we might coordinate a universal government under God, a unification of a divine principle and the release of that knowledge which mankind terms metaphysical so that individuals who presently follow any number of different endeavors, who presently have a number of different concepts may be able to unite under our banner and therefore present a united front to those individuals who are presently a part of the Christian, Muslim or Buddhist movements of the world.

It is very distressing, beloved hearts, to individuals who come out from one of these movements and enter into what they feel is greater light only to find that there is a division or a striving or an irrational condition existing where individuals are speaking malicious words against one another. These individuals feel, then, that they had best return to the particular doctrine and teaching with which they began as children, and they feel that perhaps they had been led astray. And therefore, it is extremely wise that we bring all men to the summit of their own existence under God.

It is not our purpose to merely bring about an organization in itself. But I say to you, beloved ones, that the Magna Carta is a great document, and the Magna Carta was actually spiritually forged at Runnymede in order to bring this great charter into manifestation so that freedom and the cause of freedom could be glorified among mankind. The Constitution of the United States, which was brought into manifestation and released through your beloved Saint Germain, was also a precious document that was brought into manifestation for a purpose.

Do you think, blessed ones, that the United States of America was brought into manifestation for the sake of the commercial interests of the world? Do you think that the people were bound together heart to heart in the stormy days of the Revolution in order to create great railroads and the marts of commerce? Nay! I tell you these are all incidental but necessities of communication and transportation. But, beloved ones, the purpose of this great nation is to bring forth freedom under God, where men can learn the power of love, the power of their own I AM Presence, that America could become an ascended master nation and fulfill the dream of the ages. How far this nation has departed from that standard is reflected in the annals of crime reported by your own Federal Bureau of Investigation.

THE PATHWAY TO EMANCIPATION LIES IN UNITY

Blessed ones, this is not the plan of God, and we declare to you this night that the pathway to emancipation lies in unity. The United States in itself would lack a great deal of its present power if it was made up of fifty struggling, sovereign, independent states who were not united. Its great strength lies in its union. Although the individual states may have their individual charters and paths of existence and their own legislatures, still there is a great unity in the central government of this nation, and it is in this same idea that we have drawn forth the idea of The Summit Lighthouse.

All the religions, all the constructive, secular endeavors of mankind are brought forth by the light, and the light is the light of God. All of these constructive endeavors have one purpose. Individuals making them up may differ in their thoughts and their concepts; they may not always agree. Nevertheless, there is one constructive purpose in all of these endeavors and that is to bring about the freedom of mankind, the enlightenment of mankind, the peace of mankind. And therefore, our purpose in bringing forth The Summit Lighthouse, as I said before, has been to produce unity.

When you therefore have a violet-flame meeting in this place or in any of the various sanctuaries of this endeavor throughout the world, would it not be a very good idea if as many of you as possible were in attendance in order to build up the momentum of the violet flame and draw forth the power of the sacred fire? Individuals who remain separate and do not choose at all times to unite themselves together are not following the will of God. Where are differences created, beloved hearts? Are they created in the mind and heart of God, who is all unity? Are they created in the mind of Micah, the angel of unity? Differences are created in the human mind and played upon by the sinister force in order to amplify the powers of separation and to divide you and to keep you from unity in the spirit of life and light and love.

In Darjeeling when we open our arms and we say, "Come to our fireside, warm yourselves upon the sacred fires, partake of our holy communion," do we not welcome all? I think so. We welcome everyone. As we welcome everyone therefore, I say, in every place where they would hold forth this light, let men come together. Some have felt that at the particular time when our messenger is speaking, they desire to manifest themselves and be in attendance. When our messenger is not present, some of them feel that perhaps because they will not hear an actual message spoken to them from Darjeeling that it is not necessary for them to make the trek.

I would remind them that a momentum is being generated when you come together for the purposes of the sacred fire and the violet flame. I would remind them that your leaders in this place have been appointed by God for a reason and have poured out their devotion. Individuals may choose to see people in a different light than we see them. Beloved ones, I tell you that every one of you who holds an immaculate concept of one another will never regret it, for then you will make no mistake. If you should hold a concept which is not light about a brother or sister of the light and this concept later be proved wrong, I think it is you who will be embarrassed; and we would not have anyone suffer embarrassment, for we would have everyone feel the power of love.

MY PLEA IS FOR ABSOLUTE UNITY

And therefore, my plea tonight is a plea for absolute unity. Let no one here think that I speak because there is any discord in manifestation. Nay, I speak in order to weld you together so that you will realize that the bonds of love, the bonds of peace, the bonds of eternal graciousness are real and tangible, that they are more powerful than any creation that the human is able to produce. I am telling you this in order that you will realize, as you do already know, that love is stronger than all hate or discord. I am telling you this so that the will of God, which we have served for so long, will attain a greater push. And the cosmic push this coming new year will cause countless hungry millions throughout the world—hungering for the law of the I AM Presence—to receive sustenance and nourishment that the planetary body may be blessed and hallowed by greater radiation from the ascended masters because more men and women will understand the Great Law.

When you first came into this light, I ask you, blessed ones, did you not feel ever so good when you sat in our radiation and you heard the messages go forth, when you felt the great surge of power flowing through your bodies and consciousness and setting you free from a consciousness of your physical form, your limitations and of all those conditions which bound you? Did you not feel great happiness? Was it not as though you were lifted up on wings? And, blessed ones, do you not wish to share this with others? I think that you do, seeing you have such an expansive heart, a heart which comes from God. It is no different than my own. Blessed ones, seeing you have such a heart, then open the doors of your heart, open your doors towards the great power of the Great White Brotherhood, towards the power of unity, towards the power where there is strength.

You have seen the illustration often of how one stick could be so easily broken, and at the present time there are so many endeavors which declare that they are endeavors of the I AM Presence. It is true all men are manifestations of the I AM Presence. All do not know the Law, all do not live the Law, all are not preparing themselves for their ascension as you are, and yet all should. I come to you tonight because, as your head schoolmaster, as your principal, as your governor, in one sense of the word, I am expected to speak words of inspiration to you. I am also expected to chastise you, which I have not done for some time. And in view of the fact that so many of you have not received any chastisement for a long time and because I love you so much, I have decided tonight that it is about time that some of you receive a little prodding.

Blessed ones, you do not want to take the grade over. You do not want to see others take the grade over. You want the power of divine love to be victorious. I would not desire to see you have fear in your world. I would not desire to see you motivated by fear. I would like to see you motivated by the love for humanity and therefore enter into your ascension with joy. Now, is it not a wonderful thing that you are planning on entering into your own ascension to take as many with you as possible?

Therefore, to present a united front to the world is to present God to the world. Can God be divided? Do you think the Darjeeling Council is divided? Do you think the Spirit of the Great White Brotherhood is divided? If so, it is a holy Eucharist. When we say, "Take, eat, this is my body," as Jesus said, "Take, eat, this is my body which is broken for you,"[4] it is symbolical of the Holy Spirit, the Whole-I-Spirit—all of God made manifest. If all of God is made manifest, I think it must all go in the same direction; and if it goes in the same direction, then we will have a body through which to work; and if we have a body through which to work, that body will be strong with our strength. It will be wise with our wisdom. It will be wise as a serpent but as harmless as a dove.[5]

HOLD AN IMMACULATE CONCEPT OF ONE ANOTHER

O beloved ones, you can believe me that "if all those endearing young charms. . . ."[6] For as I gaze on you tonight, I see you as that. I do not see hairs that have changed in color to white. I do not see wrinkles or lines upon your faces. For I am beholding you in your bodies of light substance, and I want you to think of yourselves in those bodies of light substance. I want you to think of yourselves in eternal perfection. I want you to think of all mankind in perfection.

Beloved Mother Mary, who sends her greetings and her love tonight through me, desires that you shall hold an immaculate concept of one another. This is more than a mere word service, a mere lip service. This is the dynamic power of your own mind in action, of your own heart in action. When you take the power of your mind and your consciousness and you hold an immaculate concept of another, how can individuals gossip? How can they speak a single word against the imperfection of another lifestream if they hold an immaculate concept? You cannot produce a lie and call it the truth. The truth, blessed ones, is true because it is God, and God is perfection. Therefore I say, when you hold an immaculate concept of one another, you will be moving forward into the coming year with the greatest impetus for victory that the student body has ever had.

And tonight I pray, in God's name, that you will accept my message in the spirit of love in which I give it. For though I speak the sound of chastisement, I come with the great enfolding love of the ascended hosts and cosmic beings making a plea for a divine unity which will accomplish the will of God upon this sweet earth and will cut countless individuals free from discord and confusion and unhappiness, which will serve to inspire your own president-elect* in this nation with a forward look and with the power of his young heart so that this entire nation under God shall be blessed.

Inasmuch as I guide so much the destiny of this nation, I think that many of you who were somewhat disappointed with the results of the election will understand that the Goddess of Liberty and those of the ascended hosts do not always look at outward situations. There are reasons beyond the ken of most individuals as to why sometimes various events transpire. We always try to bring into manifestation that which is best for the planetary body.

There are so many individuals in the Great White Brotherhood who serve, blessed ones, who are not identified with any particular spiritual endeavor and are unknown to anyone on the face of this earth, even to one another. Beloved K-17 has any number of representatives in the Cosmic Secret Service—some of these know one another and some do not. There are yet remaining unsolved many scientific mysteries. There are new frontiers, there is room for pioneering in many ways. But if men think that by reaching out into space and spending millions to attempt to reach out into space they shall solve the planetary needs, then beware. For hunger and pain and confusion and strife and hatred and all inequity on this planet must be corrected before this great solar system can find this blessed earth in its rightful place emitting the light which it has within itself, within its great heart.

LET THERE BE LIGHT IN THIS PLACE

O blessed children of Saint Germain, blessed children of the I AM Race,† blessed minutemen of Saint Germain, all of you who

*John F. Kennedy

†The term *I AM Race* signifies a race of lightbearers of all nations who retain the inner memory of the individualization of the Godhead identified to Moses as I AM THAT I AM (Exod. 3:13–15).

love the light and have served it for so many years, I want to pay tribute to each one of you, each one of you—you who have served leading decree classes, you who have served in sitting in the audiences and participating, you who serve as sanctuary directors, those who are messengers. It is not a matter of one being greater than another. Beloved Jesus at the Last Supper, when he put the towel about himself, said, "He that would be great among you, let him be a servant to all."[7] And I think that we of the ascended hosts who have long won our freedom and know the feeling of God-freedom and bliss and yet come down into the sordid, recalcitrant atmosphere of this planet in order to sweep it clean and pure of imperfection, I think that we know a little bit about human discord and I think that we prefer our own octave to the atmosphere of earth at times. And yet we serve.

I know that it is extremely difficult when you wear physical forms, when you receive the thoughtforms of individuals projected at you which tell you of discouragement, which tell you of man's downfall and speak of negation and pain. It is extremely difficult for some of you, and I know that at times you go to bed at night with a feeling of weariness, and you wonder sometimes, blessed ones, just why this is so. All of this is because the power and pressure of light and of your Presence is not fully entered into by your consciousness. And so tonight, by the power vested in me, I shall lower my voice and yet shall increase the power of light.

> *I, Morya El, Lord of love's first ray, speak directly in the name of God, the mighty I AM Presence, to the forces of nature and the forces of the elements and I say: Let there be* light *in this place. Let that light penetrate the mind, the consciousness, the feelings of every individual here. And let it cut them free, in the name of God, by the power of the sacred fire and the power of the sacred heart of every ascended being, from all that is discouraging and all human thoughtforms*

and human thought processes.

And let it raise all in this place upward in light to a vision of God's beauty, to a vision of the whole world as an emerald isle of beauty and perfection over which blazes the canopy of God's will like a blazing blue sky in which is a sun of divine wisdom and strength. Let this light flood the minds, the worlds and the affairs of everyone in this place. And let all be sustained through the coming days of this year by a feeling of absolute God-perfection.

YOU HAVE THE SCEPTER OF RIGHTEOUSNESS—TAKE COMMAND!

So have I spoken in the name of God, the mighty I AM Presence. So do I give you my love, blessed ones, and not mine alone but the love of all—the love of every ascended being, of every angel, of every elemental, of every deva and builder of form. All are yours to command if you command in the name of your mighty I AM Presence, if you command with firmness, with love and with the desire to see only good externalized everywhere. This is greater than all the wisdom of mankind, and even Solomon in all his wisdom possessed nothing greater than the power of his I AM Presence.

You have that power in your hand. You have the scepter of righteousness. You hold it within your right hand. Take command, therefore, and no longer be dismayed, affrighted or afraid. You are representatives of the New Age, and the masters of wisdom plan during this class to galvanize as many of you as possible in the greater light of perfection. There is no ultimate, blessed ones. You need it, and we need you. And God will use each and every one of you who will open your heart's door according to his great divine plan, his will and his love.

I thank every one of you who have traveled and journeyed to this place tonight. It is reminiscent of former days, and the days that are coming shall continue to expand and expand and expand. And you who sit here tonight and are convinced of that shall be in the vanguard of our activity either upon this planet or in the vanguard of light itself serving with our council until every man, woman and child upon this earth is God-free and ascended in the light. This is the will of God.

I AM the will of God made manifest, made manifest, made manifest. Thank you, each one. Good night.

December 30, 1960
New York, New York
MLP

CHAPTER 6

Men have free will. . . . They may turn once and for all to their own God Presence . . . and enter into the stillness of the Great Solar Quiet until, in loving adoration, they may draw forth the sacred fire within their own heart and flood its radiance through their body, their physical world, their mind and their affairs.

CHAPTER 6

THE LAW OF THE CIRCLE AND THE GREAT SOLAR QUIET

May the all-enfolding peace of the cosmic light enter into your worlds and your minds and your affairs. I, Morya El, Lord of love's first ray, greet you tonight in the consciousness of the will of God. From the Himalayas, from the realms of light, the Brotherhood at Darjeeling brings to you a consciousness of the meaning of our rule.

With great ease in their feelings, mankind embrace the idea of adoration to God. When in the outer world of form they try to externalize and project these vows in consciousness which they so lightly accept, they find sometimes it is not as easy to fulfill as it was to promise. It is not with a spirit of condemnation that I say this, for all of us in our octave have had the selfsame experiences which you now do have daily. And we are well aware that the light of God which raised us is able to supply the grace and the God-qualities that will raise you. The question in mind is, Are you aware?

Blessed and beloved ones, by your God-awareness, by your sense of our reality and the realization that the earth and all thereon are a visible part of a great whole and that there is much more which lives and declares "I will" that is invisible than that which is visible and manifest upon the outer—when you sense this, you take the first tiny, faltering steps that lead you to an awareness of our octave. And somehow or other there opens up within your consciousness a doorway into the octave of light.

Light is God. God is light. The reality, the simplicity, the beauty, the consciousness of God is ever present with all men. Shut is the door, and the knock that is heard by the God consciousness within is not recognized by the average individual today whose consciousness is diverted and turned aside into a world which becomes daily more confusing, more presupposing, more deceitful, and less like their own God Presence because the momentums that have builded and are building are destructive momentums and they cannot possibly externalize the will of God.

SPIRITUAL VISION IS NEEDED

The constructive momentums of light are taught to our disciples in our retreats throughout the world. Many of you in your finer vehicles join us at night, and there you are wearing robes of light. You take instruction in our inner classes and return with refreshment to the world of form, there to cope with the problems of the day and master them. Some of you, not aware of the great value of coming to our retreat, pass on into the astral realm and abide in the realm of dreams, there to enter in and tie into those worlds of other individuals who have not mastered but are only human individuals or discarnate entities who have not yet made their ascension.

Blessed and beloved ones, so needful is God-understanding to the earth that, in the words of the Great Divine Director, I say to you today, it is very important that you realize that even material knowledge about the earth upon which you live is scarcely externalized by the wisest individual upon the planet. For there are very few who even have a momentum of understanding concerning the various countries and nations of the world and the people that dwell therein and their customs. How, then, can they expect to understand our octave and the realm of light?

The words "Study to show thyself approved unto God, a workman who needs not to be ashamed, rightly dividing the word of truth"[1] is our benediction, coming long ago through Hilarion when his embodiment as Saint Paul made so many individuals aware of the great law of God. And the early Christian church was blessed by this selfsame Saint Paul, who brought to mankind an understanding of the law of God. Saint Paul, as so many of you know, at one time persecuted the Christian church as Saul of Tarsus. And as he passed along the road to Damascus, the beloved ascended master Jesus appeared to him in a great cloud of glory and said to him, "Saul, Saul, it is hard for thee to kick against the pricks." And so Saul arose and was blind until the word was given unto him, "Brother Saul, receive thy sight."[2]

Beloved and blessed ones, the mankind of earth who are blessed with physical vision have need as never before for spiritual vision. And even among those students of the light who have studied for years and pursue the spiritual path, there is a need for an expanded spiritual vision, a need for an expansion of the frontiers of hope until they shall realize that the God Presence of them is all-enfolding, all-encompassing, and cognizant and aware of all the problems with which they deal daily.

THE LAW OF GOD IS A LAW OF LOVE

The law of God is a blessed law. The will of God is good. And the peace of God will seal you against the intrusion of those particular thoughts and feelings which bring you so much pain and distress—if you will only make the calls and necessary applications without accepting a feeling of despair, which floats around in the atmosphere from the feeling world and thought world of many individuals who have not yet come to a place where they can realize the great cosmic qualities of God's will. The divine will, the eternal will, is omnipresent within human consciousness. It interpenetrates the cells of the body, it causes the heart to beat, and it expands our God-feeling everywhere I AM.

Blessed and beloved ones, I, Morya El, Lord of love's first ray, salute you, then, here in London. And I bring you the great peace of the Darjeeling Brotherhood. I bring you our God-feeling of reverence for the will of God, our great God-feeling of devotion to the will of God, and the intensity of our concentration that this will shall one day manifest among mankind as a flaming fire that floods the heart and the feeling world of all men until they will adore, as we do, that sacred will of God.

Mankind comport themselves in a very discordant manner, for they do not realize that their thoughts and feelings are registered upon their records in a very accurate manner and that one day—sometime, someplace—these same records will return to them for redemption. They do not realize that all the good, the virtue, and the lovely things which they externalize in their world will also one day return to bless and to heal them and every part of life. Such is the great law of God. But there is a greater law. It is the law of love.

The law of God is a law of love when correctly understood. It is true that men have free will. It is true that they have abused this free will. It is also true that they may return from this abuse and turn once and for all to their own God Presence, their mighty I AM Presence (depicted solely there upon this beautiful chart*), and that they may realize and enter into the stillness of the Great Solar Quiet until, in loving adoration, as does every great angel deva, they may draw forth the sacred fire within their own heart and flood its radiance through their body, their physical world, their mind and their affairs until the peace that is produced is the peace of which Jesus spoke and the peace which all the Brotherhood continually adore.[3]

*The Chart of Your Divine Self. See www.SummitLighthouse.org/IAMPresenceChart.

YOU SHALL ARISE ON WINGS OF GRATITUDE

O thou victorious will of God, thou radiance of the snow-capped summit, as I gaze upon the loveliness here at Darjeeling, the peace that comes to me and to our Brotherhood in our retreat and passeth and externalizeth divine understanding,[4] I AM grateful for thy being! I am grateful for thy existence, O God. I am grateful for thy will. I am grateful for the hearts of men that are receptive the world around to our vibration, to our vibratory action, and to the knowledge of the sacred fire. I am grateful for humility. I am grateful for gratitude.

Blessed ones, on wings of gratitude you shall arise into the will of God, you shall revere the will of God, you shall externalize it. And one day, when mankind have won their victory, those of you in the vanguard of light's perception shall be grateful forever that you rendered a service to the earth and assisted the other evolutions who came behind you in entering into the joy of their perfection.

Individuals today who through crass commercialization produce in mankind a feeling of frustration and fear, who produce in mankind desires that are inordinate, who produce in mankind hatred and strife—these too shall reap, as they have in the past, the rewards of their own doings.[5] But I am certain and confident that those who love light as we do will realize that we speak in reality and in truth. We are divine beings living still, eternally living within the sacred fire, and eternally manifest upon earth.

ENTER IN TO A NEW ERA OF DEVOTION

As I said quite some years ago, I have stood in many dingy halls, I have stood beside many a lecturer upon the platform. Blessed and beloved ones, tonight I am standing here in London blazing a consciousness of God and God's goodness out into the atmosphere of this city. And I ask in the name of God, calling now to the angels of divine goodwill, to carry abroad the glad tidings of God's will to all the earth that mankind may lift their head from a sense of lethargy and frustration until they shall realize that all that man has done has never put out the light of God, has never bedimmed the radiance of the sacred fire, and never shall; until they shall realize that that which men have externalized that is not virtue has only returned to their own doorstep by the law of the circle, having come again for redemption back to them.

And I ask, therefore, in the name of Almighty God that those of you who have the reverence and the desire to be that which God the Father, your Father and mine, would have you be shall enter in to a new era of devotion, a new era of God-peace, a new era of love when you shall recognize that the power of light is far more glorious than the power of the night; for this is but an absence of the light.

And one day the shadow shall disappear in the supreme glory of our radiance, and you shall know what it means to walk with the Brotherhood at Darjeeling. You shall know what it means to walk with men whose hearts yearn only to see men free—free from limitation, free from a sense of discrimination, free from ego, free from human consciousness, and manifesting the powers and the victory which is given to all who love the will of God and will take the energy and the time to externalize it among mankind.

I AM YOUR FRIEND

I thank you for your attention, I thank you for your love of the light, I thank you for your presence here, and I ask you to remember that I am a cosmic being, that I am an ascended master, that I am your friend so long as you adore that will. For there is no other power in the universe that can act except the will of God, which goodness surrounds you now.

I seal you in a mantle of Cosmic Christ peace, and I bless you tonight with the love of those who join me in chanting—unheard by your physical ears—a chorus of infinite devotion to the eternal purposes themselves; for these purposes are worthy of your attention.

People of this earth, thank you. May the angelic hosts and the ascended hosts surround you always and keep your goings and comings until you enter that state of consciousness equal to my own. And I care not if you surpass it; for in adoration to my own divinity, I give all that I AM to the service of the light—to the service that raises, that lifts, that transmutes, and makes hearts reverent, happy, and God-free.

Thank you, and good night.

April 1961
London, Ontario, Canada
MLP

CHAPTER 7

The will of God is ever present, never still,
constantly moving, progressing man
minute by minute into all the glory of eternity,
the never-ceasing reverberations of the Cosmic Voice
which originally reached forth into the void
and sounded forth the Word:
"Let there be light: and there was light."

CHAPTER 7

THE WILL OF GOD: A PRECIOUS TREASURE MINED FROM THE HEART

Good evening, ladies and gentlemen, and greetings to you in the name of the infinite, all-pervading Spirit of God. From the heart of our Temple of Good Will here in Darjeeling, I am speaking to you and breathing out an infinite sense of the will of God.

Among you are some who have gazed upon the sea, and in gazing upon the sea you have observed a crest of light upon the waves—this crest of light composed of the spiritual fragmentation of divine energies pouring from the sun or reflected by the moon, as the case may be, but composed of light. I would like to bring to your consciousness this night a sense that you are also projected forth from the Great Central Sun, fragments of divine substance, fragments containing within them the seeds of the will of God. Sacred, then, to the Father are you. And as you envision yourselves as made in his image,[1] you are able to obtain and retain that divine sense which will enable you to walk the earth as God.

Each of you was called, as was the Christ known to you as Jesus, to be sons and daughters of the Most High God. The Spirit of the Great White Brotherhood is abroad throughout the earth tonight as the Spirit of the Cosmic Christ. To enfold mankind in an image of themselves, of their spiritual selves, we come that men may obtain the inheritance of the elect, that they may wear those robes that are white,[2] that are pure, that are sacred, for which cause they came into the world and for which cause they obtained the divine energy of God and that eternal substance which gave them and does give to all a sense of being and be-ness.

Ladies and gentlemen, you are not your own. You are composed of the sacred Eucharist of God. You are the great leaven of the Christ. You are a manifestation of his perfection. You are called in this hour to a realization of the will of God made manifest in every atom and cell of your being. To manifest the power of God is to blaze forth light. To blaze forth light is to give no dominion whatsoever to that which is less than the perfection of your own immortality.

I AM INTENSIFYING THE SPIRIT OF LIBERTY

I am a blazing being of light, and yet today while I am speaking to you I am simultaneously able to appear in the home of a peasant child who is ill in India, not far from Darjeeling. And I am appearing in this home in the physical form, and yet to them I seem but an enrobed ascetic. For while I am speaking to you, simultaneously I am removing the scars of a leprosy from the body of this child that is before me. And a perfect healing is being performed and yet the people who are witnessing this are considering me to be but a wandering mendicant. They consider me to be but one of many of those unascended masters that wander about through the land of India.

They do not know that I am an ascended being and that shortly after I walk outside the doors and portals of this home my body will dissolve into pure ascended master light and my form, which seems so solid now, will not even seem to be. And yet simultaneously, while I am doing this act of mercy in the name of God, I am projecting the mighty light rays from Darjeeling onto the continent of North America to this city close to New York, where so many teeming millions of lifestreams are manifesting, and I am intensifying the Spirit of Liberty—the Spirit of Liberty, which is God.

As it has been recorded, "Now the Lord is that Spirit: and where the Spirit of the Lord is, there is Liberty."[3] I am intensifying tonight, therefore, the Spirit of Liberty to do the will of God, cutting mankind free from the idea that the will of man is superior to the will of God, because mankind have given substance and energy to their own wills for a long period of time and have generated thereby a momentum in much the same manner as a spiral of smoke rising up. But when the power of the infinite grace of God rushes in like a mighty rushing wind,[4] it dissipates this column of smoke which is merely human will. And it brings in the transcendent power and the light of God which does not and cannot fail, and all human will evaporates before the divine manifestation of the will of God.

This is in accordance with the divine law of being which is the same in India as in America, which is the same in China as in Peru, which is the same in the Inca Empire as in the empire of America, which is the same law that manifested upon Atlantis and upon Lemuria and in the days of old, and also is the selfsame law which manifests upon other planets—upon beloved Hesper, known to you as the planet Venus, from whence came Sanat Kumara long ago—or upon other systems of worlds and stars not even known to your astronomers.

THE BEAUTY OF THE WILL OF GOD

Blessed and beloved ones, the beauty of the will of God is in its unfolding expression, its outreach everywhere, and yet it is being made manifest, always being made manifest. This is in sidereal time. It is in mankind's consciousness, in the consciousness of man which gradually assimilates the divine nourishment and gradually emerges from the mortal image of a small and tiny child unto the immortal image of a Manchild, a living Christ, a transcendent immortal being no longer wearing the swaddling garments of mortality and mere human fecundity but manifesting the propensities of heaven—the beauty, the wisdom, the love, and the compassion of God.

All this I AM, but all this is implanted within your hearts and within the hearts of all mankind as a diamond surrounded by coal, surrounded by carbons. The precious treasure must be mined from the heart of the earth and then polished by the jeweler's craft until, by the cut and by the power of discrimination, mankind learn to polish the diamond brilliance of the will of God and there emerges into manifestation a beautiful jewel of a life's perfection, of a Christ, a Buddha, a shining orb to appear upon the surface of the earth and to spread the light upon the sea of humanity, the crest upon the waves, the shining garments of immortality, and all the beauty that cannot be bedimmed by human tears or human thought. All of this comes into manifestation because of belief, faith, love, and the power of love in action.

The will of God is thus ever present, never still, constantly moving, progressing man minute by minute into all the glory of eternity, the never-ceasing reverberations of the Cosmic Voice which originally reached forth into the void and sounded forth the Word: "'Let there be light: and there was light';[5] let there be love: and there was love; let there be wisdom: and there was wisdom"—the triune omnipresence, omniscience, omnipotence of God all sealed in the triangle of perfection within the sacred circle of the will of God, the hallowed precinct of divinity within which are all things and without which nothing exists.[6]

GIVE YOUR ALLEGIANCE TO GOD

In the name of God, in the name of the Great White Brotherhood, by the power of the sacred fire, I, Morya El, Lord of love's first ray, speak from the Darjeeling Council (for I have now returned here to the council table), and as I stand before the council table seeing before me the record of mankind's frightful misuse of energy and knowing that the time is short for this civilization—I urge again the intensification by mortal consciousness of invoking and submitting the supreme fiat of the will of God as ruler over all human mandates. I ask you and urge you in God's name, give your allegiance to God, your own mighty I AM Presence. Give your unshakable faith to the masters of wisdom. And externalize in this land and throughout the earth the great kingdom of God, the immortal kingdom of love wherein the constitutions and the mandates of man, the Magna Cartas of man, become the charters of divinity.

As Columbus charted his course across an unknown sea, so all mankind by faith today in my word, which is not mine but the Word of God, shall accept the gift of God and under the aegis of the Father, under the crown of life, shall externalize among the family of nations a perfect world, a utopia, the paradise of God among men. And then upon this mansion, which is but one of my Father's mansions[7] and your Father's mansions, the will of God will be done and brother shall no longer hate brother but love shall permeate all life and the animals themselves shall no longer express the ferocity of man but the will of God shall be done everywhere. And then untrammeled through the great continents of the air shall come the mighty rushing wind of the Holy Spirit to crown this civilization with all that science alone could not give, with all that education alone could not give, and with all that human romance alone could not give—the Father's love manifest as the Father's will.

With this sacred vibration, in the name of the Council of Light, I, Morya El of the Darjeeling Council, say to you all in the name of Christ: Peace, peace profound.

September 16, 1961
Long Island, New York
MLP

CHAPTER 8

We cherish the victory of each individual manifestation of the God flame. . . . For we are one with the Father and one with thee; therefore thy ascension is ours—our victory, the expansion of the God consciousness within us as well as within you.

CHAPTER 8

WE ARE ONE WITH YOU IN YOUR VICTORY

Heart friends of the ages, my beloved ones and cherished chelas, I speak to you today through the threefold flame within your hearts by the mighty radiance and power of the flame of the will of God focused here in Darjeeling. I manifest within you the power of my love and my being, my heartfelt consideration for your lifestreams, that mighty blue-flame power which enfolds you and shall continue to enfold you until the hour of your ascension day. The Father of thy being—the mighty Father of Light who knoweth that day and hour of each individual manifestation, the hour of victory—is manifest within you through the flaming power of good will which I am flooding forth, then, into thy consciousness this day.

O children of the one eternal flame, rise to acknowledge that flame, the threefold flame within you, and realize that it is your certain victory. [Audience rises.] Realize that you are magnificent God-beings at this hour and that as God-beings, you are held within the chalice of our attention, our consciousness. Beloved Saint Germain has brought to you this day a manifestation of his love through the freedom flame which you have invoked.

And abiding within this flame, therefore, you retain the flame of his will and the good will within his heart. Mother Mary surrounds you also with her love, her immaculate concept of thy victory.

We cherish the victory of each individual manifestation of the God flame; for it is, in a sense and in truth, our own selves in manifestation. For we are one with the Father and one with thee; therefore thy ascension is ours—our victory, the expansion of the God consciousness within us as well as within you. Realize this, that your victory of each hour of each day then is our victory, too, and we are standing and upholding that victory within you. By the power and the flame of the mighty God Victory from the planet Venus, we enfold you and we flood into your worlds each day that power of victory which sustains you unto your ultimate completion of the ascension. (Won't you please be seated.)

As I gaze upon the hills from our retreat in Darjeeling and I see the glistening white light of the peaks as they rise to the heavens and the blue of the sky, I am reminded of how the flame of good will is manifest in the world of form through the hearts of the people aspiring unto heights of greater loveliness, nobility, and truth. And so it is. Each heart flame rises to the summit of its own capacity in the heart of the mighty I AM Presence and floods forth the radiance—the fountainlike, scintillating rays of the blue-flame will which descend, then, as the gentle rain and fall unto the place beneath into the hearts of the people who have not yet reached or attained that divine summit but who feel the precious offering of those hearts who have.

And therefore, remember the lesser manifestations of God upon earth in your daily thoughts and meditations and decrees, and realize that as you pursue the summit within you, you are helping and assisting those lesser forms to rise also and that as you rise, they must rise. For you are one, even as we are one with you in your victory. So you must hold up and bring up the earth as you go forward in the light. And so you see that all life is one, and the victory of each individual is the victory of every other manifestation of life.

Feel this closeness with the hearts of all, with the leaves and the plants and the flowers, with the very earth and the air you breathe. Feel your consciousness as one, one with the earth—the Mother of the earth, beloved Virgo—one with the air elementals, for they are a part of your being and so your victory assists them. You are one with the flame of the Holy Spirit which beats the hearts of all. You are manifestations of that one eternal flame of the sacred fire.

Therefore, claim it and manifest it as your own and know that every decree which you send forth with the flame of the will of God is a fiat unto all life and connects you with the hearts of all mankind and with the flames upon the altars of elemental life. Realize that you are intimately associated with each manifestation, with each flame, and feel your momentum of God-victory and of mercy qualifying each one, releasing and freeing each part of life to manifest the God-dominion of the mighty flame of victory.

As I take my leave of you this day, I seal you, each one, upon the forehead with that mighty flame of victory manifest as the will of God—the will within you to do God's will, to carry forward the work of beloved Saint Germain, beloved Mother Mary, started so long ago and manifest in consecration throughout many embodiments. I seal you in our God-momentum of victory.

Bear it, uphold it, manifest it, and glorify God in each step, in each walk as you pursue the way of the summit, the way of God's divine victory upon earth.

I thank you, blessed ones, for your consecration. And I bid you good day from the halls of Darjeeling.

April 4, 1964
Holytree House
Fairfax, Virginia
Elizabeth Clare Prophet (ECP)

CHAPTER 9

Yours is the pure spirit of evolution—evolving from a pinch of dust to become a star, evolving from a drop of water to become the atmosphere of a planet, evolving from a pinch of dust to become a gem that fills interstellar space with a magnificence of spiral nebulae and all its sparkling rainbow color. You, then, are charged with the holy atmosphere and breath of life.

CHAPTER 9

MINARETS OF OUR ABODE

Gracious ones of the light, the penetration of the heart by arrows of light bringeth no pain to the soul but assuages, in part, human grief and brings awareness of the will of God before the screen of consciousness.

History, the dust of the century, has spun a human snarl. And we are left to untangle the threads? I think not. For we are not alone, being somewhat less involved than those of you who wear mortal garb. Yet all are linked to the planetary destiny whose responses of soul, mind, and heart can consecrate each day as a burst of new endeavor for and on behalf of immortal principle.

As we discuss principle, we are aware that the area of the principle is like a plastic or elastic balloon. For some it is limited to the size of a marble or a pinhead, and for others it expands to take in the cosmic domain. More is the pity, then, for those who have shrunk in size. And blessed be those who have the expansion of soul and the principle to maintain it, that in this hour and in this solemn moment are aware of the great cosmic need for perseverance.

As I contemplate the outbreath of the holy will of God, as I perceive the vestments of his love trailing from eternity into the dust of the present moment, I am saturated—not with self-pity but with compassion for the Infinite One, who has given so much unto his creation and received so little bonus in return. Yet, as a part of the infinite band, I am constrained to hold with that almighty hope which has kept alive the feeble and flickering aspirations of mankind at those moments when it seemed as though the thread of destiny would be broken and the very vessel of reality dashed in pieces before the eyes of mankind, as a potter's vessel, and broken.

But the great wheel of life has continued to turn, and the urn has been reshapen countless times. And so, to the present moment we hold with that earnesty* of soul and resolve that shall reinforce the destiny of the planet and reconsecrate mankind daily to the holy will of God that is above and beyond the mortal dream, spinning both now and forever those concepts of which the immaculate perceptions of life are made.

Mortal concepts, then, pale into insignificance. And as the flowers of the summer fade in the fall and mingle with the dust, so mortal concepts continue to turn and return to the screen of manifestation without accomplishing the illustrious purpose of becoming an immortelle.

Yet the children of God's heart have gone forth robed as in springtime with the splendor of color, the splendor of hope, and the radiance of God's appearance. The little parts, the small externalizations and portions of the great cosmic dream which all have expressed, are cause for rejoicing in cosmic octaves. And so the gleam of hope in the eye of a child is more illustrious to the heart of God than the most beautiful gem locked in the mountain. For behold, from this gleam in the eye of a child is born new hope

---

*At times the masters use language of an earlier embodiment. The word *earnesty* is now archaic.

which shall expand to conquer the world and the universe.

Maturity, then, comes to all who will reach out hands of aspiration and grasp our own. The years that seem to pall upon the senses are but the result of human vanity and involvement in senseless egocentricity, whereas the beauty of the appearing of the Christ arrays each day in the splendor of the morning. And the radiance of golden hope is shed abroad with the mellowness of soul which saith unto all: The fruit of the spirit is the earnest fulfillment of striving. And without it, thou canst not but avoid riding upon the camel with his humps across the mountain and receiving the jostling of the spirit in the marketplaces of life, crowded with the aspirations of men who, in banal competition, understand not the way to our abode.

A NEW HOPE

We come, then, today with the tinkling bells of joy and cosmic merriment flooding our soul. We see here, in the great spiritual marts of God, a new hope born as hearts mount up with crescendos of divine harmony and realize and cognize that the strands of spiritual substance, which seem to be invisible to many, are indeed of greater strength than all of that fiber which mankind can muster in the hemp mills and jute mills of life.

Most gracious ones, uphold then the beauty of the divine concept. Perceive the light upon the mountains. And feel the essence of the Rose of Sharon borne on the soft winds of life that sweep the soul into the rapture of attainment and free mankind from the senseless amusements that pall upon the senses.

How beautiful, then, is the light of God within the heart. How beautiful is his beauty trembling as mercury in the cup of the mind. Thus, there is flashed across the existence of man the meteoric rise of the Christ image, and man is transformed by the image from day unto day. And all are called but few choose to externalize. And as children, they prattle to one another saying, "Come and dance to our tune." Yet they have nothing to play except human discord.

Why, then, will the musicians of life continually pipe to one another that which is banal, that which is without the element of cosmic suspense? The great unfolding drama continues to thrill and enthrall the heart of the angels. Why will the hearts of men, so close to the angels, continue to outpicture human banalities and retreat from the great challenges of life?

I think it is high time that the soul no longer shall shrink as a pea in a pod, dried out upon the vine, but it shall expand and expand and expand to take in the lustrous splendor of our abode, the renewed hope of consecration and freedom from the densities of mortal thought. You must cast them aside, else your heads shall be as gourds rattling, rattling, and rattling with emptiness. After a while, precious ones, it shall come to pass that even the dried beans within the head shall cease to rattle, for they shall break apart their substance and nothing but emptiness shall remain.

It is, then, very senseless for mankind to be asleep. It is most important that mankind shall be awake and envision the worlds to conquer! The time is now, and this is ripe for the picking. Mankind must recognize that the harvest is at hand. They must become imbued with the Spirit of God.

THE HOLY WILL OF GOD

And now, moving aside from one manner unto another, I come to you to speak of the holy will of God. The will of God is not a limpid pool. It is not one in which men contemplate suicide. It is not one before which men stand and say in holy awe, "This I cannot fathom." For the will of God is plain and simple as Puritan victuals.

It is given to mankind to recognize, then, that simple virtue in the heart of a knave or a peasant is the same virtue as in the heart of a king, and all can imbibe the crumbs that fall from the Lord's table. And perhaps, then, as they partake of these morsels, they shall grow up to sit at that table and to eat the marriage feast of the Most High God.

The Sacred Eucharist is at hand. Those who will discern the Lord's body are able to partake of the Grail consciousness. In the image of the Holy Grail is the symbol of the Table Round. And as in England of old when I, as the son of Uther Pendragon, withdrew the sword, so to the present hour I uphold the sacred will of that sword of the Word that cuts both ways—quickening mankind in their aspirations and also quickening them in their spiritual aspirations. For mortal aspirations also require quickening. For many among mankind are lethargic, and as molasses in a jar they turn only when heat is applied and begin to run.

Let men, then, recognize that the honey of life is always preserved immaculate. And the honey of God's will spoileth not but tasteth as sweet to this hour as it did the day it was released from the hive on high. And the divine bees continue to do the Lord's bees-ness.

And I hope that mankind will recognize that they also ought to be about the Father's business[1] and cease to be so overly concerned about their own. For when they identify themselves with the Father's business, they are less concerned with their own, for they have made the Father's business their own. And then they have that right concern which can mount up without limitation and expand and expand and expand, as a treatise which I would like to release but never find the auditors who will be content to listen as long as I would like to expound (except at levels celestial where they are somewhat, as students in a classroom, confined to their seats when I preside at a presidium).

Therefore, I say to you today that I shall take fullest advantage of this opportunity to expand and expound upon the will of God and the great frustrations that might have been if God had been other than himself and had been manlike, rather than a manifestation of pure and holy will.

You see, precious ones, mankind have so much envisioned God as an image of themselves that they have created a God and a will made more in their image than in the image of God and his likeness. And in this almost dolorous concept, at times they have been unhappy, and rightly so, with that which has been evoked.

But God is none of these. Being fashioned, then, as a creator rather than a created being, he is diligent still to release of his substance to those who love his will in preference to their own and are content to relax their vigilance to guard the citadel of their mortal self when they are confronted with the great power of holy truth and its radiant release.

Preferring, then, the truth of God to the truth of themselves, they make that truth their own, and they are content to be consecrated to God whilst they are within the aura of our radiation. And then, subsequently, as they pass into the marketplaces of life and become once again imbued with the contaminating influences of the outer selves of mankind and mortal concepts, they become somewhat as a knave rather than the king's son. And they find themselves once again running as a rat in a maze, and they find in that maze no divine amazement or wonder but a continual concept which they call a "rat race."

And I do not think that your beloved Saint Germain is at all content with this idea. For he would not have mankind express the treadmill existence of a rat race, but rather would see mankind express the regenerate powers of a holy Christ going forward to accomplish a mission in the holy name of God without ceasing.

Pray, then, without ceasing. But let it not be a "preying" upon mankind or one another but a praying forth of light unto light—a praying that the rainbow of promise which God envisioned in the Beginning will cycle out throughout all ages and produce the perfection of the unfailing light of God that might continually reconsecrate those who are indeed knights of the Table Round.

Those ladies of the courts of heaven should also be consecrated, then, to the nobility of Saint Germain and to the outpicturing of the celestial aura and the adorning of mankind with the radiant jewels of life's perfection, which are not of necessity outward. But when worn as outward symbols, these are only symbols of the renewed grace of the heart which is continually the adorning and fashion both of womankind and mankind.

For the jewels of life which are before us are congealed cosmic energy. And they hold an immaculate pattern, if mankind will recognize it, which enables those who employ these jewels properly to advance according to their use of these congealed light rays, according to the sacred-fire instruction which is hidden in the lesser mysteries and also is expounded on at greater length in the greater mysteries.

A MIGHTY RADIATION IN YOUR MIDST

Now, the Brotherhood would invoke a mighty radiation of the will of God in your midst this morning. And I am, therefore, calling unto the blue-flame angels to surround this place with a sacred-fire jewel, scintillating in all of its splendor. In the center of this jewel there is projected from the Godhead a fiat, the fiat of the lost and creative Word. This great fiat of light that pours forth to the universe, from the beginning unto the end, from the heart of Alpha unto the heart of Omega, is then being released in the eternal Now to surround this place with an aura of azure blue and the deeper blue of the magnificent love of God which is the sacred-fire power of the holy will.

Let me, then, ask you: Do you wish to retain in yourselves the memory of pain and of unhappiness? I think not!

Will you, then, take your hands and hold them at about the level of your heart and shake from your fingertips those drops of dusty substance which, as mud rather than light, have caused you all so much grief and pain throughout your many embodiments? Shake them off! They do not belong to you, they have no part of you, they are no part of reality!

Stand erect then! And do not feel that the ravages of age have caused you some pain. Are you not immortal spirits rather than individuals who have come under the power of burden to cause your backs to resemble the hunchback of Notre Dame? I think not!

Cast off, then, all these burdens! Whose are they? Do they belong to God? I think not. Do they belong to the angels? I think not. How would they, precious ones, fly throughout the wondrous atmosphere of heaven if they bore burdens such as these? Whence come these burdens, then? They come from the weight of the mind.

Remember the words of the Christ: "Take my yoke upon you and learn of me, for I am meek and lowly. Take my yoke upon you and learn of me, for my burden is light."[2] Does light have weight? I think not. But it has energy, and as energy it can cause you to feel the pristine power of the holy will that saith unto all: Go forth and do! Be accomplishers in this world of form. Do mighty works in this day!

For mighty men and women still inhabit the earth and they can sit, as with the Christ, at the council table. They can sit with all the ascended host. They can sit at this mighty Table Round and fill the pledge of old—the pledge to the sword of truth, the pledge to righteousness, the pledge to consecration itself. And the holy will can expand and expound in heart and mind until the cherished ideals which God has thought become also the property of every mind!

These thoughts, these ideals are not confined to God alone. He has freely given them unto all who will receive, to all who thirst for that high adventure which he desires and is constrained to give. Day after day he releases this substance. And yet, as I remind you, you drink it in. Why not partake of it often? Remember, it is the communion cup of your own identity. You are no part of the miasma of the world. You are no part of that condition which mankind have absorbed into their feeling worlds with such disastrous results. (Will you please be seated.)

Now, then, may I take you with me upon my magic carpet into the land of India to our abode? Come, then, in your spiritual thoughts and see the minarets of our abode—gleaming marble, ivory white, like the tusks of a giant elephant. As in Mogul days, I see these minarets thrust high into the azure blue. I see the twinkling stars and the silvery moon beam down upon them. I see the waxing and waning of light. I see the cycles of life passing by.

But of what substance are these made? Grains of sand, grains of sand, the passing of the centuries through the hourglass of life —are they composed of these? I think not. For in atomic structure, wherever it be—whether it be anchored in thy physical body or anchored in the energies of thy mind—all substance that is given to thee, O mankind, is imprisoned* as splendor within thy being.

And so the tiny elementals, the body elemental, and the elementals of life serve the crying needs of this lusty planetary body. They serve and serve and serve and continue to serve, imprisoned as divine splendor within the orbits of your world—whirling electrons serving you day after day, hour after hour, moment after moment, without ceasing.

What, then, is that substance which composes our towers, our minarets? It is free electrons—electrons continually renewed by cosmic luminescence. No imprisoned electrons are in the minarets and substance of our buildings. In these etheric temples and in my home at Darjeeling, there is a continuation of a phosphorescent and fluorescent release of immortal glory from the heart of God.

And as his great heart pulsates with diastole and systole, there is the continual blinking, so rapidly that the eye cannot follow it, of the renewal which we call at times in jest "the changing of the guard." For these electrons do not remain fixed in one place as

*i.e., confined

yours do, but they continually return for repolarization to the heart of God. And they dance with joy and they dance with splendor, for so is immortal substance! In God there is naught but freedom and a continual release of *light, light, light* dancing with *joy, joy, joy,* whereas here men are prisoners and ploys and pawns upon the chess tables of life.

In the holy name of freedom, then, I say: Let us raise high the Holy Grail! Let us let the light from that Grail stream out before the eyes of humanity as the power of the regenerate Christ! Let us raise them in this age to the banner of freedom, the Maltese cross of your beloved Merlin, your beloved Saint Germain, the Great Alchemist of the ages! For two thousand years the banner of freedom is unfurled in his name, and I joyously in building this kingdom stand beside him.

I expect that the energies of mankind, bursting with hope, shall continue in this day and age to make their play for freedom! I believe that the ladies and knights of my court shall expand, and new men shall enter the lists* and new women shall take their place by their side. Noblesse oblige shall expand. And the jousting shall not be the mere ribald games of the court, but the jousting in the great field of life shall be for the upholding of cosmic banners for the par excellence of divine victory. It shall be for the achievement of freedom to elemental life, and for the thrust for the purpose which is the divine ideal as it stands enrobed in strands of descending holy light substance from the heart of Almighty God!

You say that you are vessels of clay. I say you are more. You are the imprisoned lightning of exiles, of the Mother of Exiles, of the heart of God, of the eternal Sonship. Yours is not the viciousness of revolution. Yours is the pure spirit of evolution—evolving from a pinch of dust to become a star, evolving from a drop of water to become the atmosphere of a planet, evolving from a pinch of dust to become a gem that fills interstellar space with a magnificence of

*an area for combat, as for jousting

spiral nebulae and all its sparkling rainbow color.

You, then, are charged with the holy atmosphere and breath of life. The great Paramātma, the out-breath of God, is your heritage! You join with me as I fling down the gauntlet of life before you! Will you accept the challenges of this hour? Will you go forth with renewed power, rightly disciplined by Wisdom's mind?

In the name of Almighty God, I say to you all: Do you think that Christ behavior is always epistled* in the lives of those who would be our followers? I think not! For if we were to submit to the tomes of mortality, we should often hang our heads at those who seem to represent us and do not.

We are Sons of the Most High God! Do you think that there is any room in us for calumny? or viciousness? or vindication? We would vindicate the law of God! We would vindicate the righteousness of God! And it needs no vindication, for it stands! And mankind will be broken by the rocks that will grind them to powder[3] if they do not rise to the summit of their being and evoke the pure radiance of the light from day to day so that they can stand the great glow-ray of the incoming golden age.

Why do you think, O mankind, the prophecy was made that mankind would call for the rocks to fall upon them?[4] It is because they could not stand the emerging light of the golden age. And they would seek to hide within the caves of materiality and conquest of finite things. Those who will keep their own spirit are greater than those that can keep a city. And I say to you, as the Christ did of old: They who will be faithful in a few things will be made ruler over many things.[5]

Think you that Almighty God is a man? Think you that the power that framed the universe is subject to the puny edicts of an ant race? I think not. And if men will be as the rock of ant concern, they will find themselves in a Lilliputian world. If they will rise from that, by dashing down the clay vessel upon the mountain

*i.e., recorded, written down in a letter; a word used in earlier centuries, now archaic

altar, they will find the summit of achievement is possible for the humblest child, who can be uplifted to behold God and Christ perfection.

This is the ascended masters' vision. Will you make it your own? It is possible. This I tell you today. And if you fail, it will not be because the powers of light are against you but because you have not availed yourselves of the opportunity presented now and each day.

I come today, then, not only to remind you of that which you already know, to declare some things that you have not properly understood, but I come also to make a compact of hearts.

Some of you are familiar with the Mayflower Compact, and there is one gentleman in this room who was present on board ship at the time the Mayflower Compact was written. I say to you, then, that you must understand that we would make a compact with you today to bind you to the holy will of God. And then, for Saint Germain's golden age, we can hope that it may flourish, that it may flower, and that as pilgrims you will go forward to make of America and the world—because ye are more than the holy twelve—a place of beauty, a paradise of perfection!

The power of heaven, the power of the angels, the power of the elementals is released, and I think the people of this state and the people of the world shall know, in due course of time, that it has been done.

Excalibur, go forth
And make a way for the will of God!
Excalibur, go forth
And make a way, as Aaron's rod!
Excalibur, go forth
And, with winged sandals, shod
The souls of those who seek to rise
And to apprize the opportunity before them.

Open their eyes that they may see,
Give them vision that they may be.
Purify and consecrate them now,
For to the light within them
Even I shall bow.

I thank you.

June 6, 1965
San Francisco, California
MLP

CHAPTER 10

In each blade of grass, in each flower,
in each dewdrop, there is holy purpose!
Do you think God creates for naught. . . ?
God creates for purpose.

CHAPTER 10

HOLY PURPOSE

Thy Word, O God, is a lamp unto my feet, a star of light that leadeth me unto thy Presence!

O God, in the temple of thy holy will, we salute thee this day. And I, El Morya, Chohan of the First Ray, do emanate forth the rays from the heart of the Father unto all men this day from our retreat in Darjeeling. And those brothers of light who serve with me here stand today in honor of his Presence, in honor of his coming, in honor of the Christ whose light bathes the earth in its iridescent radiance, the Christ light.

As on that Christmas Eve so long ago his star shone above to guide us to the place where the Incarnate Word was made manifest, so we salute that light this day, the light of the mighty I AM Presence, which shines above each manifestation in this world of form as a beacon pointing to the way of their divinity. And the Christ—the babe in consciousness, the babe in arms, the cradled one, the cradled lifestream in manifestation on earth below—must rise and rise again to become the child-man, the Manchild who shall go forth to rule the nations with a rod of iron.[1]

Beloved ones, you must determine to let the Christ in you arise and expand to manifest and to overcome all the senseless delays of the physical and the mental and emotional and etheric bodies which detain you and keep the Christ in you but an infant. It is time to arise, time to think, time to create, time to go forth—not as children but as men and women of light who have received the Word, who have received the penetration into the night, into the darkest gloom of consciousness, who have heard the call and seen the beacon, who will then rise and go forth to declare the word unto all men.

Beloved children of my heart, I who have stood with you throughout your many embodiments—I have stood with you and I have walked with you. I have been with you in trial, and I have been with you in time of testing.

You think that I do not hear. You think that I do not know the lispings of your hearts. You think that we who dwell in the tabernacle of God's holy will in Darjeeling do not perceive the lispings, the thoughts of each one upon earth. We do. And when each one upon earth rises, then, to a perception of the Christ, we are ready. We are ready to stand forth and to bestow an even greater impetus of the will to do that holy will of God, which was implanted in you in the beginning.

Sometimes we have been blocked for many a year concerning your lifestreams, and we have had to stand back and say, "This one will tarry for a while until he overcomes that condition." And we wait. And you think perhaps you are making progress, but we wait for the day when a certain concept, a certain idea, can be revealed unto you.

And when you accept that holy idea which is the gem of life, the gem of the will of God, when you receive that perception, then we can come forth and open wide the gates of your being to a greater dawning of illumination's flame, of the flame of divine love in manifestation. And we can say, "Ho! Here is one who is ready to go forth, to step through the veil, to come apart and to follow the divine calling as a priest or priestess of God at the altar of the Christ." And then we can take you by the hand once again and bring you onward in the march in the caravan of light, which ever moves forward toward the Central Sun, with many souls and many sons of God being brought into captivity.

Think not, precious ones, because you are called and in a heart center or in a holy activity that you have arrived. Many in the outer world who pursue the pathways of the world, who perhaps are in the churches of the outer world, are also upon the Path. Sometimes they respond even more to our proddings than those of our most intimate chelas, for they have not heard the spoken Word. The word that is the lamp unto their feet is only in written form, as the Holy Bible and other great writings of the world. They have not heard our voice and so they seek and yearn even more than do those who sit at our feet, for they have not yet seen the risen Christ or his appearing. They have not stood in his radiance to receive his mighty outpouring as you have been so blessed to receive.

And so, they push onward—onward and onward, through their own misconceptions, through their own untransmuted energies. And some of these among mankind are brave indeed! They are not dismayed by the forces of darkness or the forces which block them in their own worlds. They do not know the names for these nefarious conditions, but they know that they have the desire to do the will of God—and they do it despite all obstacles. These are our chosen ones also. These, also, comprise our starry band.

Therefore, think not that you have nothing more to do in this activity but to wait for your ascension, for you must push forward toward the mark to achieve the prize of your high calling.[2] For as you have been blessed with the higher responsibility, so you are responsible for even greater things than those who are in ignorance. But we have given you our love, beloved ones, and it is with you constantly. And so you have the power and illumination and the cohesive force of that love to go forth and to do the bidding of the holy will of God.

And do you know that as we rise to the dawning sun each day here in Darjeeling to receive the rays of the Holy One—to receive the essence of the sacred fire, that we may pour it forth unto men—that you who are our chosen ones may also receive that light? You may stand in attunement with your God Presence and receive from Darjeeling each morning those emanations which we have captured from the Father's heart, which we are ready to bestow upon all who are receptive.

Therefore, mark the dawning of God's holy will in you each day as the first ray of sunlight that you see through the glass of the window when you arise from bed. When you wake from sleeping consciousness and perceive the first golden-orb radiances of the sunlight, remember that from Darjeeling we are beaming to you the sacred-fire essence of God's holy will, those emanations which will give you the impetus, the power, the joy to go forward into the divine plan* which is prepared for you by your mighty I AM Presence and Holy Christ Self for each day and each hour, from this time forward, even forevermore.

For each erg of cosmic energy which goes forth has the pattern of God's divine will impressed upon it; and as you receive it, you can perceive its divine plan, also, and your holy mission to use that energy for that which God gave it unto you.

Holy purpose, to thee are we dedicated here in Darjeeling—the holy will of God, the purpose in all life. In each blade of grass, in each flower, in each dewdrop, there is holy purpose! Do you think God creates for naught, for idle time, for idle conversation? God creates for purpose. To find and know and keep that sacred covenant of his purpose is our holy charge, and we pass it unto you, even as ye are able to assist us in this mission.

*The divine plan is the plan of God for each soul. It can be released to the outer consciousness through application to the individual Christ Self, the I AM Presence, and the Great Divine Director.

We know, precious ones, that nothing can interfere with the divine plan in heaven and nothing can interfere with the divine plan upon earth—*if* mankind unascended so will it, *if* there are among mankind those who will stand and say, "I AM come to do thy will, O God!"

To find that holy will, to know the holy will—how it has been the love of our being for ages and ages—to serve the Presence of God, to serve his holy purpose! What higher calling is there? For God's will indeed illumines the plan of every ray of the divine spectrum. Every phase of divine appearing is governed by this holy principle, rooted in the mind of God, outpictured in the Christ mind in man, blossoming as the flower of the heart, the holy threefold flame.

Who can know how to use his talents without first perceiving the flame of God's will? It is indispensable, precious ones, that you know the heart of the Father as it pertains to your life and to your going forth.

You cannot choose a way upon earth and then say, "O God, is this thy will?" after you enter into contracts and circumstances which cannot be altered because of karmic reasons. It is before the fact that you must invoke the will of God, not after the fact. For how do you expect that we shall help you once you have used your free will to do as you please? This is not divine order, and this is not good thinking, precious ones, to expect that we can alter your lives after you have taken the decisions.

Therefore, when you arise invoke that flame of holy will, before you go forth, to determine your actions for the day. Once you are embroiled and enmeshed in the outer world, we cannot interfere with the cyclic course which you have set up within yourself, for it must unwind according to the cause-and-effect pattern which you yourself have set up. E'en though God hath set the greater pattern, it cannot come into focus within you without your call, without your beckon, without your heart's attention to the flame of God's holy will, which we are so privileged and blessed to hold and nourish for you until such time as you are ready to call upon us.

Let this sacred ritual, then, become part of your daily offering to the Most High God—that you reach to his heart to perceive and know all of the wonders of creation through the pathway of his holy will. And if you can remember but this sacred trust I give you this day, I shall not count my saying to have been in vain; for then I shall see and know that lives will be transformed, that many among you shall be sons of God brought unto captivity at the end of your embodiment through the ritual of your ascension. For if you truly walk the way of God's will, you cannot miss the Path, you cannot miss the calling of each of the seven rays, for each ray does follow that ordered cycle from the Father's heart.

And so, this is my message to you this day. Even as we followed the star to the place where Jesus lay, I come again then to point the way and to say to you that if you follow the star of your mighty I AM Presence and pursue it well, if you heed not the whisperings of the Herods and the earthly kings and the earthly powers but move on to find the Christ Child where he lay, you shall find your divine calling and your mission. You shall perceive it and you shall know it.

And in its knowing, the fiery essence of the will of God shall make it so beautiful and wondrous and magnificent in thy sight that thou shalt nevermore be able to refrain from outpicturing it in action. For this is the beauty of God's holy will—that it is so wondrous that man, once he has perceived it, cannot help but outpicture it! And if students of light are not outpicturing the holy will of God, it is because they have not perceived it to begin with. For to know God is to know his will, and to know his will is to perform it upon earth.

Beloved ones, you cannot separate action from knowing—they are one. And he who does not act does not truly know. I say this, and every ascended being says it with me, whether he be upon the first ray or another. For we know this to be true, and we have gained our ascension through this mighty precept.

And I say unto you: if you know not what to do, then pause and seek the flame of God's holy will, and then move forward and continue the race. Follow the star and arrive at the place where you will be the full outpicturing of the Christ in manifestation for all mankind to see and behold the only begotten of the Father come forth again in the second appearing and the third appearing and the millionth appearing, after each lifestream shall have also manifested likewise, until the entire earth shall become a diadem of stars—stars in such number that the entire universe shall see and know that the holy will of God, the will of the Christ, is come in each man into manifestation.

To this end do we serve in Darjeeling. To this end do we stand with the evolutions of this planet. Will you stand with me this day? [Audience rises.]

I thank you.

October 17, 1965
Beacon's Head
Vienna, Virginia
ECP

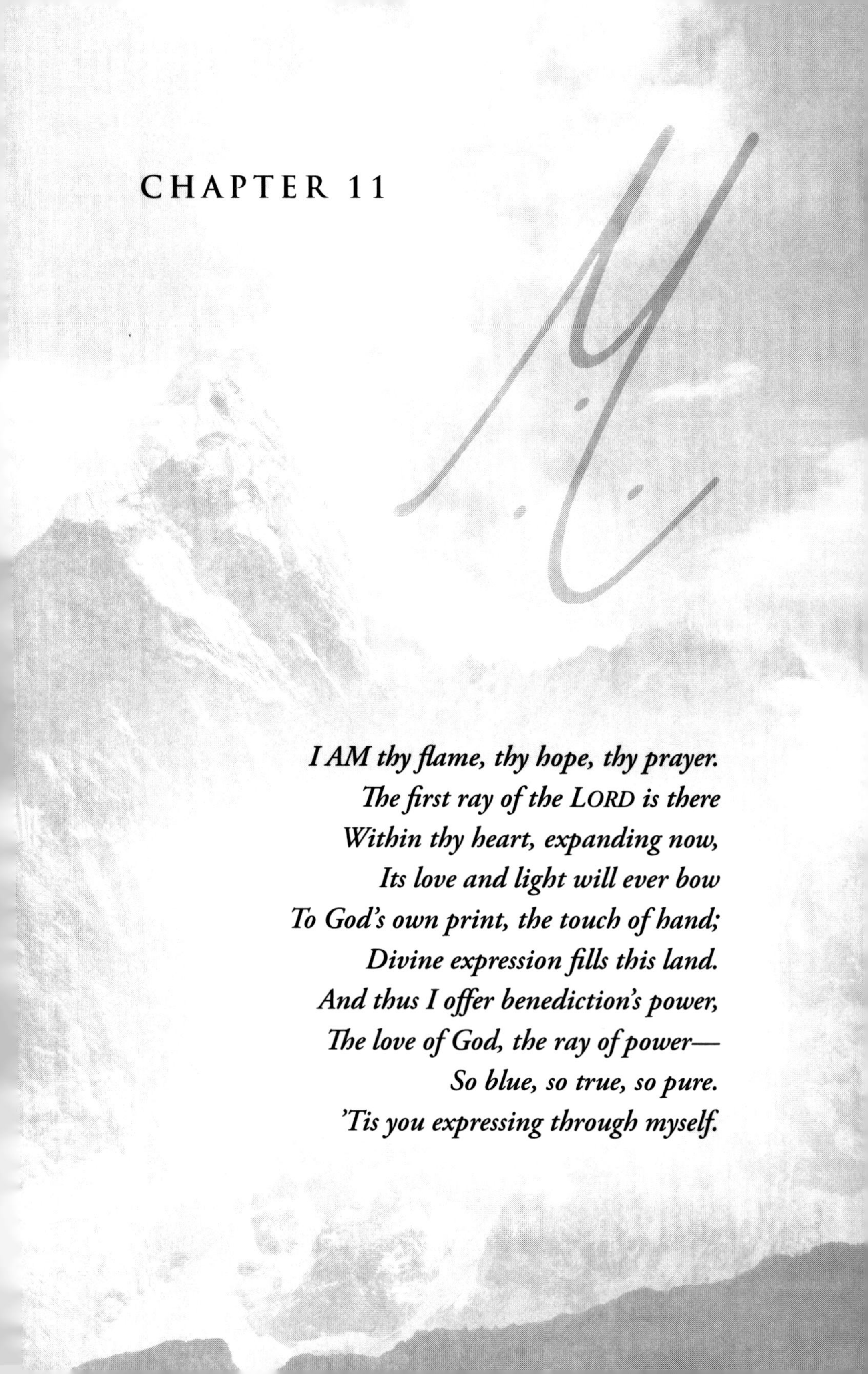

CHAPTER 11

I AM thy flame, thy hope, thy prayer.
The first ray of the LORD is there
Within thy heart, expanding now,
Its love and light will ever bow
To God's own print, the touch of hand;
Divine expression fills this land.
And thus I offer benediction's power,
The love of God, the ray of power—
So blue, so true, so pure.
'Tis you expressing through myself.

CHAPTER 11

BENEDICTION:

A PULSING FIRE SURGES THROUGH THEE!

The camels kneel,
The joy bells are ringing,
And in our retreat at Darjeeling,
The love ray is singing.
The melody of infinity
Directs the heart to rise;
The melody of infinity
Is beamed from holy skies.

I AM thy flame, thy hope, thy prayer.
The first ray of the LORD is there
Within thy heart, expanding now,
Its love and light will ever bow
To God's own print, the touch of hand;
Divine expression fills this land.
And thus I offer benediction's power,
The love of God, the ray of power—
So blue, so true, so pure.
'Tis you expressing through myself.

I act as Lord of love's first ray,
To take the pain from hearts away.
And with severe expression bold,
I hold the light of heavenly gold—
Infinite wisdom.
Flaming then,
The pink ray expands with blue
And then transmutation for the few
Expands, the many to free.

I AM thyself in action for eternity!
The hosts at Darjeeling thank thee
And the camels continue to kneel,
As the lower expressions of life
Carry the burdens
Of the higher expressions of life.
For there is no servility
But only the opportunity
To raise the life expressions
In their myriad manifestations.
Bear with me,
For soon you shall be free
From radiations strong
And enter into higher song
If you care to retain
The flavor of the Lord.

The world awaits
And with it, are you bored?
'Twould be a good thing, methinks,
If at times you would cease to drink
Of all the goodliness of earth
And feel the weight of cosmic worth.

Within thy hand it is a key
That life commands—
Be free, be free, be free!

O thou thy Great Divine Director,
Majestic were thy words.[1]
We are grateful for thy presence
In the universe
And for the courage,
Which like a lion did express
A roar of worlds afar.
Thou didst inflame our heart
As radiance flooded from thy Star.
Come now and benediction make!
Let earth her vanity forsake
And take the joy that is the LORD's,
To be adored forevermore.

O Presence great, Divine Self renew
Our covenant for the sacred few,
That the Brotherhood in White
May take delight tonight
By initiating many of these blessed chelas
Into the octaves of power and peace,
And service bold
Made for God, the Ancient One of old.
Free mankind from fear and every tear
And let them know that God is here,
His love is near.
His flame so great will triumph make
For all the expressions of the LORD.
Grace, grace, O grace adored.

I thank thee, and I call forth
The benediction of the holy seven Kumaras
Upon all that are here.
As each flame is extinguished upon this altar,
A flame shall rise, a measure high
Within every individual in this room
Who will believe and receive
This message that shall chase all gloom
And make them know that God is here
And know the way to cast out fear.
Watch, then, and behold,
And see how God will be to thee,
Not only now but for eternity.

Accept the flame within thy heart
That makes a new and fresh start.
Right now accept it!

As I extinguish this one flame,
A pulsing fire surges through thee in God's name.
And when the fourteen candles rare
Have flashed their fire through thyself right here,
You shall know a freedom for this hour.
Whether you hold it or not
Will be determined by the power
Of your intent to hold it.

April 9, 1966
La Tourelle
Citadel of Freedom
Colorado Springs, Colorado
MLP

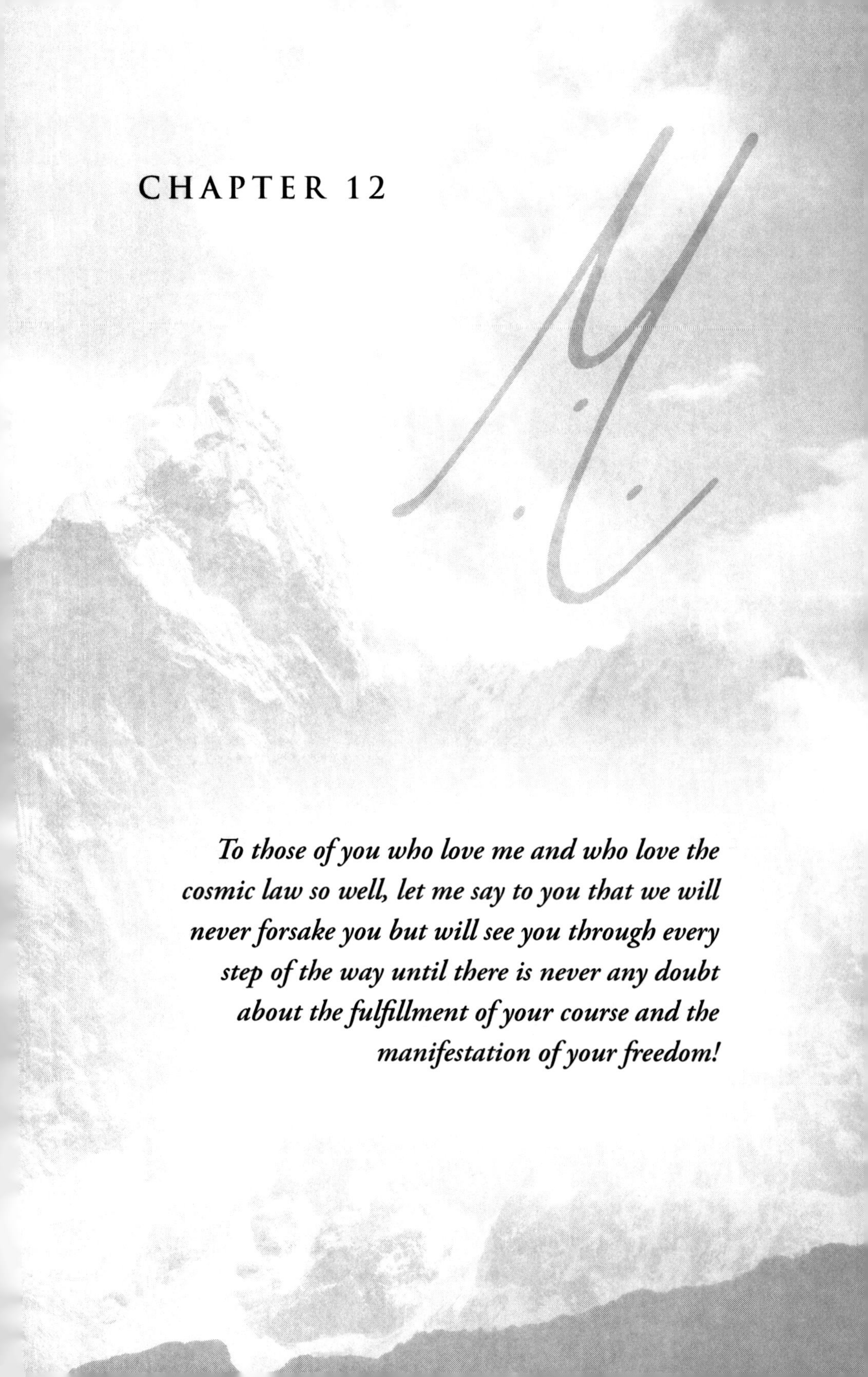

CHAPTER 12

To those of you who love me and who love the cosmic law so well, let me say to you that we will never forsake you but will see you through every step of the way until there is never any doubt about the fulfillment of your course and the manifestation of your freedom!

CHAPTER 12

THE ETERNAL VOWS OF YOUR SOUL MADE UNTO GOD

Thin are the chinks in the armour of men. The need for mankind to straighten their spines, to understand straight knowledge is great.

The wind from Darjeeling blows and brings the will of God into prominence. It comes as a white cloud. It is manifest all over the earth and yet men see it not, for they are not looking. Their eyes have turned away to other things, and in the den of the cockatrice mischief is created in their mind.

But the great ring of karma and the wheel of the Law breaks forth. And for the old, the tears upon their cheeks do speak to them of other times and other places when violations of the law of divine munificence took place and swept them away into the abyss, the abyss of mortal thought and feeling.

We hold the divine image. We hold the purity of the great white cube. We hold the purity of the Law, and the city of God is before us.

Tender is the hand of God over mankind, and yet the hardness of their hearts has prevented the infiltration of his love. His love is very great. His love is the ageless memory of himself in those days when the soul of God leaped for joy and the creation of all things was brought forth by the power of that love in action. Tender is the purity of God. Tender is the purity that soars in the soul as truth that makes men whole.

I come to you tonight, ladies and gentlemen, not as a phenomenon but as a real being, one who understands how you have cried out in the night for assistance, one who understands the secret places of your heart, one who understands, for I have known all human vicissitudes.

I have known the terrors that fly by night and the anguish of the soul by day. I have sought and I have been nourished by divine grace. And the milk of God's word has fed my soul until I have grown to become elder brother—yea, to become one whose love is manifesting upon this planet to assist men to understand the evocation of the will of God.

THE WILL OF GOD IS A MANTLE

The will of God is comforting. It is a mantle of great strength. It is woven out of the power of your aspirations. When your aspirations arise and the power of light within the atoms of your body come to a place where they desire to escape, there is a great surge as of an electric spark and there flashes forth from within your flesh form that which desires to reunite with the Greater Self.

Then there is an activity of peace. There is an activity of rending the veil. There is an activity that is pure because it exalts the soul, and the soul is glad to attain its freedom. Bound, thrice bound—yea, down through the ages in the vicissitudes and terrors of the flesh—the soul flies free and rejoiceth.

O ladies and gentlemen, in all peril that comes to mankind, the comforting presence of life is at hand. If only you will open up the power of faith within your world and understand that we speak in this basic simplicity in order to stir your souls and evoke therefrom a response according to the magnitude of your own heart!

I find here in this room some whose hearts are great and some whose hearts are small. In examining the auras of all of you, I commend you to your Divine Self and I say unto you all, your Divine Presence is your salvation and your light.

When you will understand the simplicity of a child, you will be able to come out from among mankind. And the things that now matter so much to yourselves will no longer matter, and the things that at present do not concern you will suddenly come into full concern. You will perceive upon the Path before you the great dawn of cosmic possibility when the realities of yourself will, as shining gems, be sought after, when the glory of the great cosmic law will come forth into fresh reality before the screen of your mind. And you will treasure it and you will ponder upon it and you will perceive it.

Behold, it shall come to pass that joy shall fly out over the waters and joy shall be like the shimmering sun upon the waters. And there shall be heat and a flash of light and you will find a reunion with the Higher Self—Principle of principles, divine principle fulfilled beyond the ken of mortal mind, beyond sense consciousness, beyond the stimulation of outer senses.

Therefore, the way will become clearer and clearer to you. And you will rejoice in the clarity of the light, as the light makes manifest to you all those hidden things that have been kept secret since the foundation of the world.

The world today knows not the power of our light. The world hungers after our light, and the world is thirsting after our light, yet mankind know not that which they seek.

The youth of the world today flash forth their consciousness in a flaming fury. They flash it forth in search of purity, and yet they are lured by the traps of sense consciousness until there is no reality that comes into their world but a vain search that is pounding, pounding, pounding in their ears like the surf itself upon the sands. And as the sands crumble away, so does their consciousness with the passing of the years crumble away into dissolution until there is nothing left but vanity.

Now, then, stands the great towering Christ image, the power of light which God envisioned, the power of light which is the faith that causes life to come into manifestation as God intends.

UNDERSTAND WHAT ARE THE ETERNAL GOALS, THE ETERNAL VALUES

I come this night by dispensation to talk to you of things that are the eternal vows of your soul made unto God in a day before you knew the dimness of human sense perception, in a day before you were entrapped and snared, as a fowler has trapped and snared the game. I call to your attention that the light of God that does not fail is the great reality of life.

(Oh yes, I am able to perceive your thought, young man, so clearly, so sweetly. But I shall not tell it or embarrass a soul, for I shall maintain my course. There are those who cannot do this, but they are swayed by the winds of the human mind.)

The fickleness and vanity of mortal thought has caused any number of individuals to tremble because they are afraid of what others will think of them. Let me tell you, precious ones, for you are precious unto God, that it does not make any difference what mankind think of you. What really counts is what your own Divine Presence and the Lords of Karma, the great lords charged with the reading of your karmic record, think of you. This is what is important! It is the requirement of the Great Law! It is the manifestation of eternal victory! It means your freedom and the freedom of every man.

I think that I have stood in the courts of kings. I think that I have stood with the great of the earth and I have perceived the thoughts of their heart and minds. I am not concerned with the puny ruck of mortal ant concern, but I am concerned with the soul, that like a bird in a cage it becomes free.

Open the doors, then, of the birdcage and let the soul fly free to understand what the eternal goals are, what the eternal values are, and what is the tranquility of life that will rock you to sleep, as a mother rocks a weeping child.

I tell you, precious ones, that the magnificence of God has fled from the souls of men, and yet there is a kindling and a sweeping of the earth, stirred by regenerate powers, powers of cosmic light.

Do you know that before this convocation and service began, there were legions of mighty angels gathered round this building, there were angels of blue-flame substance and angels of the beautiful substance of holy illumination, and there were angels of divine love and others who came to protect the mighty blessing being conveyed to you this night?

Ladies and gentlemen, a tribute to God is deserved from your soul, a tribute to God that will make you whole; a tribute to understanding that will unfurl the banner of our flag; a tribute to understanding that you need not create a drag upon the energies of others who would find their freedom now.

The day and the hour is come. The hour has struck.

The light of God does not fail!

The light of God does not fail!

The light of God does *not* fail!

The vision which I would give to you this night will not escape your mind if you will determine now to anchor it and to posit it in your world as an eternal value. It is the conveyance of one who has mastered life and would guide you with a flaming torch of progressive reality into your own fulfillment of cosmic destiny.

THE NEW CULTURE OF THE AGES

The light of God is around you. The light of God is around this city. And although there are those who are immune to it—by reason of the insulative force of their own consciousness, connected as it is to lesser things—I tell you that we are opening tonight a doorway in this city where great light can flow in order to expand here in Detroit and throughout this land the new culture of the ages, the culture of the feeling of regeneration as it stimulates the soul to search eternally for the flame that is within all. Let all evoke it, then, and derive therefrom its benefits.

Ladies and gentlemen, I did not come to you upon a camel, but I came to you on wings of light. And although I have ridden many camels and have traveled over many desert sands and sat upon many a hump, I assure you that mortal thought and feeling has no interest to me, nor does human opinion and vanity. For I have clean escaped from all that the flesh is prey to, all ills and all substance, and I stand for your freedom today as never before. The day will come when those who do not understand me now will understand me as they see me face-to-face, and I will clasp their hand in the bond of eternal friendship, in the reality of the eternal foreverness of God.

To those of you who love me and who love the cosmic law so well, let me say to you that we will never forsake you but will see you through every step of the way until there is never any doubt about the fulfillment of your course and the manifestation of your freedom!

For behold, the law of God is around you and the law of God is within you. And the law of God is the law of his love, the law of eternal manifestation descending from above.

Ladies and gentlemen, I say to you these words from out the mystic East, which is within thyself and is the great banner of peace. Shalom.

August 10, 1966
Detroit, Michigan
ECP

CHAPTER 13

I come to speak to you of the magnificence of the will of God as a manifestation of purity. Have you thought upon it, precious ones, that the will of God is pure?

CHAPTER 13

THE WILL OF GOD: A MANIFESTATION OF PURITY

In the tower of cosmic purity burns the unquenchable blue flame of the eternal will. Honored by every master, every deva, every builder of form as the consummate aegis of manifestation, this unquenchable blue flame pulsates throughout nature and is the blessing and boon of all who espouse the first cause.

Men speak of the absolute, but we speak of the first cause. This is because primal substance, released from the heart of the grand Great Central Sun, has established its pulsations which refuse to be quieted even in mortal realms, where the smothering aspects of man's consciousness seek to quench this unquenchable flame.

The pulsations of divine ideas continue unabated. Yet some may say, "This seems to be an enigma, for there is a quenching within the consciousness."

"What consciousness?" we reply. For the consciousness of God is eternal; the consciousness of man is but the consciousness of opportunity. Shall blighted opportunity and failure be recognized as having existence? I think not! The pulsations of God continue unquenchable. It is only the grass that is consumed, and lost opportunity is as straw or chaff blown by the wind.

I say to you, then, today, how few in the world have actually entered the realm of ideas in order to behold the ideas of God pulsing in the ethers and to know the realm of the Mind Eternal.

Men are so lost, so caught up in their own thoughts and in the turbulence of those thoughts, that they seldom repose long enough to create the grand key that opens the door to the eternal realm. There the will of God can be seen as a cosmic waveform that is released in the ever-present majesty, tranquility and valor of cosmic light. This cosmic waveform can be seen as riding forth as the Son of God—cosmic purpose on a white charger going forth as the nobility of the Father's ideals. Men today are often caught up in a net of their own creation, their ideals being the products of the mores of civilization and they are not actually going back to the first cause—the pulsations of love, immortality, and that which dispenses the water of Life freely to all who thirst.[1]

I come, then, this day, to speak to you of the magnificence of the will of God as a manifestation of purity. Have you thought upon it, precious ones, that the will of God is pure? Recognize, then, that while purity in its own realm (supposedly a separate realm) has within itself those buoyant pulsations of pure purity, the will of God is not absent from purity nor is purity absent from the will of God. And therefore, one of the most magnificent concepts in all creation is the white-fire periphery of the will of God and the white-fire core!

Some may say, "I did not know of the white-fire periphery, but I knew of the white-fire core." Do you know, precious ones, that the tip of the blue-flame torch is actually a white-flame manifestation of purity? And it is by this purity—which first enters the white-fire core and obtains the necessary heat for the cutting process—that mankind is cut free from the tentacles of his own self-created opposition to the will of God as well as from the opposition in the world itself to the will of God (which bids man to do those things which most surely do destroy him).

We are concerned with the magnification of the beauty in man, which seems to be but a pinpoint of cosmic idealism. The magnification of this pinpoint of pure white light, this steely white light that surrounds the blue flame and the magnification of the blue flame itself, is not the activity of a moment but is the activity of foreverness. For, precious ones, the will of God that was sent forth in the Beginning was not the aspect of that moment alone but of every moment that would *ever exist* in the timeless realm as well as in the realm of time.

Still your minds. "Let not your heart be troubled: ye believe in God; believe also in me"[2] is the admonishment of the soul to cognize the Christ-reality of the self. It is to understand that God, in giving the gift of his Son, gave that Son-radiance,

> Imbued with holy will
> To every part of life to raise and instill
> The radiance that eliminates strife
> That pursues a goal so noble and so grand
> And gives to men on earth
> A footing on which they can stand,
> Effortlessly breathing forth
> The pulsations that God fanned
> Into reality at the moment of the Beginning.
>
> "Let there be light" is a challenge
> Of the bright white radiance of the Holy Spirit
> Caught in the splendor of a cosmic Grail.
> It causes men to understand that God does not fail,
> And they need not either.
> For to them is given a lance of light
> To penetrate the darkness
> Of the abyss of night,
> That they also, as knights of old,

May seek the glow of spiritual gold
And understand that the treasure
In this land is within themselves.

I say, then, to every aspirant of the Holy Grail:
To see the ruby rays pour out, blending with the gold,
That I AM of old one who represents
The will of God at this table round
At which the knights may gather
To hear the sacred sound.
"Amen" or "Aum" makes little difference to those
Who can see and understand the alchemy
Of old that causes man to claim his own to be,
"Esse," to see, "essene," to understand the sheen
Of cosmic fabric, mantles of white brilliance
Surrounding soul and form and causing men to esteem
That cloth of cosmic radiance
Not be forlorn, forsaken by it all!

Oh, understand the will of God and call.
For lo, the will of God draws nigh.
It comes pulsating through the sky,
The heaven-radiance in the mind ideal
That by his virtue flame does heal, does seal,
Creating understanding as the miracle bells
Of Cosmic Christ perfection peal out
The joy of God over all the world and reveal
On highest standard, our great flag of purity and love
Unfurling to the world a new hope, regeneration
Leading all to proper understanding of emancipation.

O gracious ones, the cords that bind must be cut. The discord that has maimed and hurt mankind must be cast out. Men must come to a point in their realization and search where they can have perspective. The perspective of the will of God does not need to create in consciousness some barbed revelation that is pseudo in manifestation and in intent because it is not the will of God—the will of God that manifests in the twig that's bent toward heaven and its pulsations wise.

Let all understand God's law,
And let none despise its action in ye all.
God's law is the purity that frees.
God's law is the love that enters into hearts
And frees them from their sense of smallness,
Making bold the small and raising all
Until they can extend their hands
In loving aspiration, as the knights of old,
To this pulsing Grail chalice which does hold
The power of true being!

I AM the power that's freeing, amen;
That is the love from which ye all were made.
That is the perfect love that is unafraid
To do God's will and be a captain in the realm,
Eternally free where I AM,
Where every ascended master is.
This is the realm that you shall inhabit;
This is the realm in which God is.
There are none cast out save those
Who cast themselves without.
And all within are they who are free
From sin and sense of it and imbued
With the mission of the Most High God,
The intent of it.

For 'tis the love, the light, the life
That God is which dwells within ye all.

It is the faith that like a mustard seed
Will expand and grow ye tall,
Until ye stand right where
The sons of God have stood
And understand the meaning of
True brotherhood.
Amen.

November 12, 1967
La Tourelle
Colorado Springs, Colorado
MLP

CHAPTER 14

The will of God is a burning, fiery blue
And mighty cosmic sun.
The will of God is true.
It brings new hope to everyone.
The will of God creates the sense
Within the soul that says, "Well done!"

CHAPTER 14

"THY LAW IS LOVE, O GOD!"

What is the thought of beauty? It is the celestial fire that the hills of heaven frame. Glowing! Iridescent! This beauty is received within the heart. It is known. It is loved. It is real.

We come, then, today, that we may rekindle the fires of the heart. We would create a new sense of glowing beauty, a new sense of reality. We would have you see that the fairest, the most glorious, the purest, the most radiant is the consciousness of God.

You say this is not your own. I say it is! You should receive this consciousness as the consciousness of Self. It alone is real. The puny consciousness that mortal men consider their own is but a leaky tin vessel, and the muddied water contained therein sprays out in every direction. It creates musty odors in the world. It creates despair. We would replace this—all of this lesser consciousness—with the consciousness of the light.

My words are healing barbs. They come not to entangle but to free. They come not to confuse but to heal confusion. They come not to create despair but to create joy.

The radiance [of the consciousness of God] is everywhere, but recognition is not. The radiance lives, but those who dwell in a state of nonrecognition perish in that state.

We come to cleanse and to give life, to provide a new sense of freedom, to assuage the hungers of the soul, to captivate the emotions, yes—and more important, to captivate the mind of direction, the rudder of being, that we may steer the whole vessel to a safe harbor.

Morya asks, "What is destiny?" Morya asks, "Where are the radiators of destiny? Where are they who will fulfill the divine command 'Carry out my Will,' saith the LORD?" And men ask, "Where is the will of God?" Because they do not find it within themselves, they suppose that it is not there. Because they do not find it in the universe, they suppose that it is not there. Simply because they do not find it, they assume that it does not exist. And this is also [their view] of the very nature of God.

Let men learn, then, to externalize pathways to hierarchy. Let them learn to cultivate new currents in the air, ascending currents, conductors of God-magnificence. Let them understand their responsibility to weave the thread of contact. And if the shaft of light be from on high, embellish it and make it a true contact. Let them rejoice! But let them understand, and understand well, that the soul of man, the being of man, the consciousness of man, the full expression of the monad must itself enter in willingly and with the fullness of consecration into the idea of contact.

Humanity today seek to contact reality in all that they do, and only the few are actually those who, by reason of foolishness, can wander away from the light and rejoice. Most men today consider that they are moving toward the light even when they walk in darkness. They say they seek the light of happiness, of joy, of sense experience, of pleasure, to be recognized. But what is it that seeks recognition? It is the God within that seeks recognition.

But men cannot expect that just because the peasant bows to

the king that the king is honored thereby. For he who would honor the king brings also the gift of his highest Self. He brings the jewels of purity. He brings the gold of illumined intelligence. He brings the sweet frankincense of devotion. All of these gifts that are brought to the feet of the infant Messiah—all of these speak of the giving of good things to one another.

And whether one is king or peasant is not nearly so important as is one's consciousness. For when one has the consciousness of the mind of God, the fires upon the mountain gleam brightly within the firmament of the mind. And at those moments the world is woven together into a comprehensible whole. There is no darkness in such a one, for he cannot bear it. All that is around him, all that he sees—the full multiplication of consciousness from the One to the many—is ever an expression of the One. Nowhere can he go that he wants to escape from the consciousness of the One. For the One is all, and everything is enhanced by the beauty of the One.

Man is a monad. God is a monad. All life is an expression—a monadic expression. Why, then, will men seek to create duplicity? Why will they seek to create caves of darkness in which they dwell? Why do they seek in separation to enhance themselves, when only by consonance with the higher worlds will the fires of the Spirit reveal the reality of the kingdom to everyone?

CREATE THE ROYAL SENSE IN CONSCIOUSNESS

We come then, today, not as a tiger who stalks his prey, but we come as the raja of the Spirit to create the royal sense in the consciousness, to purvey the great ruby of immortal price.

What, then, does this mean? It means the inward fires are lit. And when the inward fires of the heart are lit, there is no darkness in that one. For darkness that comes, sometimes as an unseen and unbidden guest, cannot linger long where the heart is ablaze with the melody of the Spirit, where the melody of the Spirit is the inward song that creates a sense of worth in life, not only the worth of the individual but the worth of all.

The purposes of life, when understood, are the highest gifts, for the mind is illumined by them. When the mind is illumined by them, the Christ appears. He comes not only to the East but to the West. He comes to unite and he comes to sunder. Men must understand that when he sunders, when he cuts men free from degradation, they should rejoice! For degradation that often masquerades as though it were happiness is itself full of deceit. And wise is the man who shuns it. For life is a palace with many rooms, yet happiness should be in each room.

Wherever gloom is, we say that there is an absence of the fohatic spark of the vibrancy of life. There is an absence of reality. There is a breach in the wall through which the dust of serfdom comes upon man and surrounds him. He is no longer crowned with reality but he walks in a beggar's robe. He reaches out his hand and saith, "Help me!" but he giveth no help to any man or to any part of life. He remains, then, despondent and despairing, a wanderer in the universe. The cycles of life are uninterpreted by him, and the imaginations of his heart are but a wanderlust that seeks to find, in the curiosity of life, some new thing. But he rejects the reality that surrounds him as a mighty ocean of vibrant power.

The power of the LORD is at hand. He comes not only from Bengal but also from Singapore. He comes not only from Jaipur but also from the islands in the sea. He comes from the continents, and he is in the heart of the king as well as the heart of the beggar.

He is the LORD, and in him there is only the sound of Aum—the sound of Aum that vibrates the dust and causes the dust to raise, that vibrates the dust and makes shining worlds out of it until at last the miracle of universal consciousness is seen everywhere—a sea of hope from which men do not desire to escape, a brilliant mind that like a shining diadem, a diamond of the will of good, seeks always to convey the water of Life, not by mystique but by revelation of mystery.

We seek, then, not to veil but to unveil. We seek, then, not to discourage but to encourage. We seek, then, not to create a sense of failure for any but to create a sense of God-success for all. For when the crowning sense of Victory is recognized by man, he holds out his hands to the king and saith, "Give me, O Lord, this gift of Victory—this gift of the sense of Victory that I may be complete! For without thee I am but one who is not. But with thee I AM all things. I AM complete within myself! I AM complete within thy light, and thy light completes its perfect work in me."

This is the will of God—the building of the temple, the building of the pyramid, the building of reality and its spirals, concentric rings of light that, as cycles' stairs, are climbed by all. Little ones hanging on the lower rings gaze upward at the stronger climbers with hope and shining eyes. Those who are above gaze downward even as they gaze upward, for they see the link with hierarchy as one that must hold two hands above and two hands below.

For all of life moving onward—
Forward still, in progress bolder
Holds the glow-ray of the Lord of Life
That comes as maturity,
Not to make men grow older,
But wiser in the hands of God.
As clay or plastic substance,
Molded, then, are these
By graces from on high.
The presence of the Holy Spirit—
Fire of life flowing as a breeze,
Radiating, moving on all life,
On men that walk as trees,

Planted in the Lord's garden
By the side of the flowing River of Life.
They stand tall—

Ever present in his holy band—
Radiating a new sense of wonder,
For they understand
That God has come not to plunder
From their lives
All that they have and are,
But rather from the skies
To send new hope as brilliant star.

I AM (the Word of God that lives in men)
Declares to all,
"I will defend thyself
Against all Darkness.
Make a covenant with thee
To raise thee, set thee ever free!"

When you understand the meaning of life,
Your hearts will surge as a tempest!
When you understand the meaning of life,
The harmony of the spheres will ring you round about with fire!

When you understand the meaning of life,
Fill you then with God-desire!
No more will you be captured by the tin-cup consciousness
Of the beggar who goeth forth to beg,
But you will stand erect
Upon your very legs
And say, "O God, I AM thy son—
A star of hope to be!
I AM thy son—my life, thy own!
I AM forever free!
I AM thy Son!
I see thee in the smile
Of every child upon the earth,
Of all who are worthwhile."

For hope within the sweet
And simple smile of child
Can be transferred
To those of elder years,
Whose countenance then
God-fired and mild,
Redeemed not by human tears
Or human fears,
But by the hope that comes
Then from a distant sphere
But ever draweth nigh—
Is progress to the world!
Yea, progress from on high.

Receive then the grace of the will of God
That surrounds you
Not with shroud
But surrounds you with hope—
A hope that bows to God in every man,
A hope that exalts in all
The plan! The plan! The plan!
For in the plan—the purposed plan—
Is the will of God made known.
And everyone that understands this law
Will understand that all that he has sown
Of human discord
(Jangle—tangle round his feet)
Is but the law of karma—
Recompense that's meet—
Returning juggernaut
And fear to those who sent it out.
And God would say to everyone,
"Today is not the time to pout,
But hold your faith and face

As though it were the faith and face of God."
For then I think that
You'll rejoice beneath his rod
And say, "Thy law is love, O God!
Come now within my being.
Thy law is love, O God!
Come now within my seeing.
Thy law is love, O God!
Come now by sacred Word
And utter forth, right through my voice
The power men had heard
In elder days when elder art
Did wrought supremely then
To show the radiance God did start—
The power of his pen
To write a word that men could hear,
A sense that they could feel
A soul that they could grasp as theirs,
A power of light to heal."

And when 'tis done
The world will be one—
The tapestry complete.
The mastery of life revealed
Will bring you to his feet
And raise you up to sit beside him
On the throne on high.
And nevermore will dust impart
A sense that's futile to your being.
Rather, single eye will see
By eye that all is seeing
In the hand of Light Supreme
Where destiny is real,
Right there thy God will manifest

The power—the power to seal
The universe within the will
Of God descending now.

Oh, won't you take it by the hand
And say, "O God, I vow
To do my best to see this light
That bursts as new star in me.
I pledge to keep my faith in thee
Till I AM wholly free!"

Beloved, as I come to you today, mindful of the long way of man's becoming, it is to speak the encouraging word—the word that goeth out in the building of the pyramid of life. The cornerstone of perfection has been laid, and every man upon this planet should understand that he has a part reserved for him that no other can fulfill. When he understands this and grasps that principle, he beholds the will of God. And when he moves in that direction with all of his heart, with all of his mind, with all of his love, with all that he is, he will be fulfilling his portion of the eternal pyramid. He will be fulfilling his witness to the universe—the pledge of his faith in the destiny of the planetary body, the destiny of the hierarchy, the destiny of cosmic intent for every man and the fulfillment of the initial purposes.

DRAW NIGH TO THE TEMPLE OF CONSCIOUSNESS

The dawn of purpose came long ago. But the dawn of purpose to each individual comes as he awakens, and then, rubbing his sleepy eyes, he looks to the splendor of the morning skies and he sees there the aureate glow of cosmic fire. And as he stands contemplating all of this, it is to enshrine it within the temple of self. And this is the meaning of the word *contemplate*. It means "with the temple, sense."

And as man begins to envision that he is the temple of God,

he will draw forth—from the heart of the great magnet of life by the fires of his heart—the supreme indulgence of God's grace, a grace that creates a new sense in everyone who will receive it.

It enables them to perceive that all of the weights that beset men, to hold them bound to the earth and to a seemingly purposeless round of life—ring by ring engaged in human strife—is not at all that which the Father holds dear. In its place he sees the vision of the eternal temple of being. He understands that he and he alone, as the knights of old, must go forth on his own personal quest to seek the Holy Grail consciousness without fail. For the light of God never fails, but human consciousness, when it is not tethered to the Divine, fails often.

And the sands of time run out lifetime after lifetime. For men squander the substance of living and understand not that the purposes of life do not always come again according to some humanly conceived rhythmic cycle. They are governed by higher Law. And oftentimes (although reembodiment is true) individuals are barred from the temple of life and kept within the astral world or within the world waiting at the gates of life and death so that they may once again receive the precious treasure of embodied consciousness.

Will you then, today, draw nigh to the temple of consciousness, to the temple of light? Will you draw nigh to that temple and understand that it is by grace that you live, that it is by grace that you receive this opportunity to live, and that the purpose of all life is solely the unity of creation—to make you one with all that God is?

When you, then, squander your lives by the senseless display of egoistic desire, it is simply an emptying of your being of the cosmic fire and a dashing of that fire to the earth element, where it is smothered thereby. And Terra buries the sacred fire in her heart.

Will you then understand clearly that the Christos that is in the heart of the earth must be nourished and must be welcomed? Will you understand that you must garland the sacred fire by the gift of sacred-fire flowers, that you must make a daily offering as a ritual on behalf of self? This is so that the will of God can become akindled anew within you, as the fires of the morning sun arise. This is so that you should understand that all of the cycles of life are fountains of cosmic identity, that the pores of self must open and be cleansed (for they are little mouths), that all of mankind—the hungry body of God everywhere—desire to drink in the fires of God's love and goodwill, that God, and God alone, bestows and instills his grace in men.

Traveler, bid him welcome! Traveler, heed him when he calls! Traveler, seek him! For the hour is later than you think, and the pyramid of life rises with you or without you. Your place that is reserved for you can be given to another. For it has been said of old and truly said, "My Spirit shall not always strive with flesh."[1] Let men understand clearly, then, that the glorious bounty of opportunity given to all is one to be claimed by all.

I, Morya of the Zen—I, Morya, out of the East, speak out of the light of the heart. The Christos, the one called the eternal and universal Christ—he sings in the hymns of every sacred order. He is the chief cornerstone of the temple, immortal and invisible. He is the light of the world, the eternal, immortal, ever-living Principle by which the worlds were framed. For the dust was framed by the immortal Spirit that it should be and ought to be embellished forever by his blessing.

Take, then, this cup I give you this day and drink ye all of it as a communion with infinite Reality. This Reality lives in the will of God. It does not live in the human will, for the human will is centralized to the ego and is a sun to the human ego. But the will of God is the sun of the Divine Ego.

And all who understand this
Will cognize the flowers of Reality
That fill space and hallow space,

Will cognize the fires of Reality
That gleam from near and far,
Will cognize the fires of Reality
That by their lines divergent
And convergent are a star—
A hope to every man.

And may all men receive it!
A hope to every man!
And may no man deceived be
By outer things
Or human rationality.
For the God-flame within burns on!
It ne'er shall be quenched!
It is a part of everyone's ceaseless quest.
It is his surest living defense!
The will of God, I say,
Is everything to everyone.

The will of God is a burning, fiery blue
And mighty cosmic sun.
The will of God is true.
It brings new hope to everyone.
The will of God creates the sense
Within the soul that says, "Well done!"

My love surrounds you. Your love surrounds me. His love surrounds me. My love surrounds him. And he alone is love.

October 26, 1969
La Tourelle
Colorado Springs, Colorado
MLP

CHAPTER 15

My beloved chelas of the will of God,
among those who love the Lord
very few are willing to do his will
and to walk in his footsteps.

CHAPTER 15

THE FEAST OF THE EPIPHANY

Chelas of the Will of God!

I salute you in the epiphany of the light—the light that became the Word and the Word that was manifest in the infant Messiah.

The appearance of the Magi silhouetted on the horizon of the messianic age was the sign of the coming of the threefold flame in him and in all who would come from the ends of the earth to worship the Godhead dwelling in him bodily. And the little child whose star led us to the shrine of the Godhead at the altar of his heart was even then the great initiator of our souls.

We came with devotion, with determination, and with the native light of our own divinity which mirrored his own. By the light of God within us, we perceived his light. It is ever thus. And no manifestation—human, elemental, or divine—can perceive his love except it be endowed with that love.

Our appearing, celebrated throughout Christendom as the Feast of the Epiphany on January 6, is the sign that the kings and the priests of the gentile nations and the lowly and humble of heart, one and all who come to his birth bearing the gifts of the Trinity—tokens of devotion, determination, and, most importantly, divinity—may be received of him unto whom it is given to transfer the light of sonship.

My beloved chelas of the will of God, among those who love the Lord very few are willing to do his will and to walk in his footsteps. And the path that was made so plain, from the plains of Bethlehem to Bethany's hill, has become of noneffect in the lives of little children.

Those kings and princes of the world who had no light within them have come to adore, though they themselves contained not the flame of God's adoration. They came determined to have his light, though they had no light within them whereby to receive his light. They came with the sense of their personal divinity that was nothing more than the self-importance of the not-self. They had no cup to receive the transfer of his light.

They have come and gone a thousand times. Empty-handed they come, empty-handed they go. But the folly of it all is that they know it not. And their ritual both blind and dead, though not altering the Godhead one iota, has fooled the foolish instead. And the delicate thread of life and the spark so tenuous in the infant souls of humanity has not been quickened by those who could not be quickened because they had no life in them. Such is the state of affairs in Christendom.

While the top echelons of the blind leaders of the blind argue by what manifestation he is come, as though by their conclusive arguments they could procure salvation unto themselves and the masses, the saints led by his Holy Spirit gather around those very special souls of light who are anointed to keep the love fires burning in the heart of the body of God.

He received us then,
The little Christ Child,

He receives us now.
He looked into our eyes,
Reestablished the ancient ties
Of a brotherhood so far beyond
The moment of an appearing.
Yet the star above and the star below
Made the sign of the cross,
And we crossed the desert sands
Bearing to our native lands
The light to rekindle a world.

We shall ne'er forget
His penetrating eye.
It has never left us
In all of these centuries.
We saw that day
The eye of God upon the world
And in his face an expression
Like unto our Father,
The Ancient of Days.

It was the eternal recognition
Of the members of our bands,
And we are ever one across the sands
Of time and space.
There are no compartments in heaven or in earth
That can separate us from the memory
Of that eternal sun shining in our midst,
And in our hearts forever echoing
The mantra, "We are one, we are one."

We held the balance for his life. We held the star of the east which in the fullness of the cycles of time and space he would follow to the retreats of the Brotherhood—to Egypt, to Persia, and to the shrine of the World Mother in India. There he came to consecrate his life to the salvation of the root races of earth's evolutions and to receive the mantle of their Manus.

> He alone
> Is the connecting link
> Of East and West.
> His willingness
> To do the will of God
> Is yet remembered
> By the rishis and the saints.
> And the fragrance of jasmine,
> Lotus blossom, and frankincense
> Remind the devotees of God's will
> That he came from out the starry bands
> Of heavenly hosts,
> Trailing light and glory,
> Proclaiming the mantra and the story
> Of the bodhisattvas of God's will:
> Lo, I AM come to do thy will, O God!

In the full remembrance of the Ancient of Days and the Lamb sent unto the hundred forty and four thousand,[1] we come to the heart of every true believer of the Word and we celebrate the epiphany of Christ. Now it is the Second Advent and the hour of the appearing of The Lord Our Righteousness[2] in your heart.

O chela of the will of God, pause in your evening prayer to receive us. As you look into our eyes, remember that we are remembering the look of the Holy Child as he received us so long ago.

We recognize the guru of your heart. We are ever chelas of the Great God whose light is also come unto you. We set the example of devotion, determination, and essential divinity. We tend the altar of your heart. We prepare your soul for his coming. With us bow low before his presence.

O Holy Christ Self, pure stream and issue of God unto the beloved, receive now thine own. Assist to atone. Establish thy Word. Lo, he is come!

And make them one as we are the Three in One—

El Morya

with Kuthumi and Djwal Kul
for Brahma, Vishnu, and Shiva
in the secret manger of your heart.

January 6, 1980
ECP

CHAPTER 16

Realize, then, that the image of Father in sternness and wrath . . . and a certain remoteness from life or even from family is not the truth— not of my own being nor of Alpha.

CHAPTER 16

A GLOW ON THE MOUNTAIN

Circles of Chelas Gathering for the Mysteries of the Sacred Fire

I stand upon the place where Alpha has stood. And so, you should also. To be in the record of the aura of a saint or the mighty one is to absorb and reabsorb light's essential purpose.

For this reason, devotees of the will of God meditate upon the perfect light of the aura and the halo of Christ. For in that dimension of the mind of God, there is contact through the Wayshower of the invincible freedom that one day shall be bequeathed to the soul who exercises right dominion in these octaves.

I come as the Father of the messengers—and your own, if you will allow me. Call me Bapu, if you will—"Little Father"—that I might not displace the role, nor of the All-Father, nor of the Great Guru Sanat Kumara. Receive me as Father, that I might sponsor you and also displace in your lives many impostors who have positioned themselves in flesh, role playing—and badly at that—the office of our heavenly Father.

Be comforted, then, in the understanding that wherever there is an impostor standing in the place of Alpha, standing in the position of Lord Gautama Buddha, one of us is always available to clear the air—to manifest the tender love of our Father which we, as his sons, have entered into in the fullness that the ascension affords.

I have listened to our messenger's discussion of my report.[1] And I have watched as you have gained greater understanding of what we speak of when we speak of criticism, condemnation, and judgment. This afternoon she will deliver to you yet another lecture, directed by Kuan Yin, on the nature of that form of condemnation which comes under the heading of "imperil."[2] And soon you will have another plume of illumination concerning worldwide forces of anti-life.

Realize, then, that the image of Father in sternness and wrath, nonunderstanding, and a certain remoteness from life or even from family is not the truth—not of my own being nor of Alpha.

THE TENDERNESS OF OUR FATHER

Surely the tenderness of our Father needs extolling when we have come into the cloister of the heart of the nun and therefore discover the holiness of her communion. It is not the communion of the fallen ones who falsely report the anger of God, his banishment of his own to the depths of hell, or all of the doctrine that has effectively removed the presence of Father even from church theology.

Let us contemplate the sweetness of our Father that has all of the capacity to release the white fire in defense of the most tender violet, that has all of the lightning and the thunder to separate the octaves, and yet the most tender touch of love that assures each soul making his way on the path of life—sometimes plodding and sometimes prodding others to move faster, depending on the position of burdens of light and darkness.

This tenderness, then, be with you in the hour when I draw to my heart, in the true sense of the divine family, all who have been a part of my thrust for a purpose for aeons and aeons of service to life.

I CALL HOME THE CIRCLE OF MY FAMILY AND CHELAS

The close circle of my family, lived in East and West, I call home. And the larger circle of my family who count as chelas of the sacred fire I also call home. I would make you my own sons and daughters. I would show you at the Inner Retreat*—where I trust we shall meet—teachings and mysteries of life that are for those who have passed beyond the initiations of human pride and spiritual pride, of human stubbornness of that stiffnecked generation who have come out from the yoke of their own karma and have decided to be the regeneration of light and light's perfection.

Circles of chelas who are entitled to have the mysteries of the sacred fire must gather. And for the gathering, there must be the gathering place—the right vibration and the right spiritual as well as physical climate and environment.

The gratitude which I have penned to you in my letter of this week[3] goes beyond the boundaries of the word and must be expressed to you in many, many ways. As Kuthumi and I with Djwal Kul have contemplated the possibilities, we cherish most the onward and upward movement of aspiring chelas, the personal contact, the protective forcefield where happiness is the entering in to that close association that Gautama Buddha can and shall afford those who can make the physical trek on occasions—for seminars and retreats—to the land he has consecrated,[4] to the ivory castle, to the inner etheric city, to the memory of the first fountain of light that was Shamballa.

If I sound soft in my speech, it is because I am in a contemplative mode, musing upon the hearts of all of you—your strivings, your incarnations, your experiences expressing valor, courage, faith, charity to all. I know these moments; for I am, you might

---

*The Inner Retreat is a spiritual-physical forcefield consecrated by the ascended hosts as a place of great light and holiness, where souls seek the higher Path, the spiritual truths and teachings of the ascended masters; a place of great encounters—with God and fellow seekers; set in the spiritual community of the Royal Teton Ranch in Montana.

say, a history buff. I enjoy reading the history of your lifestreams. I enjoy picking the forget-me-nots from the fields, separating them from the weeds that have also grown in those days of infamy that are to be no more.

Thus, I gather the flowers of the best fruits of your own life's offering. And when you see the joy upon Mother's face in greeting you here at Camelot or any place, it is my joy and my smile as I look upon you and remember moments when your soul has risen to the point of the peak of the fountain of expression, transcending itself and delivering to the world a permanent record of your own heart's charity.

Again and again, these jeweled offerings of your incarnations have brought together a crystal mosaic of a life pattern. When I contemplate these victories, I know each one can come again and also multiply our presence in your midst.

As we file before this Altar of Invocation, we of the ascended hosts deliver a light that each one of you then multiplies by the unique character of your own Christhood. Your very presence here, your assent to our coming, your loving attention creates the arc whereby that which we deliver to you is uniquely multiplied for the increase of the magnitude of your Star of Being. And as chelas, you send back to us your multiplication of the "talent" we lay upon your heart.[5] And therefore, we in the office of Guru also increase in magnitude and together we become a galaxy of light that all of us will one day lay at the feet of beloved Alpha. And from all of this collective round, this *manvantara,* we will say to him:

This is our increase.
This is our offering.
This is the distillation of holy purpose!
Take it, O beloved Alpha.
And let the Great In-breath
Seal it in thy heart
Until our next going forth
From out the white-fire core of Holy Cosmos.

It is indeed harvest time. And I am chosen, how gladly, to contemplate the harvest of good fruit rather than the "fleurs du mal." Therefore, I leave to Saint Germain his discourse on the world harvest that is yet to come,[6] while I tenderly enfold you in the nearness that truly is the safety, the inner assurance, and the security of our bands on earth.

Tender moments you spend with me in Darjeeling become the very essence of courage and your going forth into harsh conditions as well as the great challenges that beset you as you continually thrust into this planetary body greater and greater intensity of light.

I am well pleased with your stand for God, for me, for our messenger. I am well pleased that the onslaughts of the fallen ones have not moved you. For you have also been tested. And if you know your history, you know that Yahweh has always used foreign powers and alien beings to test the will, the fervor, the mettle of the seed of Sanat Kumara.

Thus, we understand how to position the pilasters. We understand how to position the pillars in the temple of God. We understand those strengths that can withstand great weights; and we understand how others must not be given so great a weight, for the building would collapse were we to lay foundation with the untested souls or those who in the midst of test do not endure the onslaughts of life.

Co-measurement gives to you, in this hour, the sense that all that comes to you in the 360 degrees of the circle of your being must come at these 360 angles to your own Christ consciousness to test the strength as well as the weaknesses of your own Christ emanation.

When you meet victoriously the sign of friend or foe, light or darkness—there is a strength, there is a widening of the total circle of being. And you find that the same test need not be repeated, and you have actually transcended a plane and gone on to new worlds to conquer.

When you think about it, there are certain conditions upon earth today that trouble many hearts and lifewaves which you yourselves never encounter. In many instances, it is because of the past mastery of your soul in previous incarnations. In other instances, the test is the sign of the future, and you are given the opportunity to see how others meet those tests for the hour when you yourself must give accounting as to your own strength.

The perspective of life as a schoolroom and all things to be dealt with as measures of the individual integrity will allow you to make swift progress. It will allow you to see in weeks and months and short years a considerable degree of self-mastery of the "undifferentiated suchness" of the Buddha,[7] of the entering into a certain level of consciousness that contains the God-desire to move mountains—and therefore *will* move mountains!—and yet remain supremely unattached and therefore not connected to the astral stumbling blocks. The astral stumbling blocks, as grains of sand or pebbles beneath your feet, would (if you would allow them) prevent you from moving great mountains of light as well as adversity.

Let not the grains of sand disturb you from your flight. Let not the grains of sand produce that irritation which manifests as imperil. Let us consider the grain of sand as the cornerstone of victory. Let us consider the grain of sand, a single one, as capable of causing your defeat only if you allow it to do so. It is the proverbial making of a mountain out of a molehill. Many a path has been lost for an entire incarnation because of the single grain of sand. Correspondingly, great causal bodies of light have also been created as the single grain of sand is the nucleus of Alpha and Omega.

It is good to be philosophical in those very hours when the acceleration of light and God's power entrusted to your care hangs heavy—to pause for a moment to contemplate all that has gone before and all that is to come as you are rocked in the cradle of the Cosmic Virgin's opportunity to give birth to new sons of deliverance.

The stability of our movement is the stability of hearts aflame with love.

A SPIRAL OF PILGRIMS

This is a spiral of pilgrims mounting the mountain! And, you know, for a time there is a thinning of the spiral until it is completed and every turn upon the mountain is occupied by a Christed One. And one day the whole mountain and the spiraling of pilgrims becomes aglow with fire! And there is a roaring within the earth, there is a movement, and there is a great light that is emitted from their hearts.

It is then that all of the people in the valley look up for the sound of the thunder and the movement and the brilliant light. It is then that a new dispensation of two thousand years, the new *avatara,* and all that has been proclaimed becomes the new religion of the age.

It is at that moment of magnification, of the maximum release, that there is the drawing of a planetary body and evolution into the new light and the new consciousness. All that you do is preparation for this moment when there is the turning of worlds.

Devils Slide, renamed Angels' Ascent, is our focus at the Inner Retreat of The Summit Lighthouse and of the spiraling formation kept now in the etheric octave by angels in white bearing candles aflame.[8] They do keep this victory vigil—and you will feel it as you approach the land. It is for that spiraling of the pilgrims that many have dreamed of, whose archetypal matrix is a part of the planetary body. Though it be not the place where the actual physical spiral shall take place, it is the etheric matrix for the drawing of the pilgrims who are a part of the assembly of the components of the capstone.[9]

THE MARRIAGE OF THE LAMB IS COME

The Emerald Matrix is set. The marriage of the Lamb is come.[10] And your soul is caught up in the bridal garment of your own anointing and communion with your Christ Self.

I desire that you should meditate upon this ritual and initiation which Lord Gautama and Lord Jesus have given to you in this year in the hour of Wesak and the celebration of Jesus' ascension.[11] For it is not good that you only contemplate the entering into and the assimilation with your Christ Self, but that you accept it as done and as sealed. For it is only condemnation of the world or self-belittlement that tells you that you have not arrived at the portal of the Lamb! It is only condemnation creating procrastination that tells you you are among the wise virgins keeping the flame but the Bridegroom has not come and is not coming soon, for you are not ready.[12]

Let us draw the line! Let us remember that I have said the past is prologue—that Alpha has said it is a new era.[13] Will you not accept the will of God that proclaims your union with your own Christ Self? Will you not realize that the saints who longed for this union did not have the violet flame—did not live in an age of such intense acceleration sponsored by Saint Germain and Mother Mary and Portia and the archangels?

Therefore, to hesitate to step in to the holy union of your own God Presence is surely an act of human will and even deceit of the carnal mind practiced upon your own soul. Surely it is a denial of your own Great God Self, of the Presence of the Father who sponsors this union.

Be not beset by the condemnation that tells you if you make a mistake or misqualify energy or do something wrong that your Christ Self has cast you down and cast you out and rejected you as unacceptable! You have an ongoing relationship with God—if you will accept it. And when you do not, it is the greatest travesty that has ever occurred in all of human history!

Contemplate this mystery. Remember that Archangel Michael has declared, over and again, "I AM for the Union!"—and it is the union of your soul with the Lamb who is Christ the Lord of your temple, the Lamb who is Sanat Kumara. In this perfect union you are also wed to the Mother. You also have the fusion with her heart, for there is agreement of cosmic purpose and there is love.

Love must be defended. Any brittleness or rigidity in your personal outlook denotes extreme levels of fear in your own subconscious.

This entire community worldwide is ready for the journey to the sun—is ready for an acceleration into etheric dimensions. The violet flame and the blue lightning of God's love is our offering, as we offer it to you, for the clearing of the condemnation of the gift of love. All that is left, then, is your initiation under Chamuel and Charity for the defense of perfect love in your very midst and the realization that wherever it is not, there is not the cohesive power to hold together our body of world servers.

Truly it is the Holy Spirit that binds together all members of the Great White Brotherhood in all octaves, worlds without end. Let us not allow the enemies of the light, the misuse of the press, the false report of the false witness to deter us from the love of God in Christ Jesus.

HOW WE CHANGE THE COURSE OF HISTORY

There is an hour of crucifixion. There is an hour of persecution. But there is a resurrection. It is at the point of the resurrection, not only of the individual messenger but of all members of the community, that the world finally acclaims the light that is resident within it. They do not perceive God through these initiations in which all the sons and daughters must pass. But when the victory is finally forged and won, when there is a glow on the mountain, when Christ steps forth from the tomb—then there is acceptance.

Thus, the dictations have told you it is the hour of the Mother's crucifixion.[14] And she is where she most loves to be—that is in your heart. And it is also a security and a sense of love and being loved to be within the heart of the chela during the hours of this initiation.*

The prophecy is that the resurrection will come. And this is the moment when each one of you, together with all of us who have gone before and with the messenger, will indeed step forth from the tomb of world condemnation. And that light precipitating out, manifesting the eternal threefold flame, will be for the conviction of all souls who also have that threefold flame. It will be for the judgment of those who deny it—but they will not be able to undo it or to turn it back.

When you are students of history, of the lives of the avatars, you understand where you are on the spiral spiraling up the mountain. You understand victory and you understand adversity. And you take all of this philosophically—not losing your guard in the hour of victory, not being bowed down by the usual waves that move against the ship of life.

Let us chart our course according to the courses that have been charted. Let us move onward together, expecting that the cycles of history of the saints shall repeat themselves and that it is our opportunity in the violet flame to see that when the cycles of history are repeated that something more is also added—our free will, our input, our dynamic decree, our exuberance, and the collective momentum of our victory! This is how we change the course of history! And in so changing its recyclings, we transmute the path of the past.

I have directed the messenger to review the incarnations of our own Mark.[15] It is for your understanding of these very cycles of history in the life of one. It is for your own compassion with

*i.e., the testings and burdens from the fallen ones that God allows as initiations

yourself as you must go through similar episodes. It is also for your realization that condemnation does not stem merely from the present, but that you now stand to conquer the entire momentum of condemnation that has ever been placed upon your life in all previous incarnations. And though you may balance all of your karma, you must realize that the records of that condemnation still reside in those who have not balanced their karma. This is an added weight with which you must deal.

History as well as historians may condemn figures. And thus, they stand judged and condemned by the pens of serpents who judge and write. And future generations may never appreciate the light that has been manifest nor the fact that our Father tenderly forgives his own and that the soul has surely atoned for those sins long, long ago.

It is time to consider the great light. It is time to consider the meaning of bearing it in a darkened world that must also be turned to light.

I seal you in the light of my heart and my momentum of victory over every foe and condemnation, because I would like you to know and to feel the aura and the presence of my heart as I have stood face-to-face and nose-to-nose with the fallen ones *not giving an inch!* —not retreating. I would like you to have the co-measurement of my own lifestream and my own momentum of overcoming.

It is as it has been said: You come to a place in life where you have been stepped on once too many times. And in that moment, you suddenly look back to all previous occasions when you have been the doormat of world, collective and individual condemnation. And suddenly you realize that it is no one's fault but your own. You did not have to make yourself a doormat for world energies. And you thrust forth, and you extend the will, and you say to the proud wave: "Thus far and no farther."

This is the seed of attainment. This is the sign of those who have gotten the victory over the beast.[16] Thus, in the crucible of life are born those decisions of God-determination to have and to hold a greater God-freedom.

Sons and daughters of light, *be emboldened!* For you are winning!

October 10, 1981
Camelot
Los Angeles County, California
ECP

CHAPTER 17

Let the joy of God be upon thee,
for he hath established in thy midst
the fount of light, the fount of forgiveness.
And the violet transmuting flame surely
is the gift, surely is the gift *of the Holy Spirit*
for the removal of every transgression of the Law.

CHAPTER 17

REJOICE, O PEOPLE OF GOD!

Be Grateful for the Gift of the Violet Flame

Rejoice, O people of God! For a light is arisen in thy midst. Truly it is the light of the Holy One of Israel. Truly the Lord hath anointed thee.

Rejoice and be glad! Let the joy of God be upon thee, for he hath established in thy midst the fount of light, the fount of forgiveness. And the violet transmuting flame *surely is the gift,* surely is the gift of the Holy Spirit for the removal of every transgression of the Law.

Why, people of light, you ought to be among all people the most joyous and the most gifted, the most grateful of all; for God has vouchsafed to you the secrets of the seventh ray, even the mystery of transmutation whereby ye know that that which is placed in the flame of fire of the heart on this day need never appear again.

Therefore rejoice, for this indeed is more than the forgiveness of sin: it is the transmutation of karma. And therefore such a holy gift ought to be met with that wondrous joy that overflows the boundaries of the stream of identity as bubbling brooks inundating life, going forth with the living proof that the God of Israel does keep his promises unto thee and that this is the fulfillment in the latter days of the vision of Daniel and of the hope of Isaiah—and truly of the promise unto Isaiah and Jeremiah of the coming of the One, the coming of the God Immanuel.

Children of the light and sons and daughters of God, let your light shine! Let your rejoicing be the promise that the LORD shall have them in derision[1]—those, then, who defile that sacred name, those, then, who are the heathen! Let it be understood that these fallen ones who have sent the serious tones of their condemnation unto thee in this very week, they shall be brought low. For the LORD shall have them in derision.

And "Vengeance is mine, saith the Lord, I will repay. . ."[2] in this Dark Cycle of the Kali Yuga! I will return by the light of victory; I will return by the wisdom flame the joy that is bounding, the joy that overflows from the very heart of Alpha and Omega in the Great Central Sun! Roll them back into that native nothingness and let joy abound midst the Keepers of the Flame!

For truly it is the hour of victory and Mighty Victory's coming, and the joy of that victory is the joy of a mother's heart. And it is my own, for in the very hour of the sounding of their brass and their tin in their eternal damnable din there is the presence of sweetest child and the bursting forth of the Word, even the Coming Revolution in Higher Consciousness going forth as the printed page,[3] as the Word that is writ that can be read, that can be known, and that does indeed atone for every sin.

You who have come to deposit your sins, remember that I have told you, *remember* that Morya has come to rejoice with you in this hour that the only sin that can be forgiven and *permanently* removed from your lifestream is the one that you *permanently surrender!* Therefore, go not away from the altar in those moments of tender and tenderness to render unto thyself once again heaps of coals of condemnation. If you have not surrendered the condemnation of the sin, then where is self-forgiveness that descends from the mighty I AM Presence?

FORGIVE THYSELF AND OTHERS

Why, ye ought to be of all people upon earth the happiest, the most deliberate, the most serious, the most loving, the most giving and the most forgiving, for light has come to thee. Therefore, *we* await thy forgiveness of thyself and of others. For some of you we have waited many a year and we have had to recommend your going forth to forge a chart of victory in the disciplines of life because you failed to forgive yourself, as the beginning step on the path of Camelot.

You wait upon the LORD and we wait upon the soul's perfect formation of the gift of love unto God. It is the gift of flowing forgiveness, of violet-flame freedom and joy, of happiness, of transcendent, *buoyant* resilience that looks into the very teeth of error and declares:

You have no power over me—
For I AM in Zadkiel's heart!
And with a thrust and a roll and a ho! ho! ho!
I AM here to start anew
A victory spiral I once knew
In the very heart of God—
Whence he thrust me forth to challenge
Those fallen ones!

I AM here, O God, in joy!
And there is a fire in my eye
And there is a twinkle of sorts.
For I know the mirth of Morya
That is always needed on earth
And I can laugh them in derision as well—
Those mockers of the Word!

They have no power over me!
For I AM a son of the Union and the Union Jack.
Yes, I AM a son of the Union and I will give my *whack*
To those fallen ones by the power of flaming light!
It is the all-power of God!
I roll them back!

And I have my joy and I play in the meadows of life
And I stamp my feet upon the demons with Shiva
And I shout, "Shiva!" into the night
And I *bind* those murderers of the Word
By the name of Sanat Kumara.
He is my Lord and I will have none other!

Thus, I AM Morya and I *expose* the Nephilim* in Moscow and in Washington. I expose those interlopers. I draw my lines of force around Poland and I give my heart to the people of light who have their devotion to the Diamond Heart of Mary. Mary the Mother of the One. Mary the Mother of the union. Mary the Mother of Christ within you. Speak the word into her heart, open the door and speak the word unto the heart of Mary: "Let my people go!"

Thus, the word is spoken. Thus, the word is heard. And the power of the Archeia Mary before the throne of God and before the nations of the earth is supreme. And I tell you, the giving of that rosary is strength and it is victory and it is the sacrifice that we require.

The will of God is good. It is boundless. It is joyous! It leaps from heart to heart. And whatever you have been before, I *implore,* now see yourself in the image of the living Christ.

Beloved ones, the fallen ones are very long-faced, and they are very serious about your sins. And they will count them one by one until they must go through many fingers and toes in order to make

**Nephilim:* [Hebrew], "those who fell" or "those who were cast down." The ascended masters reveal that the Nephilim are the fallen angels cast out of heaven into the earth (Rev. 12:7–10, 12).

the long, long list of your sins of all past ages. Well, beloved hearts, I would gladly wear the banners of your sins all inscribed on tiny flags all over my temple until I should become a yogi of flaming waving flags across the sky.

Beloved ones, if it would serve the purpose, and it does, I would have them pin the tail upon this donkey, for I require that donkey, and the Lord requires the donkey. And thus, if it is a donkey that is required, I will serve! For, blessed hearts, these fallen ones—they have their councils and they have their determination.

But, hearts of light, the flame of the living God dwells in you! What more can you ask? What more can you receive when you have not fully received this most precious gift of love, God's own valentine to you, year by year and day by day?

I AM Morya in the heart of the joy of the violet flame. I AM Morya in the heart of the will of God. I stand for every son of God who has been slain in battle by treachery and intrigue, by assassination or war or the murderous intent. I stand by the flame of the living Word. I stand by the sword and I say, Let the laughter of God and the laughter of sons and daughters ring! Let it ring across the face of the earth and let these fallen ones know they have had their day! Their day is done, and the children of the Sun are on the march!

O beloved hearts, take seriously the teacher and the teaching. But *let go* of this sin and sense of sin and recognize how these fallen ones would leave you in a shroud of condemnation unto your very death: the death of the soul itself, the death of spontaneity and the leaping into the air as you wield that sword with care and thrust it with a ho! into the very nadir of the cause and core of Evil on this planetary body.

Why, the demons tremble when I speak because they know *I* tear the veil, *I* expose, *I* pierce through, *I* will have you for my own! And I call to you to rejoice this day in the violet flame. For, beloved hearts, there is no place for brittleness in this activity. There is no place for schism.

VIOLET FLAME: THE UNIVERSAL SOLVENT

When you have the violet flame you have the panacea, you have the universal solvent, and you have the fountain of youth! Thus, alchemists and those on the quest of life have sought these three and all are given unto thee.

Blessed hearts, I know of some across the face of the earth who know not of the violet flame. But if they knew it, and you will see to it, they would do better with it than you do. Blessed hearts, let us not leave it to this conclusion. Let us rather affirm that we who are the firstfruits shall make abundant use of the violet flame in joy, in laughter, and in spreading abroad in the community the good news of the Everlasting Gospel of the violet flame of transmutation!

And therefore, let the violet flame pierce the veil! Let arrows from the heart of Saint Germain, that cosmic cupid, now be sent to the hearts of those who are waiting, waiting for the Alchemist, waiting for the violet flame.

Violet-flame hearts the world around, I address you. My love abounds, and I make you a promise in the name of my chelas of the will of God at Camelot that they will deliver to you in this year 1981 that valentine box, that gift of the violet flame. Let it be thrust! Let it be hurled by the Coming Revolution in Higher Consciousness. Let it be thrust by the ingenuity of your heart because you have devised a new way to teach and preach the word! Let it come because you dare to invoke and accept the gift of the Holy Ghost.

O precious hearts, no sin so ancient is so intense that it cannot be removed by the violet flame, [the outcropping of] the immensity of the mind of God. Let us leap for joy! Let us welcome the beginning of the celebration of Eastertide and let us enter into the Lenten season in this hour and in this year with a full understanding of the meaning of sacrifice: to be emptied that we might be filled.

I come with a blessed joy. Now let us see *how* you will *prove* this week that you are a chela of El Morya, worthy of the name, and a devotee of the violet flame, an alchemist in the laboratory of the soul and heart that *knows* how to use the gift of life, how to bring forth the light of heaven for healing, for resurrection, for the sheer joy of living!

Hearts of light, why do you tarry in this fight? Let us *deal* the final blow to error! Let Truth appear. Let us see mighty conquerors here lest Morya fear that he must look elsewhere for responsive hearts to the chord of Camelot. Indeed. Indeed! I plight my troth with the chelas of my heart across the face of the earth. I will not let you smart against the acid and the acrimony of the fallen ones. Their word is turned upon them as their own judgment. Let your word of neglect of the violet flame not count against you, and let that sin be forgiven too.

For I place my life upon the altar as I once placed my own son upon the altar of God.[4] For truly I come in the name of Sanat Kumara. Truly I come in the name of Abraham. And I come to *remind* you of who you are and whence you have come, your noble descent, your lineage out of the heart of the Cosmic Virgin.

O blue-flame Mother of the Universe, O blue-flame Mother of Lights, let these stars appearing know the inner strength of God in them! Let that strength be unleashed. Let it be as the power of Hercules. Let the mighty sacred fire go forth. And let us see what stalwart sons and daughters of light will prove in Morya's name, in Saint Germain's name to America, to her people, to the press, to the politicians, to the power elite and to all those who stand with the intent to defeat my little ones.

Clear the way for the children of the light, I say! Cheer and clear the way for the incoming souls of light! Let angels cheer them on. Let mothers of light and fathers receive them. Let teachers *be prepared* and let there be the ennobling of hearts as a true celebration of Valentine's Day. Be therefore ennobled. Be therefore ennobled by the messengers of the Great White Brotherhood, ascended and unascended, by all who have gone before. Be ennobled because God lives in thee!

I stand in the courts of kings and presidents. I stand in the homes of the humble. I infuse with light and I am a preacher of righteousness preaching the good news of our God who is ever One. His will is good for thee. Drink ye the cup and rejoice.

Rejoice, people of God!

Rejoice, I say, and be grateful for the gift—O the gift of the violet flame!

February 15, 1981
Camelot
Los Angeles County, California
ECP

CHAPTER 18

We are here to make a statement! You have chosen to be born to make your statement—and some of you your final statement, as your final footprints on this earth.

CHAPTER 18

MESSAGE OF THE CHOHAN OF THE FIRST RAY

Our Statement

Ladies and gentlemen, attention. For I AM the Darjeeling trailblazer. And now there come to mind those words I penned so long ago: The trek upward is worth the inconvenience. Now you know just what I had in mind.

Welcome to the end of this trail and this trek. Welcome to the very Heart of our Inner Retreat. For I have had my eye on this Heart and this sun for many, many a century—when it was a wilderness, when the land was not even peopled, before its discovery or even the ancient coming of the Vikings.

Long before, from the heart of the Royal Teton or the heart of Sanat Kumara, I saw the destiny and the future of that race. And that race is indeed something that can be earned and won. For the whole meaning of Christ our Lord is that the crumbs of the Lord's table may also be for those who are first servants in his household and are yet to become his children and joint-heirs.

The possibility of the inheritance of the Christic light of all evolutions is this mighty message whereby each one in whom there is the I AM Presence, by the very preaching of the word, can convey the sparks that fly on a summer's evening—sparks from a campfire here at our ranch, sparks that fly into the sky! They disappear in the night, but some may ignite a heart—a heart that begins to beat for him, for him.

You all remember the story of Pinocchio—a path of initiation of the winning of a heart. Thus, blessed ones, who can measure the heart of any soul or of a man? For only God does know. The wise assume that the heart requires the burning lamp.[1] The wise assume that not knowledge alone but a fervent devotion harnessed to a love star is needed—and then, of course, the will to be: the will of the tiny grasses and forget-me-nots and many wildflowers, the will in every life. You find that will in the heart of every part of life that beats with a cosmic heart, with the Central Sun.

Therefore, I welcome you to the place of the Heart, which I dedicate in this hour to the path of the initiation of the heart. Let none enter here who will not feed my sheep! Let none enter who will not give to my sheep the true soul nourishment—those who cruelly transfer not the leadings of the soul but a dead doctrine, a serpent philosophy that leads the nations to self-destruction, destroys their economies, and makes all the world to know the meaning of hopelessness when hope should abound, for he lives and walks yet with his own.

I welcome you to the retreat, the retreat of the seven chohans of the rays, for we have somewhat to speak to you in this hour of the worlds turning. And it was necessary to have a place apart that you might see the perspective of the cities of the plain. How low and far below the vibratory level of the etheric plane do the cities of your own homes seem. The places of your embarkation seem far away in this hour. Why, you almost have the perspective of the angels who grace the mountaintops. Is this not a little bit of heaven? ["Yes."]

For some of you, it has been many a year since you came apart, not only in the spirituality of the contemplation of God but in a place of nature when and where the overlapping of the aura of the teeming cities has not been within at least a few tens or hundreds of miles. This is not only far away from Los Angeles and New York and Chicago, but it is also a secluded spot and sealed, that you might know what it is to live in the etheric plane for a while. It is like the first step into a conscious remembrance of the ascended masters' retreats.

You are not far in space or inner activity from our Royal Teton Retreat. All of a sudden it is like the contemplation of the stars. The trivia of life, the problems, and the burdens resume their lawful perspective. They are far, far away in the valley, and you are in the mountains of God, here to contemplate life and destiny and what you will do with the flame that God has placed in your hand as the gift of life and another tenure upon earth.

As you look into your campfires or into the stars or into the eyes of the messenger and beyond, it is well and good to think about the distance of past and future, and then beyond these into the recognition of the personhood of God with you as the Immanuel that is your Real Self.

MY GIFT TO YOU: A VISION OF IMMORTALITY

A vision of immortality is my gift to the messenger and to you. For I awakened her one night this very week to sense the limitless quality of our abode, where thoughts instantaneously become action and the density of flesh does not deter the buoyant spirit from the will to be and all those things you planned and saw as the purpose of this life.

I recall you to the ancient Tablets of *Mem*—the soul's memory and all that God has written for your destiny. I recall you now. For some of you it is the hour when all that follows hence must truly be in alignment with the perfect Self.

Many changes are in order for earth. But of these you ought not to be concerned, but rather dwell upon the changes in order for your own life. For only if you change, you see, will you ride the crest of the wave to victory instead of to self-defeat, as some have already done.

There is a power in the four elements that is an initiation itself. The land rejects those who try to possess it. The land rejects those who lack the givingness of the ever-flowing stream. The land is typical of the ruggedness of the path of initiation and that there are lessons to be learned if you are to embark upon a wilderness trek.

THE SPIRITUAL PATH

You may easily liken the spiritual path to preparation to face the most rugged conditions of earth. The intrepid mountain climbers and those who hike and camp all over the world are those who are in training for a higher and even more rugged spiritual path. You meet them in Nepal or in Alaska, at Mount Hood or Rainier. Each makes his choice as to how high he can climb.

"Climb the highest mountain" is a challenge to climb the highest mountain that you can climb. And therefore, year upon year is a new vision of a new mountain you never knew was there. You have already seen mountains you have never seen before, and these have translated to your souls the vision of other goals. Each one of you needs a little bit of weaning from city life—a little bit of consideration that, after all, the cities have come and gone, have disappeared, continents have sunk, and they shall rise again. But the soul moves on to its fiery destiny.

The plains of Mamre[2] are the plains of the ancient memory of Sanat Kumara—the backdrop of the Middle East, the austere country, man against the sky. Here you have a more succulent vegetation than some parts of the Middle East, though the tall cedars of Lebanon have always been a source of the contemplation of the majesty of God.

I come, then, with my heart full of gratitude, as a chalice brimming over at the lip, that you might drink of the water of a mountain stream near Darjeeling where I like to go in the Christmas snow that lasts a good part of the year. I like to see the flowers that peep through and the life that is yet vibrant, that yet rings with a determination—as across the Himalayas we view Tibet, China, and millions of people who know not yet the meaning of the igniting of the heart with the Christic light.

WE ARE HERE TO MAKE A STATEMENT

Here then, as I sit with you in an old armchair, I would speak to you concerning your own personal analysis of your future and your path. I ask you to make your own personal and family feasibility study in consideration of economic, educational, and cultural opportunities that may be found as the crow flies from the Inner Retreat in a number of directions. I ask you to consider alternatives that you may not have considered before.

Tempus fugit. I observe the turning of the stars and the cycles of a cosmic astrology. I see the amalgamation of the light of the lightbearers in one Lighthouse of Love. I see a powerful beam that is a beacon to the nations. And the tribes of the I AM Race will see that beacon because it has a great magnitude, a great mantle. And the sacred fire that blazes can be seen because you have understood the law of the One—that many heart fires produce a greater candlepower than many separated across the miles of earth.

We are here to make a statement! You have chosen to be born to make your statement—and some of you your final statement, as your final footprints on this earth. Some of you, at the conclusion of this life, will never again walk this earth to leave a physical footprint, but only blaze a fiery trail perceivable by those who are the sons of fire.

Therefore, realize that when all the world is an amplification of noise of one sort or another, making a statement is a mighty test indeed. The statement of the I AM Race must be as a banner of Maitreya billowing from the mountain—a statement of the I AM Presence and the logic of each one's unfoldment of the inner Logos.

When you are a part of the dharma to make this statement, you must realize that it is a collective statement. Those of us who are a part of the Great White Brotherhood realized long, long ago that our stamp upon the material cosmos could be made only as we would find ourselves one, one in this eternal light. No single vessel of identity contains the all in the Matter spheres, but many cups filled may approximate a single note of the infinite.

Therefore, beloved, the inescapable dharma is the inescapable collective. But our collective is never a commune. Our collective disappears into the mystical body of God, as Christ is one in us. And not one cell of this body forms a lump of discord protruding from the perfect sphere.

Discord and displeasure among the brethren is the sign of the intrusion of those who have not the seed of light. Beware the discordant ones and the complainers who crack the whip upon the chelas and complain when they make one fault—who they themselves do not enter in to sweat and toil for the raising of the canopy of our tent.

Beware those who come with the sense of injustice into our midst, who point the finger but bear not themselves the burning lamp of justice and who fear to contain in the belly the smoking furnace* that would have long ago consumed all their injustice and made of them a worthy vessel for the LORD. Beware the spoilers, then, who demand perfection in the flesh when they themselves have not the perfection of the heart.

Let the Law reveal, then. And let those who have sinned be self-revealed and quickly turn from their condemnation to a brighter love, a more perfect love, and an understanding of bearing one another's burden.

---

*Gen. 15:17.

Would it not be music to our ears if one would say to another, "Brother, I fear that perhaps the problems of your recent service may be the burden that you bear. Let me carry your karma for a day, that you may go to the hills and pray and be with God and be refreshed and be nourished. My brother, you have served and worked long in the Lord's vineyard. Now let me take thy place for a day. Go—be with the angels. I will keep the flame."

Would that not be, then, a gracious way of letting another know that perhaps the burdens of the hour have brought him not to an excelling expression of his own Christhood? And then, of course, you see how much virtue would come to you to understand the initiations of another that are not your daily mete.

The tests and tasks of other chelas might be far too hard for those who consider themselves so advanced along the way. Let us change garments for a day—not for etheric octaves, but with one another—and thereby learn a measure of compassion and flow, the ability to interchange and be ready to man any post of the watchman of the night; and in this flow, somehow to understand that the mystical body of God is oneness of hearts united, no task too great, no chore too lowly for anyone to perform.

Oh, the sweetness of our sweet communion when heaven and earth kiss in the heart of the chela! Why, much more of this heaven and you will say to me, "Morya, what need have we to ascend when all is here and our bliss is so great in the Inner Retreat?"

Well, my compassion for thee, my beloved, is that you have labored long in the weight of the karma of the cities of the world. Some of you live and move and have your being, not in Horeb's height but in the auras of ten million lifestreams and their entire karmic evolution. God has not saddled you to this beast but rather accorded you an opportunity and a path.

You must not lose your head and drop everything and run to the Inner Retreat. Life is not so easy in these parts. You must understand how to carve out of the rock a way of life and a livelihood for your own loved ones. You must move with study and care and consideration and a level head. This is why I have used the term "a feasibility study." There are a number of towns and cities as well as farms and ranches in the area. There are many services needed and goods to be produced that are the mutual requirement of a community of light.

I am still waiting for those who share the dream of a type of Utopia to realize that many of the elements of the path of chelaship do contain some of those considerations that I set forth in my life as Thomas More as both challenge and mockery to the inequities of that hour.[3] In that book, you can read and go beyond to a realization that, as I had a vision of the etheric cities of light, so did Francis Bacon[4] and many more of the brothers who labored a labor of love under the aegis of Pallas Athena.

In each of you is a divine memory of other octaves and the longing for a golden age, and all know that the beginning of that age is love. And therefore, you know that the age of Aquarius as the age of the love of Saint Germain must surely be the sign of the coming of a new horizon and a new lifewave.

Why not be the forerunner? Why not have it here?

Let only those who love such a dream with all their hearts even try. For if you have not the love of sacrifice for a goal and a dream, you should be of all men and women most miserable in the unceasing task of the building of a community of light.

I do not summon all, but only those who have the understanding and an inner fiery furnace whereby a heat is generated. The snows are cold in winter, and the winds that blow. And those who love the winter are those who have the internal fire. And in the snow and the wind they see not the cold but the fire itself. To them, the snow is sacred fire and the inner heat is a source of warmth and the burning lamp of light.

Thus, you see, God made a rugged clime for pilgrims. Rugged lands of Tibet and of other centuries and continents have summoned those who are not the lazy serpents sunning in the tropical heat, for they have no heartbeat to provide them with the inner glow. You must therefore understand that fallen ones tend to gather where the life is easy. And the individuals who are looking for something else other than more and more materialism, come apart and find in nature that which the greatest technology of all ages—which you have not even seen in this century—could not afford.

The heights of Lemuria and Atlantis, when devoid of the Mother flame, came tumbling down. Only those who have the power to endow Matter with a flame can successfully use technology to conquer Matter. And those who have not the flame build in vain.

OUR GOAL

Our Goal: To take, then, the best of a dying world and the highest of the world to come. To synthesize the old and the new and to understand the soul, perched upon the mountain. The flight upward is into God, to delve into the mysteries. And the descent is for the more perfect union of Spirit and Matter on earth.

May the violet flame in you all transmute that which can be transmuted in every area of the world. May the resourcefulness of those who drink in the prana and magnetize the fire of the rock be able to reinfuse America and the world with a new grace and a comfort and a light. But I tell you, ere the world is ready to receive the fullness of the Lord's cup, changes must come about.

I have seen the measuring rod given by the angel to John the Beloved.[5] Do you know, beloved ones, that in the archives of Almighty God it is known the exact count of individuals upon earth who have sworn ultimate defiance of the Almighty unto the end of their own limited destiny? Do you know that there is a vow so intense that has been taken by millions upon earth to never, never bend the knee before the Almighty God? Therefore, you see, a certain destiny of the future can be calculated by their very commitment to death itself.

We must only say to them, "If that is your free will, die then! But do not take with you the living and their children." We desire not to see the contamination of these little ones of the death culture, the death wish. And yet, little by little, this death culture is accepted as the norm. Every chemical that dulls the brain and the senses is a taste of sweet death. Every downward beat of the rhythm of the rock is the descent of ascension's fire—every turn against the heart of God. So many applications of science lead the individual to death.

The horror of death yet the fascination of its horror, from abortion to murder itself, is a way of life for many. And if they are not engaged in the very act itself, increment by increment in their own world, then they are glued to the endless, endless scenarios of television or the motion-picture industry or science fiction. And therefore, the way that leads to death on earth is broad, and many, many follow the gurus of death in Church and State. It is so subtle that many do not realize that common, everyday occurrences are a little bit of the taste of death itself.

Here you breathe life. Here you feel the invigorating pulsations of the earth. The fire in the heart of the mountain is not far, and as yet it is not disturbed. I say then, considering those who have made their vow, I am grateful that you have listened well to the understanding that God has already made *his* vow with the I AM Race and sealed it with a covenant that cannot be broken except by man himself who turns the way of the fallen angels.

Let there be light! Let there be perspective! The invisible hand that moves the destiny of this nation and of the course of your life writes now the geometry of your soul. There are coordinates. There are stations where you must meet other lifestreams. There are works to be accomplished. There are dreams to be gathered. There is a seriousness in the days ahead.

From the hour of July 4, 1981, I gave to the messenger four years to define the place prepared.[6] And in that hour, this property had not yet been secured. You are the ones who have secured the down payment and one of four equal fall payments that are to be made until this land is wholly secure against the ravages of the economy or the ups and downs of fickle minds and tempted hearts.

Well, children of the sun, I vow to express my gratitude to you in your personal life and action. By your call to me, I will show you the plan of making your place secure in or near this Inner Retreat. And I will show you how your life can be complete and full, productive, and how it can become a part of a great beacon —a statement that must be made by every available means of technology and by the chakras of your body temples, by this wavelength and that, by satellite, by television, by radio, by the heart's communication, by initiations here and teachings whereby you learn to expand the flame of the threefold light and send to your brothers and sisters in all lands the message of freedom.

Why, if you choose, you can bring to a culmination together all that has gone before, that patriots and pilgrims have laid across America—that is about to be lost but is yet to be saved by the lovers of Mother Liberty, by those who care enough and know that there are yet millions of hearts that can glow in this nation, if you can but add your own heart to theirs for a season until they learn to fan the flame and expand.

Why, the unsolvable problems of El Salvador or of a city's police force or of the crime rate or of marijuana that hangs heavy as black sheaths upon our children—these unsolvable problems can only be solved by an acceleration of the fires of heart, by a willingness to meet God face-to-face.

PLACE OF GREAT ENCOUNTERS

That is why we call it the Place of Great Encounters. It is not for those who fear to meet their God along the way or to be blinded as was Saul until he received the new name Paul and was given his commission;[7] it is for those who do not fear the consequences of their own karma and its challenges. Why, has not our messenger shown you that she would go anywhere, do anything, submit to any burden to balance that karma so that we could have a finer servant? Well, she will tell you herself, she is not any worse for the wear and tear but far better and wiser a bit.

Blessed hearts, be ongoing, for many saints have walked the path that you are reticent to walk—the path whereby you face the canyons and the deep of your own subconscious and the specters of the night. Why, just read my book *Chela and the Path*.[8] Gird up your loins, put on the whole armor, study the recipe for winning. And when you are all set and have all your gear, simply charge forth and slay every last beast so that you will not have to come again and find still there a serpent's egg and in it, a serpent's tooth. After all, it is the tooth of sin that bites, and it must be extracted as the whole beast must be gone.

Well, as I have always said, the path of the first-ray chelas is to get on with it—to draw a straight line, walk in it, look straight as an arrow to the highest peak, and watch the gleam of the sun at dawn glisten there and know that at the summit of every mountain is a diamond waiting, waiting for you to take it and make it your own.

Oh, the wonders of nature and God in nature! But you see, many have gone to nature with drugs, with stimulants, for all sorts of reasons. They have missed entirely elemental life and the Holy Spirit.

Nature is a great challenge. It defies entrance into its heart unless you come with a flaming spirit. In fact, beloved ones, the effect of this land upon those who are not ready is a greater densification of the human consciousness. It is exceedingly possible to become more dense in this terrain and life. . . .

Do not think, then, that the land itself transforms people. People are self-transforming, and they have a way of outplaying their lives—going down or up. And they do it, whether in heaven or hell or anywhere on earth.

Therefore, what is the Place of Great Encounters? It is a place where the secrets of God are locked in the atom. It is a place where those who understand the meaning of the solar fire in the heart *can* accelerate to a greater extent—if they have a will to do so—than those encumbered by ten million auras interpenetrating and sending ten million different signals. Is it any wonder you feel a bit heavy at the end of a day in New York or Los Angeles or Calcutta?

Well, precious hearts, the Place of Great Encounters is the place where you meet the mountain and conquer—else it will conquer you. These are the mountains. Like the rock of Christ, one either places himself upon the rock to be broken by Christ, else in the hour of the judgment with the fallen ones does cry out to the mountains to "fall upon us,"[9] in a desire to somehow accelerate the karma and the judgment for the inner knowing that one has not compensated for one's misuse of life.

Some are running like lemmings to the final judgment. They consider, "As long as it is coming, we may as well have done with it." And others are running to the mountain.

We have built our retreats in the Himalayan fastnesses for the very reason that the mountains themselves are for the thinning of the chelas. And therefore, you see, each one must find his niche. Whether the bird of the highest rock or the gardens of the cities, there is no condemnation. Each man must know himself and know his place of overcoming.

And the striving chelas must realize that when they have scraped the ceiling of their present abode and there are no further lessons to be learned or expansion to be gained, there is a place prepared. And this place, once only etheric, can now be physical because you have dedicated your hearts to making it possible, whether or not you yourself may make it your home in the near or distant future.

You have realized that for some, this is a necessary leg of the path of attainment. And you have realized that one day in the near or distant future, your soul will require this exact combination of environment, God's chemistry, and community. And in that hour when you have need, by your good karma you will find that place prepared—here or there.

Therefore, I express the gratitude of my chelas throughout the world, on earth and in the etheric retreats awaiting embodiment, whose path of initiation could go no further or higher without this physical Place of Great Encounters. And I come to tell you that it is indeed a nexus. And you have opened the door to the seven chohans for the meeting of the chohans and their chelas here in this Heart and, through it, through the recorded word, to many around the world. There are teachings which can be given only in this environment and altitude, and books which can be written here and here alone.

It is my desire to see you who find your duties in other places yet return to our Heart once a year to become more and more skillful in living with nature, self-sufficient, and understanding the balance of the base of your pyramid—including the physical survival and thus the expansion of heart and lung and muscle and drive.

O blessed ones, just as soon as we pull together the mighty oar of the building, we will accommodate more and more. And they will come, such as you have not seen them come before. And I think of the ant and the rows of ants making their trek to the anthills. Well, our chelas are far more than robot ants, but they can follow a straight line from any part of the earth to the hearth and home and the citadel of our Brotherhood.

Yours are some of the first footprints making that path indelible. I consider that you are the writers of history and that history is being recorded in the rock and the mountain. And elementals, enjoying their lessons in reading and writing from the angels themselves, in their first little books of handwriting, have asked their teachers, as they are perched on these mountains, if they may write the story of the pilgrims who have come to the Heart. They are delighted beyond words! And for them, they have a new zest in learning their letters—these little elementals who want so much to be like you and to be a part of Montessori International.*

You see, all of life dreams and has goals and has a level of striving. And a little peek into the life of the nature spirits would bring tears to your eyes. For you are their hope. As Pelleur long ago said, "You are our hope."[10]

The hope of God is great this day. And I must speak to you again before I bid you adieu from this Heart. For this is my welcome and this is my love. This is my cup and the beginning of our celebration.

I hold you to my heart, each one. And in that embrace in this hour, I take to my being the problem you have brought with you, the burden that you would like to transmute so that you might do more for Morya.

Blessed ones, we *will* do more together. This is my promise.

May you always be blessed by the bread of angels, as I AM.

August 25, 1982
Inner Retreat
Royal Teton Ranch
Park County, Montana
ECP

*Montessori International was a private school, founded by Mark and Elizabeth Prophet in 1970, for children preschool through twelfth grade.

CHAPTER 19

Our memories are very strong of our encounters in this world—our awareness of the oncoming Light and of a Darkness that also must be swallowed up.

CHAPTER 19

BETWEEN TWO WORLDS

"We Can Count on Our Chelas . . ."

O presence of the will of God in the diamond heart of the chela, I welcome you to Darjeeling! I welcome you to the infinite splendor of the path of goodwill.

How goodwill begets more in kind! And I, El Morya, am inclined to discourse with you this evening upon a subject most favorite to my heart. It is, of course, the path of personal Christhood that is the way out of the planetary dilemma. But for the time being, it is the point of identification of every son of God caught between the love of the Father and the love of emergent souls.

Thus, the Path is amply depicted on this Chart of the Presence.[1] For, you see, the one who is mediator, Christ in the flesh, is indeed caught between two worlds and therefore must love the Above and the below, translating in both directions—the great macrocosmic need and the microcosmic need.

Truly, the meaning of the cross and being fastened to it, beloved hearts, is to occupy, until the full coming of the Lord into his temple,[2] that position between the I AM Presence and the evolving souls of humanity. For the one who is at that point of service understands one must not approach too close to the God-head lest one leave the evolving souls bereft of one's presence; and one must not descend too far and lose the right hand of the Almighty One for the very succoring of souls.

And thus, the path of the Middle Way was pronounced by Gautama, truly demonstrated by Jesus; and now it is your own. May you perceive the Middle Way as the point of contact through your heart between the Father and evolving souls on earth. And may you value that office in hierarchy as none other can value it, save the one who is the One Sent—your own beloved Christ Self.

In the peace of that one, won't you be seated by my fire.

Our memories are very strong of our encounters in this world —our awareness of the oncoming Light and of a Darkness that also must be swallowed up. Our cares and concerns for infant humanity have been such that, having done all we could do, we have taken our leave of this octave only to do more.

In this day and hour of the dispensation of Saint Germain, from my heart I assure you that many more in embodiment can sustain the flame of life and of a greater mastery without losing their heads, as has so often been the case. Well, beloved hearts, we have not minded losing our heads as long as we have not lost our sacred hearts and our souls' oneness in the living Word. For if the heads roll, is it not better it be ourselves than another?

Thus, we have been willing, for the will of God, to move on. Now we are willing, through our chelas, to stay—in fact, to decelerate closer to the evolving souls, even as many evolving souls are rising higher.

There is a great discrepancy between the paths of people on earth. It is, in fact, true that the more the lightbearers rise, the more darkness and evil is also embodied, pulling in the opposite direction to attempt to hold a counterweight against the rising light.

Blessed hearts of the Infinite One, we are most concerned that this opportunity from the heart of Saint Germain—for which you are sponsors and for which there are many sponsors in the Great Central Sun—might provide you with that impetus of the union of the soul with the living Christ, that more and more souls may truly come to understand what it means to occupy for planet Earth the Person of Christ as mediator between the plane of perfection of the I AM THAT I AM and the plane of evolving souls.

When there is but one who can hold a balance in an age, you can understand that only so much can be accomplished. This is not because that one is limited. Nay, it is always because from other systems and worlds there do come the antichrists who have inverted that very light and pit themselves against the plans and projects of the avatar of the age. So has it ever been with beloved Saint Germain.

Therefore the false-hierarchy impostors of that one, as the anti-Christ and anti-force of freedom, have yet remained in embodiment, pitted against every move toward a world congress of freedom—of which, as you very well know, the United Nations has become the perversion inasmuch as major decisions can be vetoed and denied by those powers, such as the Soviet Union [Russia] or Red China, that have at their helm the forces of anti-freedom themselves.

Thus, beloved hearts, Saint Germain's own world congress of freedom has not become a reality. The United States of America has been the beginning. Saint Germain has sought to extend that union through the Pan-American Union* and an association of states in this hemisphere, but even this has not been productive to the extent that the master would have hoped by his own vision. And thus, always it is that the Christed ones, banding together, must offset that which is the anti-Christ consciousness moving against the consciousness of the age.

You know well, dear hearts, that we have seen in the union of the lightbearers—as it was prophesied long ago that these lightbearers should become the ensign to all people[3]—that in the

---

*An organization formed in 1890 to promote cooperation among the countries of Latin America and the U.S. It has been re-formed as the Organization of American States.

banding together of our precious hearts, our diamond-hearted chelas, there would be the strengthening, the reinforcing, the dipping into the Christ consciousness and therefore the forging of that Christ in the heart of community, strengthening all, strengthening to the very heights in order that there would be the balance held. And you have known that our Inner Retreat signifies the coming together of the eagles.[4]

Though Saint Germain has been the participant in the mighty action of the flame of Gautama Buddha, you must realize that the physical/etheric retreat of Shamballa has not been moved, but that the "Western Shamballa," as the additional focus of that retreat, has been established. Forevermore the Shamballa of the Lord of the World and Sanat Kumara does remain in the etheric octave over that Gobi Sea, the Gobi Desert.[5] And in this hour, the forcefield in the West is the extension of that arm and the planting of the new plant of light from the very heart of Shamballa. Therefore, the Brotherhood of Shamballa and the mighty light of Kuan Yin, who appears in the garb of the Saviouress, does establish at that retreat an open door for service and the holding of the balance.

THE NECESSARY PREPARATIONS

I would, therefore, bring to your attention certain facts concerning our projects there, that you might understand, beloved hearts, that in order for us to accomplish the necessary preparations on the schedule given to me by beloved Helios, we do require more help—help in the very physical presence of those who are capable and able to perform the necessary services, help in the form of resources, help in the form of supply.

I bring this to your attention, beloved hearts, so that you will understand that many who anticipate that all will be in readiness and waiting for them and for their families when they arrive at the Inner Retreat ought to consider that if everyone maintained that attitude, there would be no one there to prepare the place.

As it is, as we see the timetables and as we hold in the heart of the messenger those very timetables, we realize that the sufficiency of human resources as well as supply is not to the level where we may commit [i.e., guarantee] to our embodied chelas the fulfillment of the plan that we deem necessary and wise for your own lifestreams. Thus, it becomes a necessity for us to present this information to you so that you will blame neither the embodied servants nor the Darjeeling Council when you look to find refuge there and find that all is not accomplished as you thought it should have been.

Beloved hearts, I think sometimes that the winds of the age, the tides of change do affect even our best servants, and there is an absence of realization as to just how deadly a tonic fear itself can be. Fear breeds self-concern and *over* self-concern and also a mountain of indecision. Fear also breeds a preoccupation with endless details of little consequence or import save to take up one's time and attention, preoccupying oneself from the realities at hand.

Thus, you understand that those who suffer psychologically from inordinate fear at the subconscious level (as records from previous embodiments) are many of those who are institutionalized this day because the fear itself does prevent them from normal action. Thus, you can see that inaction, a failure *to act* multiplied many times over, can result in a life that is noneffective, impractical, and certainly preoccupied with everything *but* the challenges of saving a planet.

People decide to retreat and to study this or that, to accelerate a certain development of their personality or education when, in fact, it is clear that this is tantamount to Nero fiddling while Rome burned. It is a way of distracting oneself from horrendous calamity to fail to act in the hour of greatest peril or the hour of greatest challenge or the hour of the greatest victory. These are psychological maneuverings of the not-self.

How well it is, therefore, that you have perceived the necessity of binding the forces of anti-will at each point of the apertures of consciousness on the cosmic clock.[6] For thereby you will see the new day and the new ray of the will of God that is for that day—a mighty blue ray that is tinged in violet, almost an indigo. That particular blue is a special quality that I give to the very heart of Saint Germain, whereby the alchemy of the blue-flame will of God is present in this very admixture of my palette.

THE RANCH

Beloved ones of light, let there be an infinite fire descending! Let the sphere of cosmic purpose, as shooting star over the ranch, reveal to precious hearts that if the place is to be prepared, there must be hearts and heads and hands to prepare it!

If the necessary facilities are to be established, the supply must be forthcoming!

I desire, then, that you take up a discussion of these necessities and what can and ought to be done, . . . for it is most important that all realize that the plans are set, the geometry is known; the filling in of the blueprint of the mosaic itself by the fire of the cobalt blue must be wrought by those who are builders in the world of form. How well you know that Gautama Buddha is the champion of the will of God as the flame of God-obedience and that the four o'clock line of his victory in Taurus is for the action of the builders.

Thus, the builders must come, building from the very foundation to the apex of life. And those who are separating themselves for other preparations or the accumulation of wealth must realize that many souls now in the higher octaves as well as many of you in embodiment who were there in those hours when the millions were brutally murdered by the Red Chinese or the Soviets in Eastern Europe, in Russia, and in Poland—those individuals who lost their lives were obviously at the wrong place at the wrong time.

They trusted. They thought and thought again and could not believe that such a thing could happen. There was opportunity for some to escape, but they could not believe that such a calamity could happen. And therefore, in the hour of maximum danger, when souls ought to have been prepared and borne to safety, there was more of a preoccupation with those things that would no longer matter. For there comes a time in life when the only thing that matters is life itself and its preservation in the physical octave.

You have never been set on a path of martyrdom by the ascended masters of the Darjeeling Council or any other council, for the age of martyrdom is over. This is the age of full Christhood and of joy and of abundance. There is no martyrdom in hard work or the labor of the heart or the building of the New Day or in chelaship that does not fear the exposure of the sensitivities of oneself and one's human creation.

How long shall we labor with those who desire not to be corrected, not to be affected, not to be offended? Shall we forevermore have our messenger walking on eggs around certain chelas who will not forsake their old ways but would rather be comfortable as they are forever?

Well, beloved ones, it is the same principle. If you see the folly of individuals attempting to preserve their material life and status quo and you see the handwriting on the wall—whether in the Middle East or Central America—can you not see the same in your own self when you seek to preserve yourself as you are and fail to realize that every rising sun is a signal and a sign that you must rise and leave behind some portion of the old order of self and selfishness? Can you not see, therefore, that preserving the perverse way or the exception to the rule is also allowing oneself to be out of alignment with the inner blueprint?

We have said before, it is not so important to arrive physically, it is important to arrive in the spirit of the Christ consciousness. It is important to *be* in that consciousness and allow all other things to be subservient to it.

We have not desired to see you deprived of anything beautiful and lovely in this octave that is a part of the expression of your life.

In fact, we desire to see you take all of this to the Inner Retreat, even if it requires a caravan that must go around the earth to bring all of your possessions with you! But, beloved ones, this takes time and space, this takes cycles. And therefore, if you would move culture and civilization with you and the best of life and hearts and heart friends, I would suggest that you be up and doing.

And if you perceive the necessity for the building of the nucleus for the rest to be sustained, I would suggest you become the avant-garde, the advance men and women who will truly build that foundation. And if you are unable to leave your homes of light and your businesses which truly are practical and in the service of humanity, then I say, send the supply that others might do the building, that others might take care of those ingredients as you even supply more than the tithe, more than the gift, but also that extra measure that will allow us to accomplish what is to be accomplished.

A TRANSITION INTO A HIGHER DIMENSION

Beloved ones, we have always preached the path of the "life-saver." We have always determined and desired to see change come about as the most beautiful planetary transition of alchemy. Your eyes are wide open, ours are wide open. Therefore, we see that not so many of earth's people—except for a motivation of fear—desire to see a smooth transition into a higher dimension.

They may desire God in the moment of absolute need, but a golden age is not what they would want to see. They joke about not desiring to be in heaven, for none of their friends would be there. Their desires of the flesh would have no part with the higher octave and they do not desire to leave these, preferring death to change.

Their preference for death rather than change is stated every day in the hospitals of the world throughout the planetary body, as those who pass on do so because they have been unwilling to give up their desires, their human habits, their eating habits, their smoking habits, their drinking habits, their drug habits. They prefer all of this hell and fiendish life to the golden age.

These are the ones who pull a planetary body almost in two—pulling apart at the seams what ought to be the garment of God universally present. And therefore, there is a strong pull as an undercurrent moving against the great golden age. And if you desire not to be caught up in that astral tide, you must move away from the sea and go up the mountain where those pulls cannot affect you, where the consciousness of God is full and plenteous.

Let us, then, consider what is at hand. Let us understand that there are always those who would pull against our particular movement and plan and our design. And therefore, beloved ones, in any company and communion which we share, we must also be guarded. And therefore, the revelation of the Almighty One, the I AM THAT I AM, must always be at the point of the practical precipitation.

At the *point* of action God reveals himself. God does not declare, except when he desires to do so through prophecy, what his future actions will be. Thus, there are many surprises in life. Even when you give birth to your own sons and daughters, you have the complete surprise of the sudden appearing of the first smile, the first breath, and the unveiling of the image of Christ in the one God has sent to you. Thus, there are some things that remain veiled until they are uncovered.

And Yahweh spake unto Moses and said, "I AM WHO I AM."[7] He did not reveal his name, except the state of being itself. His promise to Moses: I will reveal myself in the course of events and so will the people know who I AM.[8] And therefore in the deliverance of the people, there came forth miracle upon miracle upon miracle, one by one.

Thus, the LORD God came to be known by his presence, and this community must come to be known by the action of God within its members, in the building of the Spirit from the within to the without. And therefore, we will not publish our plans to the world and allow the alchemy of the fallen ones to move against the divine chemistry, the "all-chemistry" of God. You must walk by faith, for there is no other means but faith by which you can walk.

The will of God is being accomplished and the knowledge of what must be accomplished is held directly from my heart to the heart of your messenger. And that seeing and that knowing must be respected, must be supported, and it must be realized by those who are ready to sponsor it more fully in the physical octave. The activity has needs if the activity is to accomplish the will of God. Therefore, I apprise you of this fact.

May you move in the inner Spirit of the Holy Ghost. May you understand the necessary veiling of the fullness of that divine blueprint until it takes form. May you understand that we count you and many around the world as a part of this mighty spiral that resembles an amphitheater of light. This amphitheater of light, as a spiral to the sun, contains a point and a position for every soul.

May you welcome to your hearts, therefore, an understanding of necessities. And may you counsel, for it is well to counsel with the messenger* concerning a new vantage point and position in your service to the cause. Realize, then, that we will do what we can do, and so will our best servants do as they can do. But we must have more than a vote of confidence; we must have your physical presence and we must have coordination throughout this activity.

Your expectancy and your hopes are high. Therefore, I come so that you might understand that the unknown God who reveals himself to you is the *known* God of your own Christ Self and your own Divine Personhood. And therefore, the one who shall lead the children of the Hebrews out of Egypt is the one God and the God flame *in your own heart.* The internalization of the I AM Presence, the Son of God, and your own soul in communion with these is truly the key to the divine accomplishment, the very success of this mission.

---

*through prayers or letters, as she has passed on to higher realms and taken her ascension

We are practical builders in the ascended-master octaves, and among you are the most practical of men and women in this world. Therefore, let there be a pulling together of the oars, a mighty heave, and let us understand that month by month, in this year and the next, certain things must become physical if all is to be prepared in the hour of your preparedness.

Blessed hearts, in the fullness of the will of God, I have addressed you. I have been with you through your calls this evening. I have been with you in the heart of hearts. And many planetary changes have taken place at inner levels, binding the forces of the anti-will that have moved against your lifestream and our purposes for many centuries.

We thank you with our hearts' love for your determination and your response always. Truly, the most faithful and shining sapphires of the sun are a part of this community.

Of one thing I am certain as I look into the eyes of Saint Germain here in Darjeeling as I am speaking to you: that we can count on our chelas when our chelas are apprised of the full facts and information at hand. Therefore, my beloved hearts, I seal you in the exigencies of the hour, knowing that the eternal Spirit will confirm my word and this office and the oneness of the Great White Brotherhood in the purposes at hand.

With the sign of Gautama Buddha, I seal you and I send you forth into the joy flame of the will of God and of the seventh-ray master.

In the service of the light of the will of God within you, I AM always your Morya.

October 8, 1983
Camelot
Los Angeles County, California
ECP

CHAPTER 20

"Incompletion" is the stamp that has been stamped upon many a file of many a chela whose records we keep in Darjeeling. . . . Understand that this means that the divine plan cannot be completed because of personal karma or world conditions or the separation of twin flames.

CHAPTER 20

THE MISSION OF TWIN FLAMES TODAY

How to Join Forces with Your Twin Flame for Freedom

Hail, flaming ones who have come to the knowledge of the first principles of holy love, who desire then this holiness of love's early dream and are willing to endure unto its completion.

I am El Morya, sponsor of these messengers and of the path of your chelaship through the will of God. I salute Chananda, as he has delivered the opening address from the Darjeeling and Indian councils of the Great White Brotherhood, sponsoring the light out of the East unto those gathered here on the very edge of the Motherland.*

Thus, tarry with me an hour, for I would speak to you of the mission of twin flames today.

First, I would tell you that the ascended masters always address the question of what is most necessary to the God-realization in the chela and to the meeting of the demands of urgency of the hour —urgencies which engulf nations and leaders and families and solitary souls climbing the mount—the Mount Olympus or the Himalayas, Mount Shasta or the point of Everest.

**Motherland* refers to Lemuria, lost continent of the Pacific.

Blessed ones, climb the mountain to the I AM Presence and understand that the need of thy soul complementing the urgency of world need is for a greater wholeness, a greater love, and a greater light.

"Incompletion" is the stamp that has been stamped upon many a file of many a chela whose records we keep in Darjeeling. "Incompletion." Beloved, understand that this means that the divine plan cannot be completed because of personal karma or world conditions or the separation of twin flames.

Understand that at one point in the career of your messengers their reuniting hung by a thread. Its possibility was present by a thread of contact and a thread which, if broken, could become buried deep 'neath the tides of the sea, as deep as the transatlantic cable.

Thus, realize that not all have found one another. Some have passed as ships in the night, producing tension, frustration, sweating, bad dreams, psychological conditions, the sense that all is lost, and ultimately the obsession and more severe psychological problems which in fact are not truly resolved in the presence of the beloved but often exacerbated.

THE UNION OF TWIN FLAMES

Thus, I come to pierce the illusion that all problems are resolved by the meeting of twin flames or even soul mates. But I come with a statement of truth: that all problems *may* be solved by this union when it is founded upon the rock of divine Reality.

We come, and we sponsor because your hearts have yearned, your souls have prayed, your minds have sought—sought to fulfill the reason for being in this life, sought to attain oneness with the perfect one. We will connect those for whom the connection results in a positive force for one another and for society. And where it would be detrimental in all ways or some, we recommend the accelerated path of the chela, humility before the teaching of the Great White Brotherhood, which does give to you the knowledge of the violet flame and the call to Astrea, which is the most powerful mantra to the Divine Mother that has been released in this octave.[1]

The power of the universal Mother carrying the circle and sword of blue flame that is released in this mantra is great indeed, capable of fulfilling every manifestation of the Mother, East or West, and capable of driving from you evil spirits that lurk, addictions, self-indulgences and all pettiness that snatch from you that precious love which comes so gently, so powerfully, and yet is as fragile as crystal and can be broken and will be broken by the forces of the night unless you keep the tryst with Astrea and Archangel Michael and Kārttikeya, whom you know as Sanat Kumara.

Understand that the highest and most perfect love begins with your individual expression of the heart, the expansion of that flame of love until all irritation is consumed and pride is not, and you stand before your God truly worthy of whatever blessing can be given.

Inasmuch as personal karma is the key factor separating twin flames and inasmuch as it is desirable that twin flames unite in service, the x factor that can make the difference is the entering in of one of the ascended masters or of Padma Sambhava or Gautama or Sanat Kumara to sponsor that union by pledging to take on the karma that does keep apart those souls. This sponsorship is like the sponsorship of the individual chela except it is the joint sponsorship of the twain.

PLEDGE OF TWIN FLAMES TO BALANCE KARMA, SERVE IN HARMONY

This, then, is a call you ought to include in your prayers. It is a call that says:

"O God, I desire to perform the best service and to fulfill my inner vow with my twin flame. If it be that karma does separate us and therefore our service, I pray, let the LORD God set it aside for an hour and a year that we might show ourselves worthy, plow the straight furrow, enter into the service of our God and our country and of world freedom that together we may choose to balance that karma. And we do choose to do so, LORD God.

"We pledge, then, no matter what may come, that if we be united, we will serve in harmony by the grace of God to first balance the karma taken on by an ascended master that that one need not carry for us the burden that is truly our own."

Thus, having so said, it is important to record on paper in your own writing this prayer and whatever you have added to it with the date carefully inscribed and with your signature. You may insert it in the book of the Everlasting Gospel.*

You must remind yourself to call to Archangel Michael to defend the highest encounter and to bind all impostors of your twin flame. For as soon as the desire is set and the sail is raised on your ship, the false hierarchy will send in those of attraction, of glamour or of heavy karma or even the initiators that come out of the depths of darkness posing as the Krishna, the holy one of God that is thine own.

To prepare for the perfect union, one must have the vision and the inner tie to God that tells one of the lurking danger. Thus, keep the prayer and the call. And when all tests have been passed and the one sent is sent, remember that the purpose of that togetherness is truly first and foremost the balancing of that karma and the setting free of the ascended master that indeed has sponsored you and paid a price, the understanding of which will not be yours until one day you stand to offer yourself to pay the price for another.

---

* *The Path of the Higher Self,* The Everlasting Gospel (volume 1 of the Climb the Highest Mountain series), by Mark and Elizabeth Prophet.

THE ASCENDED AND UNASCENDED TWIN FLAME

Now, it does often occur that this very call results in the ascended twin flame approaching the unascended one. And thereby the union of hearts, as Above, so below, can be fulfilled as the ascended twin flame does hold the balance of the karma while the unascended twin flame accelerates on the Path.

This union may become so great that the ascended master and the unascended chela may walk the earth as one at inner levels, and the Electronic Presence of the ascended twin flame may be upon the unascended one. Thus, that unascended one, having an aura of completeness, presents therefore to others a strength, a love, an ability to give because the source is wholeness, is oneness.

This path must be prayed for. Some of you are not able to unite in a very personal way with the ascended master who is your twin flame because of intervening personal relationships that have become, if I might tell you, all too personal. And as a result, even the most intimate communion in the secret chamber of the heart with your Christ Self is too often interrupted by the sympathetic heart that is more attuned to the sympathies of other human beings than to the Christ of those human beings. The [auric profile of the] sympathetic heart, the heart of self-pity, has been drawn in pastels, through the messenger, by Saint Germain. You can see its downward pull and the muddy aura that it produces.[2]

The antithesis of this type of misqualification of the heart is expressed in the one who is all too impersonal and therefore does not have a momentum for the release of the fires of the heart in love to brother or sister or pilgrims upon the path of life. Thus, whereas the nonexercise of the heart results in hardness of heart, its misuse makes it become emotional and bowed down with that vibration of pity—pity, I tell you, that is not able to raise up oneself or the friend.

BURDENS OF INDIA AND AMERICA: FALSE GURUS

Now understand that as I am El Morya and the Chief of the Darjeeling Council, I represent God-government and I counsel the nations. And I perceive in this hour the great burdens upon India. And one of the greatest burdens of this nation in this hour is what we have called the Black Brotherhood of India. Not only are they the impostors of the true gurus and masters, but they are the impostors in government, in the economy, in the educational institutions—they are impostors in the sense that everything they do is to oppose the divine plan of twin flames from coming into manifestation.

Much of this comes from greed or the desire for power, even if that power is impure; the desire to control—the desire even to control individuals on the spiritual path by limiting their knowledge of the true science that comes from the God Himalaya. Thus, they may entertain followers and disciples or chelas, but they may limit their knowledge of the Law and the use of the light, telling them it is for their good, even as in the West in some circles Communion is served without the impartation of the wine of the Spirit; or the teaching of Christ is incomplete because it stops before the teaching of the internalization of the Word is given.

In this case, then, the false teacher brings but a little of the Path and withholds the rest, doling it out crumb by crumb merely to keep the followers tied to himself. He, having no light [i.e., Christ] of his own, does live upon the light [Christ] of others. And thus, these mechanisms are highly refined—the enslavement of souls by the Black Brotherhood of India drawing a dark circle around them and seeing to it that they cannot press through to the Brotherhood of light.

This false hierarchy, then, has come in the person of many false gurus to America, to the English-speaking nations—to Australia, the British Isles, Canada. Through the nations of the world they have come. They have taught *siddhis** to those who have not the Spirit incarnate of the Lord Krishna. They have given the initiation of a mantra to those who have not surrendered their souls and hearts to God, who have not paid the requirements of the Law. And yet these false gurus, beloved ones, they do not—they do not indeed actually transfer the highest light.

Thus, a network of false hierarchs, false gurus, and false chelas is being built around the world, establishing the antithesis to the masters of the Great White Brotherhood by promising immediate results—the results of energies in the spine or the chakras or certain powers or certain relief from suffering—all of this without the required balance of karma or the path of reunion. This, then, becomes a limitation to the divine government of India and of America, for it is the best servants and the lightbearers who, seeking the light [the Cosmic Christ], become encumbered by and often even fascinated with the false gurus.

Beloved ones, I counsel you, then, to know that we have given to you in the path of our teaching that which will secure you and protect you from any idolatrous cult or association which has as its foundation the avowed determination to keep you separated from your twin flame but tied to the false guru. Thus, the allegiance is mandated by these false teachers to the person of the unascended guru instead of to the Person of the Godhead and the I AM Presence.[3]

We warn because we have seen the going astray of lightbearers into these avenues. And it has cost them, sometimes for several embodiments, the scheduled union with the twin flame, the scheduled initiations with Maitreya. And the world itself has suffered; for these lightbearers have belonged at the very heart of their nation's government, educational institutions, sponsorship of motherhood, and in the holding of the balance of the economies.

**siddhis:* [Sanskrit], supernatural powers acquired through the practice of yoga.

DIVINE WHOLENESS: THE MANDATE OF THE HOUR

We have called this conference, then, and we have called it for this very purpose, that you should understand that the necessity of the divine wholeness is the mandate of the hour to solve the international crisis of war, of the last plagues, of the fourth horseman of the apocalypse who rides as the death rider in this hour.[4]

Whatever you see in the world can be healed by the science of the spoken Word through the soul's union with the I AM Presence, with the ascended masters, and with the twin flame, first at the level of the Christ Self and then in all levels of being—each decree and mantra therefore being offered in the defense of this community, dedicated by Maitreya to the reinitiation of twin flames who left the Garden of Eden and did not take the advancing steps on the Path.

Maitreya has come. He has set up the Mystery School, choosing the Royal Teton Ranch as the place for that light. He has come to call ancient souls, twin flames back to the initiations where they left off on the continent of Lemuria. Here was the Mystery School. Here was the opportunity. Here it is born again.

Do not fear and do not withdraw when Maitreya recounts to you at inner levels what are the requirements of the return to this opportunity. It comes once in many thousands of years. And each and every one who hears my voice in these rooms—you must know that you are here because you need this initiation in order to be effective with your twin flame and to make your ascension.

Do not be concerned that life may be hard or situations may be painful. These are outer things and outer circumstances. Live in the eye of the flame in the center of the heart. Perform thy duties with joy. Fulfill all things. And win thy freedom, not to escape but to be free to heal the world.

WE PLACE OURSELVES AT YOUR SERVICE

Thus, we are come. Thus, we place ourselves at your service. May you know the meaning of having access to the ascended masters through Maitreya, Gautama, Jesus and Sanat Kumara—the Lion, the Calf, the Man, and the Flying Eagle.[5] So, these are the symbols of the ones who hold the divine office in the four quadrants. So, let your heart be opened to the mysteries of Christ. And do not deny them before you have tasted of the nectar of thy Christ Self.

Yes, I tell it to you straight: you have been indoctrinated, both East and West, with a false theology—at best incomplete, at worst in error; at best by the well-meaning ignorant, at worst by black magicians who have stolen the light of the universal Christ of Jesus.

Rejoice that you have found the light in your heart. Lament not the years of darkness, for these too were the karma of thine own neglect. This is the day of the opening of the temple door. Walk through, for the Lord Christ beckons thee. Fear not, for to fear the ascended masters and the Christ and to feel secure with the false pastors is of all conditions most reprehensible.

Thus, let us turn the tables. Tarry with us, then, to learn the discrimination of the heart. Take in the light, for the words of the decree are pure.

In the name of the Lord and Saviour Jesus Christ, we have come that his star might appear within you—twin stars of hope for future bright.

July 5, 1985
Camelot
Los Angeles County, California
ECP

CHAPTER 21

I come, then, to tell you that the fulfillment of my dream of the universality of Christ and his Christhood in all is truly coming true through you, my beloved chelas, and through the messenger.

CHAPTER 21

THE UNIVERSAL RELIGION

Most gracious chelas of my heart, I come to deliver to you the love of my cup which runneth over. I would speak to you of the long dream of the ages which I have held of the oneness of thought as pertains to the universal religion that must become the possession of all men.

Blessed ones, how well I remember coming to the point of the birth of the Saviour.[1] That one incarnate in the light was for me the foretelling of the universality of the Christ mind in the light of the invincible Godhead—the single-purposed will of that flame, the beauty of the countenance of the Child—and one would attend, therefore, the birth of that immaculate conception of the Divine Image in every soul born of God.

My mind moved on to visualize just how such a light would come to rest in the cradle of world movements, revolution, organization. And I must say that even then I knew how difficult it would be for the individual without light to comprehend that light.

Therefore, the Word was made flesh. And we beheld his glory, and it was the glory as of the only begotten Son of light. And yet the light shone in the darkness and the darkness of humanity comprehended it not.[2]

And we three, we knew the noncomprehension of the world. We knew of the fallen ones and the brothers of the shadow and Herod, who attempted to know from us where was this Child, where would this Child be born, and adjured us to report to him when we had found him.[3]

The fallen angels desire to be the first to know, beloved, who is the Christed One. They carefully monitor the entire world. They monitor your children with tests and accelerated programs. They look to see who will not fit into their studies of the social sciences and the chaos they have made of the textbooks. They are constantly sifting to know where is the Child who is born, who is to come, who shall be the one to disengage them from their darkness.

Beloved ones, the programming of the people of this planet, the programming of the earth is not only to suppress the individual cognition, the perception by wisdom's flame of the heart that "I AM Christ," but it is to monitor all lifewaves and to discover who is Melchizedek as soon as he should appear—who is Abraham, who is the one who will upset the applecart of their entire Edenic mirage of temptation, betrayal and subversion of all branches of human and divine learning.

Beloved ones, I went from the crèche carrying in my heart the great burnishment of the soul who was and is and shall be forevermore the One Sent as the Christ light of the ages.

Blessed hearts, so I bore it to the land whence I had come. And so, I bore it in subsequent incarnations, some Christian and some not. But in each lifetime, though perceiving him as Muslim or Hindu or Buddhist or as Christian, I would yet have the veil bestowed upon me of those traditions of the limitations to that Christhood. The sovereigns and the priests and the orders of the day who would attempt to impose these upon me would say, "This you may believe of him, this you may not believe. This is correct, this is incorrect."

And so boxes inside of boxes inside of boxes—until child-man is confined in the center of the littlest space, lest the hallowed breath and the fragrance of the soul should go forth and unfold as a rose and permeate the planetary stream of consciousness so that all should sense the fragrance and breathe in the prana of his light and know by all senses spiritual and physical that truly the Christ does glow as a rose unfolding fair of the heart.

MY INCARNATION AS AKBAR

Beloved sons and daughters, I remember well, and I would remind you of my incarnation as Akbar.[4] So Islam was the religion of my birth—Hinduism, the religion of my nation. So, juxtaposed midst all of this, I did perceive that all religions were found wanting. Therefore, I assembled the representatives of all faiths and sects within the larger religions, that they might deliberate, that they might also convince me of their way. I had purposed in my heart to lead each group to the point of the realization of the quintessence of the light of the Child whom I had seen at his birth hundreds of years before.

Thus, the memory of the Christ Child impelled me to draw others to the divine resolution of the light and to the dissolution of the barriers to the free expression of that light. And so, it came to pass that I did point out to each group the limitations that made each version of religion incomplete. And I did propose to take the best from all and leave the rest and arrive at that doctrine upon which all could agree as the basis of the new world religion. But they objected and objected vehemently. And therefore, I was left with a band of disciples, a circle of followers of my own court, who recognized God as light and saw me not only as their secular leader but as their spiritual head.

Thus, you see, I came into the office of Guru through the acceptance and love of those who respected the power and the will of God they saw within me and my devotion to the integrity and the honor of that will. Thus, all religions were free to practice in the realm and any were free to be a part of my circle.

I bring this to your attention because as you read the life of Akbar, you may find yourself in my family and circle of the court, certainly harking back to the court of Camelot and the chelas of the will of God who have been with me for so many centuries.[5]

Blessed ones, it is interesting to see how time after time we have sought through various means and vocabularies and languages and doctrines to define Camelot, Utopia, the place prepared. We have sought to understand how the light of the Christ Child that was perceived at his birth might infiltrate and filtrate through all of humanity's grids and charms and chimeras.

We have sought to come to the place where, practically speaking, in the streets of life the little child might be defended from pornography on the basis of the integrity of the light within his soul, on the basis of the knowledge of the preexistence of the light, and on the basis of the light as the person, the person as God, and the child as the instrument therefore demanding a cosmic defense, an honor guard. For the light in every man is the One Sent.

How to bring the perceptions of people from the point of the realization of the birth of Jesus to the moment of the bursting of the flame: "Lo, Christ is born where I am and if where I am, then in all people everywhere! I shall serve and adore by educating that light and that child-man. I shall serve and adore by nourishing, by defending, by teaching, by joy, by the art and, above all, by my example that I know who I am, I respect who I am, and therefore I respect who you are, both in the divine sense and in the human as your right to create yourself after your highest ideals."

Thus, beloved, from the point of respect for the light, we must come to the realization of respect for the exercise of free will, attempting to illumine where we believe greater illumination would result in a better exercise of freedom.

Beloved ones, through all of this I have discovered in all of these lifetimes that one may make great progress with the children of the light, with the seed of the root races. But the response from the brothers of the shadow is to find out the scheme, the strategy, the game which they imagine you are playing—to find fault with it or, if they believe it has merit, to turn it to their own devices.

Thus, Christianity became a universal religion based on the ambitions of Rome and a Roman emperor. Some saw fit to raise high the banner of persecution to the extreme. When this no longer served their purposes, they embraced Christianity and sealed within it the idolatrous cult that has been present ever since. Thus, Christianity has descended as a Roman religion, not as a religion of Jesus.[6]

Therefore, understand that when it suits the powers that be to create a universality of anything, you will know it is not for the purpose to which you have decreed, but to their own ends. The Great White Brotherhood sees the unity of nations under God, sees the oneness of light in government, in science, and in religion —this only when the point of individual Christhood is attained for the responsible use of these avenues leading toward the unification of all.

Beloved ones, the one-world aims and systems in the economy and the governments today can only lead to the neutralization of the power of Christ in the individual, can only lead to the destruction of the highest path of mysticism which has become your own as initiates of the will of God.

World unity today is sponsored by the fallen angels in tremendous numbers, that they might see to it that their own who are the have-nots are provided for. (And the have-nots are defined by the Darjeeling Council as those who have not the light, who are debtors to the cosmos and who only take and do not give.)

Thus, where the lightbearers have founded nations based upon the principles of light and the ancient traditions of Moses and Christ, so the have-nots have nations based not upon the light and the fountain thereof blazing in the midst, but upon institutions and orders where their only means of having light is to acquire it from the nations or the individuals who are the haves.

Thus, we see that the fallen ones desire the dispersion of light both to weaken and neutralize the lightbearers and to give it unto their own masses, whom they use in wars, political elections, revolutions, riots, and movements of various sorts that they might have the light to further the causes of the rivalrous Nephilim.

Therefore, beloved ones, you will hear people be for this and for that. "I am for a one-world religion," they will say. But you must ask, "What kind of world religion? Under whose domination? A World Council of Churches that denies the individualization of the God flame? That denies the divinity of Christ in every man? That denies the option for the resurrection and the ascension? That denies karma and reincarnation as a cycle and a spiral of opportunity and a path of initiation?"

Beloved ones, the more centralized is control, the less control the individual may exercise over his own life. Whether in religion or a universal academy of science or medicine or the government, you will see that unless it is truly God who is at the center of their sun, there can only be the red sun going down that is not of the light —however a patriotic symbol this may be for the people of Japan.

Blessed hearts, therefore understand the meaning of the term *universal.* The universal Christ, the universal doctrine, the universal God-government is a thing that exists in itself. It is that something, beloved, that is present and real as the etheric matrix, as the garment of every lightbearer, as the light upon the altar of the heart. Up to this hour, that universality cannot be outpictured. For by definition, the moment that etheric matrix hits time and space and begins to come into form, immediately it is boxed and there is the contriving and then there is the arguing and then the wars accelerating for who shall have the seat of power, who shall bear the sign of authority.

THE CHURCH UNIVERSAL IS THE CHURCH TRIUMPHANT

Blessed ones of the Sun, the Church Universal is the Church Triumphant. It exists in the etheric octave and in those in embodiment who are the devotees who have daily contact with that etheric octave in the inner temples with the ascended masters, with the hosts of the light—who have killed ambition and pride, who have killed their desire to be thought great and powerful and to be preferred, who have killed their flesh-and-blood definitions of self and other selves, who have put to rest all desire to acquire anything but God, God, and more God.

These are the ones who remain in the earth, pillars of fire. "Pillars of eternity,"[7] I have called you. For your roots are in the earth, your branches are in heaven, you remain the strong trees of life who do not allow the planet to become barren for the withdrawal of the universal matrix.

Fear not, for the flowering of your tree is the fragrance of Lemurian gardens. And the fruit thereof truly is the nourishment of soul and heart and body. Your presence in the earth is an impetus for all souls of similar vibration to come into the understanding and the knowledge of the universal law and his Christ. Fear not, beloved ones, for your presence also aggravates, draws forth, and awakens the serpent consciousness, who, sensing the light, must immediately pounce to pervert it.

Blessed hearts, therefore remember the fire infolding itself within the center of your tree of life. Remember, blessed hearts, this fire of the kingdom come. Remember, the fire will do its work —the separation of the Real from the unreal. This function is happening through you wherever you are—children, lightbearers, little ones.

If you will remember the Word of that babe whose face I gazed upon two thousand years ago in Bethlehem, if you will remember that that babe is in your heart and your angels and I and Mother Mary do ever regard that face of the Divine Image in you as well as the face of your Father, if you will remember that in the heart of the babe who said, "Lo, I AM come to do thy will, O God!"[8] there was also the commitment, "For judgment I AM come into this world!"[9] then you will not have consternation when you find yourself in the midst of controversy, in the midst of a belligerent effort to unseat you from your lawful seat of authority here or there or in the professions.

If you do not remember that you bear in your breast the newborn Christ Child who is waxing strong, coming of age, preparing to challenge the doctors in the temple with one cycle around the clock of twelve, moving toward the East, moving toward Golgotha and beyond to the Himalayas, moving to become the World Christ, if you do not remember who I AM, who is this light in you, you will not understand the reactions, strong and sharply divided to the right and to the left of the way.

When you realize that nothing that you perceptibly did has caused a fury and a controversy—when much ado is made about nothing—realize that Christ in you is working the mighty work of the ages independent of your own planning or purposing. Be grateful that the light is in you. For those who have no controversy, no burdens, no confrontations, no family problems, nothing to deal with are as neutral as the amoebas that pass in the stagnant waters.

Understand, where there is quickening there is fire. And where there is fire, some on the left will be burned, some on the right will enter into that fire and rejoice in the coming of the Saviour's all-consuming love.

BUILDING THE INNER TEMPLE OF MAN

Bear well your office, beloved hearts. Bear well all that comes to you as controversy or darkness. For we hasten your path of the bodhisattva and to our retreat. Let us test you. And expect the tests. Be unmoved. Greet the adversary with joy and the adder with the "cluck, cluck" of the joyous yogi.[10]

Precious ones, all is for a purpose. If you forget the firstfruits of the morning, the morning's delight in the dynamic decree—we call it the apricot light and wavelength and decree of the dawn that does release the secret ray of the heart—if you forget the firstfruit and the seed inside and the seed inside of the seed, then you will be found caught without the necessary defense at two in the afternoon and five. Every hour has its commitment to holiness. Holiness unto the LORD! O LORD, Thou alone art worthy, art holy, art life.

Then, beloved, we will come to you to give you that initiation again. If you are forgetful and unmindful of the pyramid that you build—the pyramid on which you stand as an initiate—then you will go back to the first step. For you see, a mighty substructure must be beneath the one who would stand on the Great Pyramid and be the capstone for the world.

Thus, we are building. The tenth lesson does not replace the first. And if you neglect the first, your foundation will begin to crumble. Order, then, is the first law of heaven as the first law of the path of initiation. Do not forget your first exercises or pieces that you have learned. These are foundation stones.

More than anything else, we desire to see the building of the inner temple of man. When your outer building ceases to reflect the inner building, then things go wrong. You are burdened. There is strife, rivalry, envy among lightbearers—else among dark ones who have crept in of whom you are not aware because you have not kept the vigil.

I come, then, to tell you that the fulfillment of my dream of the universality of Christ and his Christhood in all is truly coming true through you, my beloved chelas, and through the messenger. Therefore, it is with great joy that we feel this spring to victory. We feel this message will bring to Saint Germain the needed ingredient for the unification of the lightbearers of Europe and all nations.

Therefore, in this hour I do send this messenger in the name of Saint Germain. For it is to this moment that I called her long ago—for this gathering, for this transmission of my own cherished image of the newborn Christ. Thus, in the oneness of that flame, I send her clothed with blue fire and the blue sapphire that I have placed upon her. I send her to contact my own. And I AM the sending of the winds of the Holy Spirit that shall take her there to every heart I have called.

I AM the anointing of all who support this mission, physically and otherwise. I AM the flame of God-gratitude of the Goddess of Liberty. All our hopes are with you, Keepers of the Flame, gentle fiery Mother. All our hopes and dreams are with you!

In you, then, we see the fulfillment not alone of ourselves but of all saints of all time and religion who have dreamed of the moment of the quickening of the Holy Spirit and the Great White Brotherhood—that suddenly, as electric spark across the sky and lightning that shineth out of the East, there is a world consciousness of the universality of Christhood and of the I AM THAT I AM where I AM.

> *Let it be, O God! I, El Morya, unto whom you have entrusted the Darjeeling Council of the Great White Brotherhood, appeal then, O Father. Let this be. Let it come to pass that victory in the spirits of all faithful on earth shall result in the victory of God-government.*
>
> *For all as one and one for the allness of God in all should result—should it not, O Father?—in a perception similar*

enough to create the brotherhood on earth that we have conceived and realized in heaven. It is a brotherhood of mystics and saints and pillars of eternity and good folk who stand for light and are unabashed as they decree for its alchemy in themselves and their world.

O Father, we together—we, the Darjeeling Council and our chelas of thy will on earth—we have given our hearts, our minds, our light, our all. We await the descent of thy Spirit, thy will, the sending of thy legions, the sealing of our effort.

O God, as we have proposed and disposed of thy will on earth, so we pray together for these, these called of the light and all who are being called. We pray as one for thy divinity and thy Spirit to saturate the earth and quicken those who are to be quickened and sever the quick from the dead and bind the dead and fulfill the ancient promise.

Our Father, trusting in thy will, we thank thee. In honor bestowed by thee, we walk in thy name. Amen.

Thus, go forth illumined by his Spirit, beloved—in faith, in trust, clothed upon with that God-determination and that mighty jaw of will of the jolly good fellow who has been my own and your Lanello.

I seal you in the diamond heart of the will of God. Now it is your joy to realize it to the full, to drink all of it and more, for it is self-filling, fulfilling, refilling.

I AM El Morya. Forget me not.

October 14, 1985
Camelot
Los Angeles County, California
ECP

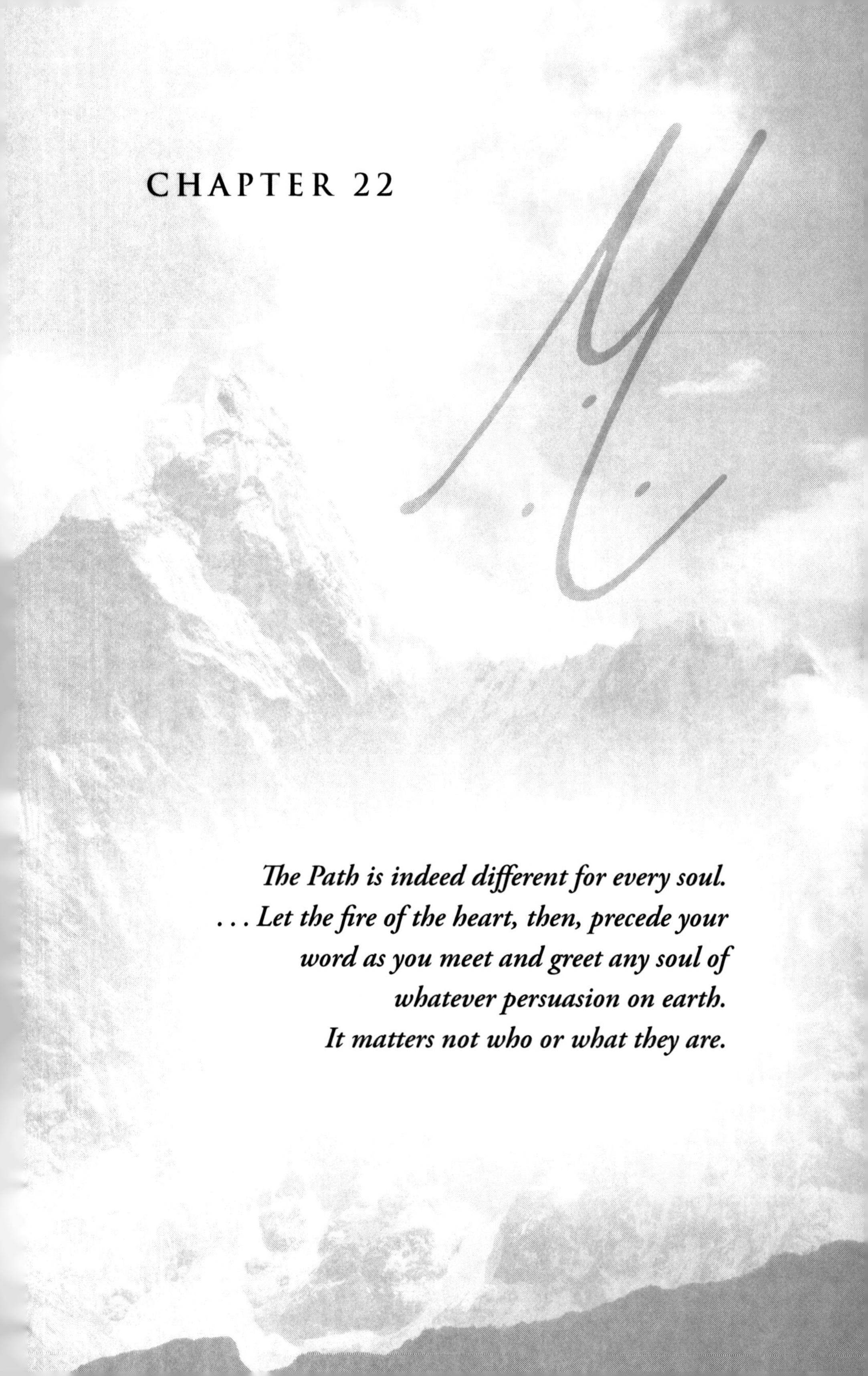

CHAPTER 22

The Path is indeed different for every soul. . . . Let the fire of the heart, then, precede your word as you meet and greet any soul of whatever persuasion on earth. It matters not who or what they are.

CHAPTER 22

TAKE A STAND FOR PRINCIPLE!

I would speak to you, my chelas, of the word of grace—how grace does indeed erase all offense, offensiveness, and the potential to be offended.

Let grace be, then, as a flame that leaps from your heart to kiss the heart flame of another. Let the fire of the heart, then, precede your word as you meet and greet any soul of whatever persuasion on earth. It matters not who or what they are.

Let my chelas be noted for the grace and graciousness of the heart that attends to the detail of comfort, kind word, interesting comment upon life—conversation that is constructive, uplifting, ennobling, supportive, placing all at ease and, by example, inspiring, then, the very possibility of nobility in those in whom the spark has not dwelt for many a year.

Therefore, beloved, by the grace of the first ray of God may you win many to the heart of Maitreya.

There are those who wear upon their sleeves those things in life that ought to be private—things, then, concerning the inner groanings and the travail of the soul. These things are not to be uttered but to be contemplated within as one's God is one's best friend and as I truly am near.

Let the fruit of the Path be shared, but let the process of attainment be held close to the heart. For to display the pain or the arduousness or the struggle of decision or the long dark night to impress those new to the Path has but one clear motive, and that is to deny that Path to those who come and will be led gently by the hand, as you have been, to the moment where they, too, may experience the bliss that always accompanies or immediately follows the difficult testings.

Do you understand, beloved, that I speak of a path that is a measured beat, specific for every individual? Prepare the soul by love and wisdom but do not display all that you have gone through in your own moanings and groanings and strugglings which have preceded a moment of surrender. For, the one to whom you speak may have no difficulty in surrender at all! But having given to that one such descriptions, you discourage and confuse and do not give a realistic picture of the Path.

The Path is indeed different for every soul and, I tell you, for the soul who loves the will of God, one could almost use the adjective "easy." It is easier by far to walk the Path in diligent striving for the will of God than to be apart from that will. Those who are apart from it, who bemoan their plight, gaining sympathy from others, do despite to the calling as well as to the answer in the heart of the chela.

Therefore, beloved, do not convey your unlawful struggles to others. And I say "unlawful," for I do believe that once one has perceived the will of God and had the benefit of long teaching and training, for that one not to follow that will but to step aside from it is truly sinful and a shame upon us all who have gladly given our lives to take a stand for principle. Let the unprincipled ones, then, be removed from being our representatives!

Principle is indeed the manifestation of God. And when you

have no other reason to be good and when you would rather be bad, the reason that is left is principle. For principle itself you move forward, drink the unpleasant cup, perform your duty and hopefully add to it love's own grace.

Thus, let us examine who indeed is representing my path to others. Let those of wrong example see and know it in themselves in this hour. And to those who are teachers and ministers and assistants to the messenger around the world, let it be known who does, then, misrepresent the teaching or the Path or myself.

For I, El Morya, am determined with you to raise up the highest in you as far as you will allow me to go. And I am just as determined to remove with you those baser elements and states of confusion that deprive you of the full cup of victory. I am also determined that those who are here in our various centers for the wrong reason may have their power trips exposed that the true shepherds might appear before any more may be lost by the wrong example.

If I am to be known by my chelas, then I will expect those worthy of the name to remember that you are truly burdened by the responsibility of my office and mantle to in all things properly represent the Darjeeling Council.

With these few words, ponderous and to be studied, I seal your hearts, sealing also all that the messenger has spoken for your edification and opportunity in this hour to come into alignment, to right old wrongs and hurts, and to fly straight as an arrow to the heart of Maitreya.[1]

In his service, I AM Morya of the first ray of the Will of God. May you so be that ray as chela of my heart.

August 3, 1986
Camelot
Los Angeles County, California
ECP

CHAPTER 23

Let the light ascend
and the soul will follow suit.
Let the soul ascend and
millions will follow.

CHAPTER 23

A SAPPHIRE CHALICE

Violet Flame for a Measure of Safety

I give myself, a sapphire chalice, to the chelas of the will of God. Fashioned of my heart, this chalice interspersed with diamonds is one that can grow as the chela grows (even as the parent who carries the child may carry a greater weight as the child does grow).

So, I, El Morya, looking with utter compassion upon my own, desire in this giving of myself to demonstrate to you the way of the diamond heart of God's will.

Therefore, out of the first ray of the dawn's love for the diamond-shining mind of God I come to you with lessons to keep you in the facets of the sapphire will of God that you might not sink into lesser vibration, my chelas, in these hours when earth becomes heavier before she *shall* become lighter—and she shall become lighter by your invocation of the violet flame and *only by that invocation.*

Therefore, in making myself a chalice for my chelas, I give myself to be filled by my chelas with the wine, the purple wine of the rich grape of the harvest. Let it be, then, an intense wine of the Spirit that comes forth by your call to the violet flame. Let the chalice of my being, with you, be the wine-bearer of Aquarius, beloved, for something must be done. Something is needed, beloved. Therefore, I propose in my heart to give myself, for what else can one give?

Therefore, I have appealed to beloved Alpha, who has assured me that in the giving of myself to those who espouse the will of God I am consistent with his proclamation of sponsorship of the lightbearers of the earth.[1]

Blessed hearts, I desire to be a chalice that does overflow with the wine that you distill by your meditations in the white light of the Holy Spirit; and then with the intense imploring and fiery appeal to mercy, to Kuan Yin, my cohort of light, there might flow through you such intensity of the violet flame as to provide our beloved Saint Germain with an extraordinary portion, even a reservoir of such violet flame as to increase transmutation and therefore provide that measure of safety that is not now present in the earth.

You tread on thin ice, beloved. This sea of glass, then, becomes a transparency not for heaven but for the pit itself that does exist beneath this city, and therefore see how a surface of glass sustained by the light only of lightbearers* does hold up a city that has turned toward darkness.†

Let us reverse the tide, the Lemurian tide of the misuse of the light‡ of the Divine Mother in holy temples![2] Let there be a turning of the tide, for God is able and God in you is able and I have seen what miracles my chelas have wrought in recent years and centuries. Therefore, it is never too late to begin.

Thus, I AM become a chalice walking—a chalice running when you run! I come, beloved, in the full measure of my heart's devotion to my brother Saint Germain, your own beloved master

*pillars of individual Christhood

†toward the left-handed path of the turning of the light to the subservience of the not-self, its pride, ambition, sensuality and denial of the Christ in the Sons of God

‡God consciousness

whose life, I tell you, is given for you. Therefore, let the full measure of this chalice be given daily, for each day I shall take that which you have deposited in this chalice and place it in the violet-flame reservoir of light on the etheric plane. Therefore, beloved, fill and let it be emptied—fill it to overflowing.

Thus, beloved, this my walk with Saint Germain may prove to be that stitch in time of Hercules and Amazonia.[3] It may prove to be such a boon to chelas that they will at last transcend these planetary karmic cycles that have produced a density within them that is not to my liking.

Therefore, *pierce! pierce! pierce!* O blue-flame sapphire light! Blue-lightning angels and devas of the diamond heart, come forth, then! For there must be a piercing of this density, that this overflowing wine of violet flame, Holy Spirit, may pour through the cracks and the fissures in the earth and yet give to elemental life the support so necessary.

Blessed hearts, now let us consider how each one does become a facet of the Divine Mother's diamond heart and my own. Blessed Mary does stand in this room radiating a healing light. You have tarried long, some longer than in many a year, longer than many have attended a church service for lifetimes, and therefore the reward is instantaneous. As the Blessed Mother has perceived needs for healing you know not of, she does anoint you with unguents of healing light. You are so beloved.

O be quickened, O be quickened, beloved! For the victory is nigh. The angels stand guard. But a victory whose cup is not quaffed is not a victory—and there are not in-betweens. Blessed hearts, it is a choice for victory or utter defeat and self-humiliation.

Let the light ascend and the soul will follow suit. Let the soul ascend and millions will follow. Have we not earned our blue-flame ribbons of light? Have we not seen and known the inspiration of millions because we have dared to ascend the mount Horeb and to know God face-to-face?[4]

Let the uncommon light be kept by the uncommon souls who do dare to be different.

I now touch by my heart's love and the fire of God's will ten thousand new chelas of the will of God about to enter in. I touch them, beloved, for my love of Jesus and his call for ten thousand new Keepers of the Flame.[5] I touch them, and I tell you I am in pursuit of the holy ones of God who know not they are holy until they are told by the Blessed Mother.

Beloved, let the flowers who are the lilies in the earth be quickened and awakened! Let them feel the gentle breezes and have hope again. Do your part, beloved, for I have secured all the dispensations that the Great Law will allow me. Now, will you not give of your heart's light* that you also might be the recipient from Alpha of a fiery mantle and dispensations that I could not receive?

In your own way, then, seek and find. Call and knock. Receive the answer and know that the door of Darjeeling is opened.[6] Come, then, my beloved, for we have the work of the Divine Mother of all ages to fulfill.

> *O ancient Divine Mother of Lemurian soil, O Divine Mother, rise again, rise once again! Thy children call thy name, see thy face, know thee once more. Rise, Divine Mother! Carry thy children to the heights of summit peaks! Bear them up and we shall catch them by the Holy Spirit.*
>
> *O Divine Mother, raise on high the Manchild ere flood tide take him from thee. O Divine Mother, many-armed Kuan Yin, blessed Mary, O Divine Spirit of Omega, O Mother of the World, receive thy children ere it is too late! Seal them in the immaculate heart that they may not lose faith or hope or courage.*
>
> *Let fearlessness flame* pierce, *then, the darkness surrounding the children of God! Angels of the diamond heart,*

*Holy Christ Flame

seal them in the fiery protection of Saint Michael that they may no longer be abused, misused, trodden upon. Father, take them in thine arms.

I AM Morya, so concerned for the little ones and the tender hearts and the little feet and the blessed hands that pray and the lispings of the tiniest child in crib.

I stand before you in this city as I have stood before. I receive you, if you will receive me, on a path of discipleship that shall lead to a practical and swift application of the Law for the defense of life. Life must needs be defended, beloved. I implore you, defend life and know your own freedom!

I AM Morya. I seal you by the sign of the first ray. Know, then, the signet of the blue rose of Sirius.

Purusha.

February 13, 1988
Sheraton-Palace Hotel
San Francisco, California
ECP

CHAPTER 24

We are in the heart of the Ashram,
for is not the Ashram the
nucleus of all energy systems?
Aye, indeed it is!

CHAPTER 24

THE UNIVERSAL ASHRAM OF DEVOTEES OF THE WILL OF GOD

Contact with the Brotherhood by the Ashram Ritual Meditations

Now I come in the ending to set my seal upon your brow, O chela of the will of God. Here in full presence yet also in Darjeeling, I AM the diamond heart of this movement. And I AM determined that it shall not fail, for the chela one by one will not fail.

I am present in the midst of the eye of the hurricane, as are ye all in this hour though you know it not, so sealed are you in the great manifestation of the will of God that is the vortex of light around this community. Therefore, beloved, when you shall go forth on the morrow, go forth arrayed in the armour of Archangel Michael. And do not flinch. And consider failure to be not an alternative.

Thus, we are in the heart of the Ashram, for is not the Ashram the nucleus of all energy systems? Aye, indeed it is! Therefore, let us chat together this evening.

The accomplishment of the publishing of the *Ashram Notes*[1] we laud. Now we inspire you to understand that this is the foundation of the cone that did begin The Summit Lighthouse.

The Ashram is ever present. It is a world order. There are many members outside of this community who are my chelas. They uphold the Ashramic consciousness;[2] and the *antahkarana** has been abuilding for thirty, forty years and more. For the understanding of the Ashram as the house of light, the dwelling place of the Guru and the chela, gives comfort to all. It is the comfort flame midst the storm. It is the light in the cabin window that is seen afar off by the traveler through the night storm.

The Ashram is the haven. It is the resting place. It is the special place that, wherever you find it, is the same as every other such place. Surcease from the struggle, entering in for the recharge, brothers and sisters of one mind and heart and purpose meeting here and there along life's way in our secluded outposts—such is the vision of the Ashram that I hold and that does exist.

Therefore, you, too, have been nestled in that place, which many have prepared by the stretching of the antahkarana of a cosmos. Feel now the thread of this antahkarana pass through your heart. It is truly a thread of light. And therefore, if you will tremble the thread by using at least one of the meditations daily (and there are indeed short ones that no one should find excuse to neglect), then you see, you will always be a part of the antahkarana. You will always be able to hear with the inner ear and hear with the heart what is the situation of all servitors of the will of God of a cosmos.

You stand to benefit much from this association; for admittedly many are beyond your attainment, some the unascended adepts, others ascended masters and cosmic beings. And therefore, you may deliver to those of lesser attainment their momentum even while you yourselves are strengthened by that impetus from above.

Indeed, the Ashram is an impulse. It is an impulse to love and to fulfill the commands of Christ Jesus. We are worshipers of the universal manifestation of the Christ. Yet we are here to fulfill the

---

**antahkarana:* [Sanskrit, "internal sense organ"], the web of life; the net of light spanning Spirit and Matter connecting and sensitizing the whole of creation within itself and to the heart of God.

words of the Saviour Jesus Christ, who is Lord and must be seen as Lord by those who would enter the heart of God's will and receive the strength to fulfill it; for without Christ ye cannot.

Shorn lambs, yes, karma-bearers, yes, and those who have vested no small amount of energy in other causes that are not of God's will. Therefore, until all of these strands be withdrawn from an investment unwise, you see, you require the intercessor in order to do the will of God. The intercessor is indeed the mantram, is indeed the meditation, is indeed the ritual! For I and my Father are one.[3]

And, lo, Christ will whisper to you, "I AM the Word and my Word is manifest in you as you allow that Word to resound through you." And so, as you do, beloved, first you become the manifestation of the words of Christ, and then, beloved, millions of words clustered together in a diamond heart become the chalice for the Word itself. And one day you will know:

I, too, with Christ am the Word incarnate,
For there is no longer separation
Between me and my Lord.
For I AM one in his words.
I have drunk his blood.
I have assimilated his flesh.
And I am that I AM, *which he is,* where I am.

Lo, it is he!
Lo, he cometh!
Lo, he cometh where I AM in the Ashram
Or in the eye of the hurricane.
Lo, he cometh.
Ten thousand of his saints surround me.
And I AM One—
I AM One in him and he in me by the Word incarnate.

Thus, the Ashram is indeed a means to an end, and that end is total identification with the Word of God. It is the strengthening of hearts that we seek, and ritual has evermore been the means to that end. The ritual itself does increase the capacity of the individual to hold mighty currents of energy. As the capacity does increase, you are transformed. Rituals are self-transforming.

Listen as I give them with you through the messenger. Listen to the quality of the voice of Lanello and of myself as you hear the fervor of love and realize that the messenger is teaching you by example how to create a chalice for light from the recitation of the Word.

The mere repetition of words will not suffice in this pursuit. Every word you speak, even as you hear me speaking now, is put forth with a power, with a fervor of adoration and gratitude to God. In fact, our spoken word does carry all of our being and the stamp of our individuality. So, when you recite your rituals, may the sacred fire breath carry into your words the light of your heart.

When these words are sent forth, there is no ending to them. They cross the matter spheres and bless all life. Such is the nature of the word of the Guru! Emulate this delivery, beloved, in your Ashram rituals so that your words, as cups of light moving on a conveyor belt, shall reach millions of hearts of light, never stopped by distance; for these words given in this fashion travel beyond ordinary wavelengths of sound.

There is indeed the light and sound ray whereby the words of the Guru are carried wherever in the universe the Guru is manifest as God. And they are shuttled across the skies from star to star, and all who are chelas of the will of God who have reached a certain level of attainment listen with the inner ear for the conveyances of the Word as power, the Word as teaching, the Word as love, the Word as the exegesis on the Law itself and the scriptures of East and West.

Now understand how the Word of Jesus Christ does live forever beyond heaven and earth. For it is beyond these octaves that the Word goes coursing on its way, nourishing life and holding the balance of the universal Ashram of the devotees of the will of God.

Blessed ones, all who have any level of attainment whatsoever must be devotees of the will of God. Thus, you begin to see the magnitude of our Ashram, that the entire Spirit of the Great White Brotherhood is a part of the antahkarana that you enter when with regular rhythmic cycle you recite our rituals.

In the Beginning was the Word, indeed. And in the ending is the Word as the Work of the Lord. And in the middle is the Word. And everywhere is the Word!

KEEP THE CHANNELS OPEN

Now then, beloved, I assure you that it would please me highly if you should seek out and find those souls of light of a similar wavelength to your own to bring them the message of the universal Ashram of the light of God's holy will, that they might understand that by a little entering in and a little joy in the vibrations that pour through the worded release of our meditations, they might find the true communion of saints and oneness with all who have ever loved the will of God.

This strengthening process is necessary. For when you do not receive from the earth currents or from the earth itself its nutrients and all that you require for the strength of the body and the mind—for clarity of perception, for functioning in the capacity of an unascended adept (as you are called to do)—then I tell you that the channels that you tie in to and reinforce by your words in our meditations will open up to you the energy and the currents of light to make up the difference against the problems of pollution of this world or any other world so contaminated.

Our God does not leave you comfortless! Our God can supply you with light and equalize your needs. But if the channels be not open, if they be not sustained, beloved, then when you have need you are not tied in to the Ashram. Moreover, through this antahkarana you experience the direct tie to your mighty I AM Presence (when in the karmic state you would not otherwise be able to sustain it), for you are perpetually in touch with cosmic beings.

What of the decrees and the decree momentum of many years? All of this does reinforce the rituals, but the rituals are very special. They are very precious. They are foundational and fundamental to all who would begin on the Path and run and not be weary[4] and complete their course.

The ritual is the means of devotion, and through this devotion and your application of the instructions for visualization, you gain a certain skill by fervor of heart, by will of the mind and by caring for other parts of life. To send light and to intensify the light ray, as you see it shoot forth from your heart, you must visualize the intensification of it and direct it for all God-good wherever the need is greatest. Thus, meditation will strengthen your vision and aid in the clearing of the third-eye chakra as you use it more and more to project only good to every part of God's life.

The meditations are a dispensation. They come from the causal body of a great cosmic being who has also been my mentor. And through my heart this release to my chelas does complete a circle that can take you to far-off worlds that are the abode of this great being.

Thus, beloved, in all ways know that we have many reasons for which we do many things. And though I could speak to you for many an hour on the realities of the Ashram and what it can mean to your acceleration on the Path, I do request that as chelas of the will of God you will accept my word, that it is so.

Accept that this bonding together of your souls with one another, with my heart and with all servants of God's will is a major key in your success and your God-victory. This applies even in the matter of the initiation at the two-thirds level of the pyramid, even in the matter of the expansion of resurrection's flame in your heart, given to you with such love, such ineffable love, by Jesus.[5] Yes, your participation in the Ashram ritual meditations will strengthen you to accomplish all that you desire by a path of self-mastery.

Thus, let the community, let the chelas determine when they desire to group together to give these rituals. Let it be the spontaneous will of all. Let their votes be made known and suggestions filed. Thus, we may commune together in these rituals when it is the free, God-given gift of those who participate. May it be your link to the future and the arc whereby the soul may pass over the dark night of the nineties and be in place in the matrix of the will of God.

Trust me that you must be in the earth yet not of it. Conquer self. Establish right livelihood. And if you do not have it as a sufficiency in your life, know that inasmuch as it is one of the requirements of the Eightfold Path of the Buddha,* there is some force of the anti-Buddha within the self that you must go after. For right livelihood is the very nature of the Path itself, and wrong livelihood will not profit your soul nor be for the balancing of karma.

Thus, if greed or any other vice color your motive in livelihood, you will not be accelerating on the Path. Consider, then, the requirements of the Buddha on the Eightfold Path and bring your lives into proper adjustment. Unless you can call to the Five Dhyani Buddhas and earnestly desire the removal of the five poisons,[6] unless you can call to Cyclopea for the vision to see what poisons bring ailments to the spirit and the soul and the mind,[7] it is difficult for me to help you.

But when you are a part of the Ashram rituals, you receive pulsations of my mind and you enter into your own mind of Christ; and you see things in yourself that you don't like, and you are strengthened to deal with them. And you will not fall apart when

*Right Understanding, Right Thought, Right Speech, Right Action, Right Livelihood, Right Effort, Right Mindfulness, Right Concentration.

you discover things about yourself that you have not been willing to look at before.

The abundant life must be demonstrated by those who espouse the path of embodying virtue. Virtue does lead to the building of the magnet of the heart, and love can only attract more of itself. And the magnet of love does always bring all things necessary to the one who carries that magnet of love to the exclusion of all lesser vibrations.

EXPAND THE CIRCLE OF YOUR MEDITATION

Now in the heart of the Mystery School I AM come. The thread of the antahkarana of the Ashram I have passed through your heart. Now I make this offer to you to establish a focus of the Ashram by giving the rituals and seeking to expand the circle of your meditation, inviting those who will come and those who would enter in.

If you establish this forcefield, even if you are alone in your home, if you establish a weekly routine of daily meditations and keep it, I, Morya, Lord of the First Ray, will sustain for you the matrix of the Ashram where you are. If possible, consecrate a place where you give your rituals and keep it holy. Even a little corner of a room will do.

Thus, beloved, the Ashram always has been and always will be without requirements except devotion. You do not need membership cards. You do not need written pledges or dues or anything else. You have the *Ashram Notes* to study and restudy.

There are souls in other dimensions who use this little book as a bible for their entering into the heart of the will of God. The *Notes* give impetus to profound meditation upon God and his Christ; they are like the bittersweet candy in the mouth that will never dissolve but always be there to savor again and again.

The *Notes* will draw those whom you include in your circle into a desiring to know more of the Path, more of the chohans of the rays, more of the Great White Brotherhood. Let them ask for more, for their cup is full as they receive those *Notes* and do the rituals. Never offer a seeker more than he is ready to receive. Let him be content to glory in the Word of God and in his presence, being so suffused and so satisfied thereby that it may take time for him to desire more.

It matters not. It is the quality of love in the spoken Word that you give that will bring that one to the heart of Christ, and this is our goal. For when one who does not know Christ Jesus comes to that point of love and profound knowing of the master, all doors of a cosmos can be opened unto him.

Thus, I, El Morya, with my chelas desire without pushing or pulling, without tugging or forcing, to bring to all whom we meet the Communion cup and morsel by morsel the bread of angels, *panis angelicus.* It is a piece[8] I love to hear again and again. Whenever you play it, I shall be there; for I love Jesus' sermon "I AM the bread of life which came down from heaven."[9]

Truly Christ is the bread of life, and one crumb of that loaf is able to transform a universe. Therefore, not in mountains of material but in the love quality of your heart will you find yourself being able to offer morsels of that bread of our Lord. And the wine of the Spirit each one shall drink in, for you cannot send forth the word of a ritual unto a cosmos without it returning to you the light essence of your immortality to be.

In truth, with my amanuensis Mark Prophet I have opened a door to thousands and millions through the Ashramic consciousness. Now, beloved, I have passed the torch, I have given you the key. The book is in your hands. May you let it do the work, and may you be its handmaid and the handmaid delivering souls to worship their God and to be free to know Christ.

This is my plea to you, beloved. For it is the true introduction to The Summit Lighthouse, which is built on this foundation. May you now go about placing that foundation in your lives, for you will need it in the coming days and months.

I desire you to know that the time allotted to us is an open span. I shall no longer define it in weeks or months, but I shall define the time available to you as opportunity. When opportunity is taken and fulfilled each day, you yourselves might provide the extensions of time and even the extensions of space.

ALWAYS BE PREPARED

Work while ye have the light,[10] yet always be prepared. Look to the future with hope but never with confidence in converting the enemy. His jaw is set against the LORD. He will not receive the conversion of the Holy Spirit, for God simply does not desire to convert the enemy.[11] Therefore, be always watchful, for the enemy has not gone through a metamorphosis to somehow become the Lamb of God. It is not possible.

Thus, prophecy has not changed. Cycles have not changed. But what you make of them and what your communion with God shall be will indeed determine the term of months or years allotted to you as a cycle to build the new heaven and the new earth, which I am certain you realize is entirely an inner building of the temple of God.

Thus, you will have to learn to plan for infinity and to be prepared for the finite world. You must in your own heart sense the timings and the cycles and the limits to your manifestation upon earth. This you can achieve as well by your meditation on the rituals.

Go to the heart of God to determine your fate. And have a heart for any fate! The future is an open door. You will not control it all, but you will send forth forces of light that may do your bidding as you serve the light.

Blessed ones, I do not avoid telling you that you may go forward with your lives, nor do I avoid the subject of whether there shall be war and what shall become of the economy. But I will not cross the line to make definite prognostications. The astrology that you have heard bears consideration; for, as you know, it is a mathematical formula of karmic forces as they interplay through this solar system and beyond. Many things can be calculated and foreseen, but what is not foreseen is the intercession of the Great White Brotherhood and the intercession of the unascended chelas of the will of God.

How you take what is given, how you lock your forces with this antahkarana of God, how you increase the resurrection fire, how you do all these things is the most determining factor of all. Not what I say, beloved, but what *you* say and do will determine the outcome of *your* life and of this community. Hear it well and know it clearly! Be practical. This is your hour on earth. Use all sixty minutes of it to the highest good and gain for God, yourself and all lightbearers.

What I say in this hour, then, is that opportunity is still at hand. Yet the enemy is fast winding about himself the coils of his own karma. And by and by he shall reap it and there shall not be any turning back of it. See, then, what the light of God can do and know that only you are the doers in this hour.

I remind you of the pay-as-you-go policy of the Brotherhood. What you give us in the decrees offered in my name through the audios, we will multiply and send back to you. Give us the light, the energy and the decree momentum. Increase your contact with the Brotherhood by the rituals, and you will see what Morya will do for each and every one of you. It is a pact we make with all who are true members by action of our Ashram.

We will not fail you, beloved. Give us the light. Give us the energy. Give us the will. Give us the faith and trust and listen with the inner ear to obey our voice. Then you shall see in full, grand display what the brothers in white are capable of on behalf of true chelas.

These are my thoughts in this hour, beloved. Watch and pray, that ye enter not into temptation, and watch the events of the world scene. No chela must ever be caught off guard when it comes to planetary events and cycles and his own personal life. You must be astute enough to anticipate the future by the signs of the times that you read and sense each and every day.

Thus, I AM with you. Thus, my Presence remains over my messenger that you might contact me at a more physical level. And I am truly grateful for her service and staying power as well as for her compassionate heart, even as I am grateful to you for your faithfulness and your striving and your devotion and your presence that continually makes possible the activities of this Church and the service of the messenger.

We of the Darjeeling Council salute you.

We encourage you!

And we say: Onward, chelas of the sacred fire!

Courage! Courage! Courage!

July 8, 1990
Royal Teton Ranch
Park County, Montana
ECP

CHAPTER 25

We find the most humble and self-effacing of souls in the highest octaves of the etheric plane—those who did good works all of their lives and yet never recognized that they were at all special in the eyes of God or man. Such ones, beloved, are indeed the salt of the earth. I count you among them.

CHAPTER 25

THE GREATER CAUSE OF DIVINE LOVE

Chelas of the Will of God:

There do come processioning across the grand highway those who are the servants of the will of God—some who are ascended, some who are unascended who abide in etheric cities and retreats, and some who are yet on the earth plane.

Thus, beloved, upon this occasion of the thirty-fifth anniversary of the founding of The Summit Lighthouse on August 7, 1958,[1] I have assembled in this hour the souls of all on earth who are committed to the will of God. I shall not tell you the numbers that make up this body of those who have elected to do God's will. But rather I shall speak to you of the fervor of their hearts, of the spirit of noncompromise that they have espoused as well as of their loathing of mediocrity and the standards of the world that are not meet for the shaping of a chela of the will of God.

Thus understand that this day I have also put together an outline of your participation with me in the lifetimes you have had with me on earth and other planets. I now place before you the record of your achievements or the void left by the absence thereof in your associations with me, and I transmit to you a soul quickening that you might remember the days of yore.

And, as you are at this moment in the aura of my Electronic Presence as Akbar,[2] some of you may recall that you were in my court. Some of you represented the religions of the day. Some of you did serve me well. Others of you disputed and did affirm the separateness and the specialness of your particular religion.[3]

It is, then, an hour to savor communion and community. And as this community of hearts serving throughout the earth has recognized the superlative nature of the mystical paths of all the world's religions, so you are bringing to fruition the great dreams we have held together not only in the India of the sixteenth century, beloved, but truly in the hours we have shared in many other incarnations.

For we have often spoken together on earth and in etheric octaves of the oneness of God and of the conspiracy—and, yes, I use the word *conspiracy*—of fallen angels who have said, "We will confound and divide. We will create contrasting doctrines that will cause men to look down upon one another's credos, upon their most cherished beliefs."

Yes, divide and conquer tactics in religion have been based upon divisive doctrines whose differences do not really amount to a great deal. As the messenger has said, the only true doctrine is the doctrine of divine love. For it is by divine love that we meet the needs of all people.[4] When that love is aflame in your hearts and you are truly enveloped in the flame of the Holy Spirit, so, beloved, you have the assurance that you are daily making strides.

And thus we find the most humble and self-effacing of souls in the highest octaves of the etheric plane—those who did good works all of their lives and yet never recognized that they were at all special in the eyes of God or man. Such ones, beloved, are indeed the salt of the earth.[5] I count you among them. But I also count you as those who might pause and consider what is the current savor of their salt, not allowing it to be diluted for any reason, especially not for spiritual pride.

That which you are is that which you know. That which you are not tells you that which you do not know and have not made concrete in your life. It is one thing to contemplate those things that one would like to do and to become; it is another to materialize those things without crossing the line of the cosmic honor flame.

Above all, cherish the honor of your name, your word, your deeds. Cherish the honor of this community and do not allow it to be tarnished by actions you may long regret. How clear it is that wrong action does follow you all the days of your life, even beyond the point where God has forgiven you and your friends have forgiven you. And so, beloved, it is well to think through any contemplated action, to plan well and to counsel with those who may offer you sound recommendation based on their knowledge of the Law and personal experience.

This is a day and an hour of completion. When you take the number thirty-five, you see that the three and the five add up to eight. And the figure eight opens the way for the causal body of each one to balance the lower self and all attainments of the lower self. It represents the Eightfold Path of the Buddha and the path of completion.

A foundation has been laid. Like the Liberty Bell, it is not without a crack and yet it is solid enough to be a worthy vessel indeed. And with the violet flame, God shall "mend thine every flaw."

VIOLET FLAME

Take not for granted that the violet flame will perform its work without your call. Take not for granted that simply because you have the knowledge of the violet flame, the violet flame will daily consume the records of your karma.

You carry burdens that you ought not to be carrying and that you would not be carrying if you would remember that it is not in the thinking about decreeing but in the actual decreeing that you will produce the violet-flame action you need. And so you must take up with great joy the violet-flame decrees and songs and decree and sing with all your heart, giving devotion to all ascended masters who serve on the seventh ray. My, oh my, how you will see such an increase in agility removing all fragility!

So, beloved, by your loyalty to your violet-flame decrees and to yourself you can come into a greater strength of divine purpose and the reality of the composite of yourself.

What is that composite?

The composite is all of the pieces of self that are worth retaining. And don't forget to cast into the flame that which is not worth retaining! You see, in your past lives you have had many moments of glory and numerous accomplishments. But, having failed to cast into the sacred fire the records of nonaccomplishment or your misuse of the light, you burdened yourself with a burden that does to this day get in the way of the ascended masters and our ability to assist you as you engage in the service of the greater cause.

What might that greater cause be?

DIVINE LOVE

Well, beloved, first and foremost, the greater cause of The Summit Lighthouse *is* that cause of divine love—love meeting the needs of people at every level, love that is understanding, love that, above all, is forgiveness. And in giving that forgiveness, one must acknowledge that one must not and will not retain a record of another's error or misdeed.

Let that which you acknowledge to be unreal be dropped, then, as unreal, nevermore to be picked up, nevermore to be revolved. As the Lord did say to Peter: "What is that to thee? Follow thou me."[6]

Let go of all the inconsequential issues of life! How these

burden the soul and waste the breath that could be empowering you with a mighty flow of prana and the raising up of the sacred fire. How precious is each drop of life! How precious is each year on the tree of life of The Summit Lighthouse and each one's participation, enrichening the lives of millions.

Blessed ones, let us know that the greater cause of divine love is served as we multiply our service by the very number of causal bodies we share. Thus, you are a part of the entire Spirit, or causal body, of the Great White Brotherhood, made up of all saints and ascended masters. By this phenomenon of spiritual oneness, you have access to the cosmic computer of the mind of God and you can tie in to the talent pool and the resource banks of all lightbearers and servants of the will of God.

Think of the tremendous strength that accrues from our combined resources! Think of the opening up of invention and the multiplication of the Word! Think, then, in this hour of how you can remove from every level of consciousness the blockages to your soul's bonding to your Holy Christ Self. These remain as record from every step and stage of this and previous lifetimes until you clear them by fiat of violet flame and soul searching. The messenger does indeed do you a service when she tells you to pray fervently that all records long forgotten, all scenes of past lives not accessible in your outer mind might be cast into the violet flame and erased—cause, effect, record and memory![7]

Just think, beloved, how happy you will be—once you have attained your immortal freedom—to have put in place here below in this octave, according to the admonishment of the apostle Paul, "whatsoever things are true, whatsoever things are honest, whatsoever things are just, whatsoever things are pure, whatsoever things are lovely, whatsoever things are of good report," and all that leads to the enlightenment of the Holy Spirit! Think of the possibilities of gathering in your heart and chakras the light essence of all that you have extracted from your tree of life and then multiplying it by your threefold flame and passing it on to others. Thus, "if there be any virtue, and if there be any praise, think on these things."[8]

THE KEY TO THE EXPLOSION OF LIGHT UPON EARTH

It is, then, high time indeed, after thirty-five years of our sponsorship and your service, that we should see projected into the living rooms of the world, beamed by satellite [or other means] at least once a week for one hour, the teachings of the messengers on the path of the ascension, on karma and reincarnation and on what was truly spoken by Jesus that is recorded in the Gnostic gospels and other writings.[9]

Should not these be made available to the world?

I tell you this day, the Darjeeling Council of the Great White Brotherhood is unanimous in affirming that this is the key to the explosion of light upon this earth and to the tens of thousands of souls who are hungry, waiting to be filled with this truth so that they may immediately come forward to reinforce your ranks. Thus, beloved, I come to ask for your vote of confidence and your approval of and dedication to our plan for the widespread dissemination of the teachings via satellite on television [or other media] for the victory of this decade! [36-second standing ovation]

I thank you on behalf of the entire Darjeeling Council and our sponsors of higher octaves. Won't you be seated, chelas of my heart.

In the past weeks I have particularly pointed out to the messenger how the fallen angels seek to subvert step by step the divine plan for this community and for the individual chela and Keeper of the Flame. I have pointed out how the forces of Darkness will not stop at any hour of the day or night to stand in the way of the progress and the victory of the individual lightbearer and the community as a whole, as a worldwide organization.

BE STRENGTHENED WITH THE SACRED FIRE

Blessed ones, I have asked you and I ask you again to take note of psychological blocks to your path, to your career and to your accomplishing those things that you have determined to do. And I ask you to be strengthened—strengthened with the sacred fire so that you will no longer allow Nephilim or Watchers or minor devils or discarnate entities to in any way dilute your purpose or steal from you moments or hours of the day or cause you to become embroiled emotionally with this or that concern.

I say, beloved, these fallen ones yet have entrée into your subconscious mind through your own dweller-on-the-threshold.* And therefore I encourage you to go over the steps and stages of development in this life—yes, to pursue the understanding of the inner child and many inner children, representing phases of spiritual and psychological growth. Come to the realization that the warring in your members[10] may be the nonresolution of your adult self with lesser levels of this incarnation, earlier years, experiences and unavoidable circumstances of the daily drip-drop of your karma that you have not entirely dealt with.

Thus know, beloved, that the lower mind is made up of many compartments, containing many records and many crosscurrents. That you might achieve the victory over these records and crosscurrents, I instruct you to recognize no enemy, whether within or without, as having power over you for a single moment. This will surely put the wind of the Holy Spirit in your sails. Remember, each victory, great or small, allows you to multiply great abundance for the purposes at hand.

**Dweller-on-the-threshold* is a term sometimes used to designate the anti-self, the not-self, the conglomerate of the self-created ego, and the negative forces comprising the subconscious mind.

THE BUDDHAS, BODHISATTVAS, AND THE ARCHEIAI

This, then, is a moment when I come to tell you that the Buddhas and Bodhisattvas, the wondrous ones who have spoken at our conference[11] and many more stand on the threshold of the etheric octaves looking down at you and offering the full momentum of their causal bodies, the full momentum of their light.

It is a day and an hour and a year and a decade where hope for humanity lies in the strong power of the archeiai. And it is upon the fountainhead of that flame of hope, that white fire, that we base our deliberations, our planning, our commitments and our willingness to sponsor those who also have that hope, who do not despair, who do not enter into levels of despondency. For these truly know that they can count on me, for one, and on the Darjeeling Council and millions of ascended beings who are absolutely determined to assist the chelas of El Morya in accomplishing the goal that is all-important to all of us. And that goal is to see to it that every lightbearer on earth has the opportunity to study our teachings in this decade—and if not in this decade, then very early in the next century.

Beloved hearts, if every lightbearer who is in embodiment on earth this day had the full knowledge of this path and teaching, think, *just think* for a moment, how this world could be turned around by the fervor of their violet-flame decrees, by their dedication to the will of God, by their understanding of the path of the ascension and by their willingness to accept responsibility for their karma and to pick up the dropped karmic stitches of each and every past incarnation.

Why, beloved, this was Saint Germain's dream already in 1930 when he introduced the violet flame through Godfre and Lotus. This is 1993 and still this teaching has not made its way to the hearth and home of every single lightbearer upon earth! We say, beloved, that this is our greatest concern.

SHATTER IGNORANCE

As an interviewer asked the messenger yesterday, "What is your greatest fear?" so she did voice what is indeed the "fear" of the Darjeeling Council, as it has been the fear of every enlightened one in all ages. It is the fear of ignorance and the consequences of ignorance—individual ignorance, planetary ignorance, the ignorance of the mass consciousness and of mankind. For out of that ignorance they do practice acts of hatred, acts of war, acts of murder, acts of suicide and the robbing of children and youth of their light, their soul essence.[12]

There is ignorance at all levels of society, whether it be in the field of medicine and nutrition, whether it be in the educational systems, in business or (and this is most regrettable) in the houses of worship—in the churches and in the temples of the earth. And there it has been not only ignorance but outright falsity in the presentation of Christ's doctrine and of the message sent forth from the heart of God as direction for the pathway of true light and service.

So you see, beloved, to shatter ignorance and to do so by the power of the Five Dhyani Buddhas, to shatter ignorance and to consume the poisons by embodying the wisdoms[13]—this, then, is our goal for you. Those who are cunning in their ignorance commit atrocities beyond belief. They know better but they do not always do better. Thus ignorance is also a matter of conscience, of willfulness, of deliberate sinfulness.

Can you not say of yourself, beloved, that as you have increased in enlightenment on the Path and become less and less ignorant as to divine law, human law and your responsibilities in life, you have been happier, you have balanced karma, you have come out of darkness?

And with the dawn of each new day that brings greater enlightenment, you have seen what a burden of the darkness of ignorance is upon this planet. You see it in the top leadership of the nations. You see it in the homeless on the streets. Yes, beloved, ignorance is yet rampant, even when so many advances in science and technology have been made—ignorance of the heart, ignorance of the indwelling God, ignorance of the science of the spoken Word.

Think of all of the teachings that have come forth from the ascended masters, many of which have been in print and are now out of print. And so I make another appeal to you who are writers and editors and to you who would learn to be writers and editors. I tell you, to have in print all that has been taught through the messengers is our desire. For, as we have said before, each facet of the teaching is for a particular person or a special group of persons.

Thus, beloved, even a portion of the teaching you have received would enable you to walk out of Darkness and into the Light. And you who were born into this community or who came into it early and have received a spiritual as well as an academic education have also seen, by comparing your knowledge to that of those whom you meet in the world, just how much general information others do not have, just how much true enlightenment is absent from their awareness solely because of what they have not been taught.

So, you do not look upon others in pride but in profound gratitude as each of you contemplates this day how by the miracle of an angel you were drawn to find a book or someone who would lead you to the altar, where you could see for the first time the Chart of Your Divine Self. Oh, what a blessing, beloved! What a blessing is each morsel of truth. It is as a seed planted that grows in a receptive and grateful heart!

May you cherish what you have, then, and not allow it to be diluted. Let not the essence of self-knowledge, of the purity of the Path and the truth of the Path and the knowledge of your own destiny—where you have come from and why you are here—be diluted, beloved, out of some desire to have one foot in the world and one foot in heaven.

Know, then, that some must lead. I well know how lonely is the role of leadership. It is lonely to be at the top, beloved, but only one at a time may pass through the nexus of the pyramid unto eternal life. Thus, when your turn comes and you are in a group of a dozen or fifty and you know that you have the mantle of leadership for that group, do not fear to exercise it.

Recognize that leadership is needed. Leadership as example is the greatest leadership of all. Let the example of all who have gone before you be for you a reason to give that level of commitment of which you are capable and to aspire to higher levels of attainment to the glory of God and to the oneness of his Presence.

As you therefore contemplate the past lives of many ascended masters who teach you today, learn something from the past. For in past centuries and in past golden ages there was a greater strength of mind, a greater health in the body. In previous centuries there was more opportunity, beloved, strange as it may seem, to excel and excel greatly.

Yes, beloved, mediocrity has become universal through the philosophies of socialism and Communism and through the indulgences of capitalism, so much so that people do not recognize the role models who are standing before them, and scarcely do they study the heroes and heroines of yesterday.

When you consider, then, what the masters have done in previous embodiments, may you realize that in this lifetime you have the opportunity to add mightily to the rings of your own tree of life and to step out from among your peers in the states and the nations from which you hail. You have the opportunity to truly show the heights to which the individual may attain when he is a servant of the will of God—when he truly knows that God is the reality and that he is the instrument of that reality.

The greater cause that lies before you is the maximizing of what you have, the multiplication of holy purpose and the fervor of the Holy Spirit in your heart that does make you desire, no matter what the price, no matter what the cost, to give to the many of the ascended masters' cup of self-knowledge and the knowledge of the Path itself.

BE WILLING TO SCATTER MANY SEEDS

Be as the sower who went forth to sow.[14] Be willing to scatter many seeds, many more than you think will take hold and grow. For, beloved, if you limit your seeds to those of whom you are certain, to those who you think will then take up the teaching, you may be in error. You may find that it is the very ones who you thought would have absolutely no interest whatsoever in the Path who will indeed be interested.

You cannot read men's hearts of a surety or know what is the fallow field or the stony ground. Therefore do not presume to be a reader of men's hearts but rather understand that God has established the redundancy of nature. There are always many more seeds than are necessary to harvest a crop.

Therefore, send out many seeds. Send them everywhere! And always be ready with a gift—not necessarily the gift of ultimate enlightenment but the gift that fills the immediate need of the one with whom you are speaking. A gift that will strike a chord, beloved, a spiritual gift that will keep that one coming back to you because you understand the need of the soul and the heart—the soul that is alone and the heart that aches. You can fill that vacuum with the same light and joy and the true friendship of the Holy Spirit that the apostles and the saints freely gave.

So, beloved, understand this. Understand the great key to being the sower, sowing the seed of the Word and yet knowing, as Paul said, "I have planted, Apollos watered, but God gave the increase."[15] Do not try to be the one who gives the increase but be the instrument, be the one who prepares the way for the Great God to nurture that seed in someone's heart until it surely becomes a mighty tree, the tree of life itself.

I am gratified that many use the Ashram rituals. Truly the antahkarana of our Ashram is being strengthened daily, even since the early beginnings when just the few did keep the hours of the rituals weekly.[16]

Rejoice, then, beloved ones, as we rejoice and yet understand that many things are out of kilter in the earth. There are imbalances in the earth. There is the accelerated and untimely descent of karma. It is all around you! Some have eyes to see it. Some say it is an act of God or an act of nature or just a coincidence or something that happens every so many hundreds of years. But, beloved ones, karma is falling like rain. Karma is descending and many people suffer.

And many who suffer because they have not learned how to follow the rules of God are now ready for a catharsis. Yes, they are ready for that purgation which karma brings. They have knocked on every door. Many have come upon their knees, knocking upon the doors of etheric retreats, asking to be admitted, for they are ready to learn and to know the straight gate and the narrow way that leadeth to eternal life.[17]

We will teach them. We will send them back to you. May your homes and centers be opened. May your hearts be opened! And may you have a burning desire to give what you are and what you know to all who hunger and thirst for the truth. May your daily desire be to serve to set life free and may all else be subordinated to this one goal.

You live in a moment of cosmic history that surely is exceptional. On one hand it is a moment of hope and opportunity, and on the other hand it is the moment of the promised descent of planetary karma. Happy are ye who have learned to balance this equation and who move on dauntless to do the will of God!

"It isn't over till it's over," as the saying goes. Until this or that happens, it has not yet happened. There is a moment when one's destiny becomes concrete and the clock cannot be turned back.

This has not yet happened for earth, though it has happened selectively in the lives of individuals whose clocks have literally run out.

Knowing, then, as you do, that there is yet an open highway of opportunity, make the most of it and look forward to adding another ring on the tree of life of your Summit Lighthouse. I, El Morya, will come to you now and again regarding our plans and what we deem to be most essential to the expansion of our organization. If you will but give me your decrees, we will deal with all legal matters pending and get beyond them, beloved. And if you will deal with matters within yourself, you will be one less person who has a tie to the astral plane.

This is important, beloved ones. The Lord Jesus' words have been quoted to you many times: "The prince of this world cometh and hath nothing in me."[18] When you make yourselves invincible—invulnerable as the lighthouse—watch and see what will happen to this activity, which is sponsored by the Darjeeling Council of the Great White Brotherhood with the approval of the Lords of Karma, the Four and Twenty Elders and the Fourteen Ascended Masters Who Govern the Destiny of America.

Long live the dispensation! Long live the sponsorship! Long live the chelas of the will of God on earth! Happily may you attain fulfillment in the Law.

I AM El Morya Khan, ever with you on the path of invincibility.

So it is, beloved. I seal you this day and I say:

Charge now and fulfill the reason for being of our Summit Lighthouse!

[44-second standing ovation]

August 8, 1993
Royal Teton Ranch
Park County, Montana
ECP

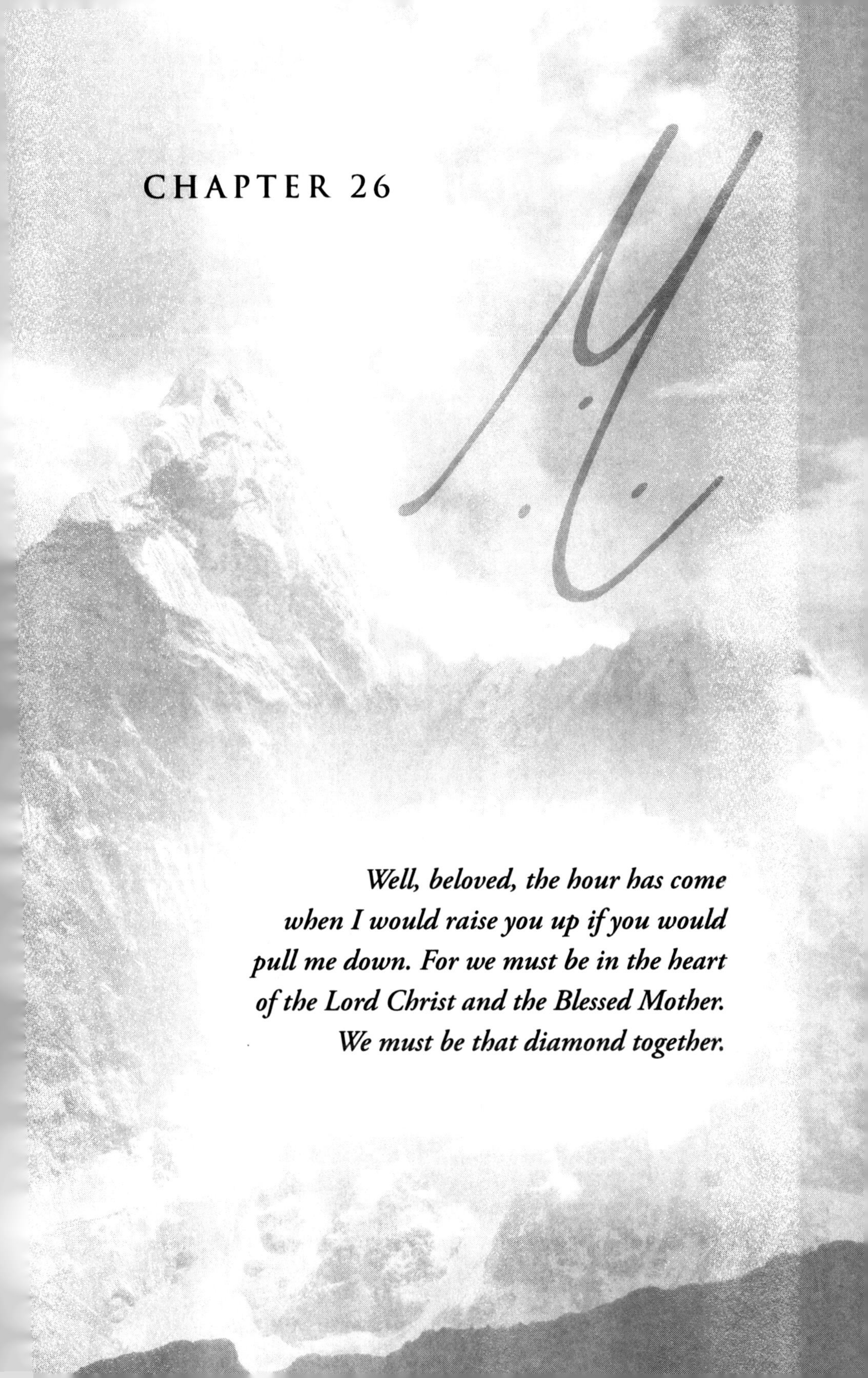

CHAPTER 26

Well, beloved, the hour has come when I would raise you up if you would pull me down. For we must be in the heart of the Lord Christ and the Blessed Mother. We must be that diamond together.

CHAPTER 26

BONDED TO THE LORD OF THE FIRST RAY

The Initiation of the Bonding of Guru and Chela

Hail, O chelas of the will of God! I am here and for a right good cause!

[16-second standing ovation with joyous shouts by the chelas followed by:]

Hail, El Morya! Hail, El Morya! Hail, El Morya!
Hail, El Morya! Hail, El Morya! Hail, El Morya!

For tonight I come to bless you and to bond you to my heart if you would indeed be bonded to the Lord of the First Ray.

["Yes!" (25-second standing ovation)]

Let there then be no more separation between us, beloved, even though it be paper-thin or thinner. Where there is a cleavage in the rock so the fallen ones drive through, thereby to convince the weak and the unbonded that we are not one; and therefore all manner of calamity may come upon you. And you look and you look and you say, "*Where* is Morya? *Where* is Morya?"

Well, beloved, the hour has come when I would raise you up if you would pull me down. For we must be in the heart of the Lord Christ and the Blessed Mother. We must be that diamond together. The capstone is placed on the pyramid.[1] Let us seal our lives and let us listen well as to what must cast out the spell of darkness, death and gloom that would separate us at all.

Blessed hearts, the bonding process is a sealing much the way there is a vulcanization in the processing of rubber. Blessed hearts, that sealing is that bonding. Therefore to achieve it you must understand the Path and its consequences. Thus, I come to speak to you in this hour when one and all we celebrate the birthday of our Mother here and our Mother Kuan Yin. This is the hour, beloved. Therefore, as Above, so below, let the Mother be one.

Be seated now, for I would speak to you of our love.

You have passed through many a fiery trial, but not all. This is the beginning but not the ending. And therefore look not for reprieve but for re-creation in your God. Look not with weariness upon what you think the morrow may bring, but rise and shine with your ritual to the sun.[2] Admit no defeat. Admit no entrance to your house of despair, worry, despondency.

Blessed ones, look only at that which comes to be conquered. Look above you and you will see Vajrasattva,[3] the Diamond One, even the unison of the Five Dhyani Buddhas.

Know this, beloved, that you must greet adversity and the adversary, welcoming the initiation and intensifying into it a release from your heart of sacred fire whereby you say:

> Where I stand, there is Morya!
> And in his name I say:
> Thus far and no farther!
> You shall not pass!
> You shall not tread on holy ground!
> You shall not enter this hallowed place!
> You shall not come between me and my God!
> My God is happiness this day.
> My God is holiness.
> My God is the divine wholeness of the Living One.
> I and my Father Morya are one!

Blessed hearts, know, then, that for the bonding to take place you must desire to become *all* of the Chela, *all* of the Christ whom you embrace and all of me, as I am one in that One. The bonding of Guru and Chela bears great responsibility, for there is no longer twain but one. Thus you see, what affects one will affect the other.

You can come unglued from this bonding by your free will, even as you may allow your mind to become unglued and the forces of insanity to enter there and to tell you that the will of God is not good. But you can by the recitation of the mantra and even of the ritual to God's holy will[4] affirm and confirm and define where you are the essence, even the elixir of God's holy will.

Not my will but thine be done. Not my will but thine be done.[5] Lo, it is my mantra all the day, as I am bonded to the heart of Alpha. And by that strength and that Father I, too, am Father; for I come bearing the Alpha flame.

My beloved, you have seen that you could withdraw from the world. You have seen how nothing in the world is of any consequence and how unencumbered you are without being surrounded by so many possessions. For you have packed them all away for another day! [9-second applause]

We have determined, Kuthumi and I, to make yogis out of you, and yoginis. Now you see how little you have to take care of when all things are put away. What a simple life! What opportunity for mantrams, mantrams, mantrams, and the wheels to spin and the cells to receive the fire of God.

Looking at empty rooms and four walls, you may perceive, beloved, that there is God, God, God, without the mind being caught on a hook of this or that knickknack or bric-a-brac that never was a necessity at all; for the God within you is all there is. And thus, beloved, hallow emptiness and fill it with the Holy Spirit.

Let us be divested of so many encumbrances and let us value life itself as a living flame. For if life be not a living flame, can it endure? I say nay! Place your attention upon increasing the flame, for the winds of darkness will one day blow and they will seek to snuff out that flame. It must burn again in other octaves and climes. And you too must climb.

Take another step and another, and accustom yourself to the rarefied air. For, beloved, holy atmosphere and sacred fire breath will restore every cell of life within you.

Beloved ones, you can maintain the bonding of our oneness in this octave if you absolutely *refuse* to entertain despair. Despair is hopelessness. It is self-doubt and fear of God.

Therefore *let* love endure. *Let* love endure as a fire that burns in the heart. And if you do not feel that fire burning, say:

> O Jesus, Jesus, Jesus, come into my heart!
> Rekindle my love.
> Let it overflow the chalice of my heart
> That I might extend the cup of mercy
> To every part of life,
> Every part of life,
> Every part of life!

Let love go forth without dissimulation.[6] Be not caught on that point where someone has done something to you that even for a moment you cannot forgive. Let God take care of it. Do not lose your oneness or your bonding. Do not enter into spirals of despair, thinking that any foul or unclean spirit may take from you the cup—the cup, beloved.

Remember, one hand holds the cup, and they would dash the cup before you have drunk of this elixir of eternal life. Therefore hold the cup steady. Hold the emotions steady, steady in the flame of the Elohim of Peace.

I AM the peace-commanding Presence. Do not allow yourself to fall below the level of that love of Christ. Take the altar with you. *Be* the altar of God! . . .

Blessed hearts, the bonding is, in fact, a secret rite and an initiation of the inner temple. I offer you, then, a preliminary bonding whereby you can come to know little by little what this oneness can mean. And I tell you it is preparatory to your entering in to the etheric retreat where the soul is truly bonded; and that soul, beloved, must be well anointed with light. For if we are to trust, we must have one that we can trust.

One by one I would see the permanent bonding, but you must know there is a place where you can no longer go. You may no longer wander in the astral plane, in illusion, in fiction fantasies where emotions are titillated and thrilled, where baser desires are ignited and the soul will lose her path again in the lesser ways of the world.

YOUR TWIN FLAME

Some of you have twin flames who are yet in lower octaves. You must strive harder to maintain yourself at the etheric level and in the Christ Presence. You are responsible to pull up that one. . . .[7]

Well, beloved hearts, if you go up, up, up, from that point of light you can summon seven archangels who will obey the command of the Christ in you. They will send their legions. They will rescue your beloved. But unless you provide the fulcrum, unless you provide in light the absolute balance for what the other half has lost in descending, there will not be the leverage, there will not be the fulfillment of the Law and you will not be granted your prayer.

Suppose, beloved, you do not know where your twin flame is. Suppose you do know that your twin flame is ascended or a great master or teacher. Nonetheless, there is always another's twin flame and another and another. There are twin flames of ascended masters yet lost in the astral plane and losing themselves more day by day. Thus, if you cannot or need not do it for your own twin flame, then I say, rise to the heights of the mountain of God on behalf of those twin flames who must be rescued to complete the mandala of the Great White Brotherhood.

There are more ascended masters in heaven than you would dream of whose twin flames are lingering at such low levels of consciousness as to make it almost impossible for them to be reached or turned around by the ascended one. Thus, I tell you, beloved, there are many reasons why you must rise up and not be pulled down to the ties not only of twin flame but of others, of souls with whom you have a service to render.

There are the lightbearers who have been aborted who must be brought into embodiment. Prepare yourselves, raise up the light and know that they cannot come through just anyone. I request that you appeal to me to be sponsored when you desire to bring forth a soul, a child of God, that you might be protected from the entering in of that which is not destined for you and not your karma.[8]

Blessed ones, by our sponsorship there may be set aside karma and you may even bring forth lifestreams that you would not ordinarily be called upon to bring forth because of the condition of your karma. I ask for this, beloved, because I know whereof I speak. And I know that there are lower souls and false-hierarchy impostors who would give anything to be able to pass into this community through the portals of birth, through those who do not keep the vigil and do not keep their consciousness as holy parents desiring to sponsor those who may therefore secure the earth for the golden age of Saint Germain.

The bonding process to my heart has begun for all of you who desire it if you will take the *Ashram Notes,*[9] if you will faithfully do the rituals, not necessarily all of them hour upon hour but those you select to give at a certain time. Be regular and rhythmic. For each time you give even a ritual that requires but three minutes, you will tremble the antahkarana of all souls who are a part of this Ashram. You will strengthen the weak. You will be strengthened by the strong. You will see how a cosmos can quiver. For everywhere you are is Morya intensifying the light.

INTERNALIZE THE LIGHT

You do not have to walk the earth in the sense of being a karma-being, a person burdened and limited. Shout the fiats! Internalize the light! And let this celebration of another birthday be a celebration of many candles lit around the world who have said, "This is the end of it! I will have no more to do with my human creation! I will *stomp* on it! I will *drive it* out! I will not be off guard. I will not catch myself in those valleys of derision whereby my own God is derided as I dally in the nonsense of self-pity and indulgence."

Blessed ones, you must reassess your leap! You can leap much farther than you think. But you truly allow yourself to remain in such limited states that, I must say, my patience does run out. And I become impatient! And then I simply quit the place where you are, for I cannot wait another moment. For life calls me everywhere upon this planet and I must be there.

And I am where the piercing of the Gemini mind may reach the very heart of the mind of the chela, where quick as a flash of light you catch my thought and then you do not dally in implementing it but you *know* it is my thought, for you *know* my vibration. You do it. You act upon it. And you know what is the process of receiving divine direction from your Guru heart to heart and mind to mind.

You must have the opening. The *ears* must be opened! The *pores* must be opened! The *chakras* must be opened! And you must have a listening *heart!* You must have a listening *mind!* You must have space where I can speak to you and you can recognize my ray as distinct from the babble of all of the other astral voices that promise you this and that and easier paths and easy rewards.

THY SINS BE FORGIVEN THEE

I have come determined that you will understand that you can be God-free beings today. I have come so that you will understand that even the cackling of the neighbors and the folly of the people will make you realize that if you are to conquer this wave, this level of onslaught, you must be higher. You must be higher than they. You must be more determined, more God-free, more centered and, above all, bonded to my heart. I simply cannot work through you when you have anger, when you have resentment, when you feel downhearted.

You must absolutely know that I have put my life on the line for this activity. Why, beloved, I have given so much to this activity and to all of you that I could not even pull out if I wanted to.

Now, this is a joke, beloved. And I wish you to understand that it is a joke. It is absolutely true! And the joke is on me. For you see, this does not mean that you have the Guru by the tail or that you are indispensable chelas. But it does mean that I have plighted my troth to you, and I am determined to stay until this entire matter is through. And I tell you that one way or another it shall be through! [21-second applause] And since I am not through with you and you are not through with me, then we know who is going to be through. [11-second applause]

Therefore, let us establish our oneness before the altar of God through and through. I mean every word that I say. And all of the love of my heart is upon each one of you.

Yes, I know your shortcomings, your mistakes, your goings out of the way. But it is because some devil, and a little devil at that, has convinced you that you are a mere crumb, that you are not a son [or daughter] of God, that you do not have the full power of the Godhead ready to descend upon you in answer to your call and by your affirmation. You allow yourself to be convinced by all manner of psychological meanderings that you are not worthy to be the embodiment of the light, and then you allow those puny devils to recite for you once more every sin you have ever committed in this life. Beloved ones, will you shut them up once and for all? ["Yes!" (14-second applause)]

On this birthday of Kuan Yin and the messenger, I say to you in the name of cosmic mercy, thy sins be forgiven thee! I, El Morya, am your Guru and I say it in the name of the living Christ and by the leave of Jesus and the Father and the Son and the Holy Spirit:

Thy sins be forgiven thee! [31-second standing ovation]

Now I, Morya, say to you, don't let me catch you picking up one of those ghosts of a former sin ever, ever, ever again! [13-second applause] I charge you, then, to walk out of this place this night as sons and daughters of God, sinless, stainless, purified and made white. And therefore go and sin no more, and forgive all others of their sins as I have forgiven you.

Be the extension of Kuan Yin through my heart and through Mother Mary. Lift your head up high and now remember that on this day of April 8, 1990, I have said it: Be free! Walk as God-free beings in dignity and do not stoop to those lesser levels.

A PATH TO BE WALKED AND WORKED

Now, beloved, understand that there is a path to be walked and worked. There is studying to do. There is a mindfulness to gain if you are truly to be the embodiment of God's holy will in Christ's name.

You will have to self-correct. You will have to study harder. You will have to decree and believe in your decrees. And you will have to give those fiats into the day and into the night to keep that dweller-on-the-threshold in submission so that the Christ can blossom forth and preach to the world the message of liberty.

O beloved, strive harder to embody this God free will that I AM. For I tell you, all of the problems that beset you, all of the negatives you can list that are set against you, those things are as *nothing* before your God Self.

Remember all the ascended masters who have spoken to you! *Remember* the dispensations! Walk the earth as ourselves! And then see how we will indeed defeat this adversary. . . .

You must remember that karma must be balanced, debts must be paid. And while you have karma that extends into the earth and debts owing to any part of life, you are tied to those of lesser vibration and to a lesser civilization. I say, cut the ties, be satisfied with less and value your independence by having an independent karma. No ties, beloved. Therefore, at the appropriate cycle it is necessary to work and work the works of light and work the labor of the hands and to see to it that you balance your accounts.

Therefore understand that as you write to me... and to the messenger, your communications will be considered at the altar or they will not be considered. And you will be informed whether there is an answer, whether you must meditate in your heart and come up with your own answers, whether there be direction or not. The Law does not always allow me to give answers. If answers be not forthcoming, know that this is your initiation and it is one that you can truly pass.

Perhaps you need a stilling of the mind. Perhaps you need a voice fast. Perhaps you need a rest from allowing the mind to continually be absorbing information, reading or watching television or listening to others talk so that from the time you awake to the time you sleep you are either hearing yourself talk or others talk or absorbing the communications of the world.

If you would speak to God in his holy mountain, you must come apart and be a separate people.[10] This was the command to Joshua: Be separated out from the Nephilim and their civilization....

A TIME TO LOVE AND GIVE AND FORGIVE

I am here this night to praise effort but to warn you that until the preparations are thoroughly through, they are not through.* It is not a time to become lax or to become self-indulgent or to feel sorry for yourself. It is not a time to have problems in the home. It is time to love and to love and to love, and to give and to give and to give, and to forgive and to forgive and to forgive. It is time to understand and to extend understanding. It is time to know that many are burdened, and loved ones must hold up the burdened ones.

Why, then, do any number of you contemplate divorce and

---

*i.e., preparing the Inner Retreat

other manners of the breaking down of your strongholds and your strength? Do you not know that the cause for these conditions lies in yourself and that sometime, somewhere you will have to conquer what you are finding to be insupportable in your household? . . . Remember not to covet what is thy neighbor's, neither his possessions nor his shelter nor his wife nor any thing that is thy neighbor's.[11]

Blessed hearts, you are wed to Christ. You are wed to me. And wherever you serve side by side with any individual, there you must conquer in love. And when you have conquered in love and you feel that the bonds between you and another are through, for the karma is fulfilled, take care that in your decision you do not injure little ones or any part of life. But if you think you must be divorced, apply equally to the altar [to be unmarried] as you would apply [to the altar] to be married.

Blessed hearts, this is a walk with God whereby God delivers you when he is ready to deliver you. And you will not set God's timetable. Do you understand? . . .

Blessed ones, conquer within the self and understand that this path is not for the simpleminded. This path is not for the weak or the lazy! This path is not for the self-indulgent who another time and another time . . . are still falling prey to the discords of their human creation. . . .

We say, seek the path of the bonding. I announce this initiation to you so that you will understand that some of you, if you do not seek a greater bonding and a greater love and a greater love of the will of God, may find yourselves cast off from the Path and becoming castaways.[12] . . .

It is time to be the Christ. And the one who will suffer if you do not will be yourself and one by one [your loved ones and then] the activity and ultimately the entire purposes for the Great White Brotherhood in the earth.

Blessed ones, staying power is a great virtue. I call it constancy.

Whatever else you may think of this messenger, I have been able to count on her with her staying power from the moment she entered this activity in 1961. I would like to be able to say the same of each and every one of you—*staying power!*

Do not take as an excuse [to abandon Maitreya's ship] the behavior of this or that chela or member of the staff or the organization. Perfect people are not found in this world. Do not in your pride take their imperfections as your excuse to fail in your own right.

It is your right to be victorious, beloved. It is your right to understand that the cycles are turning, that the time is short, that the judgment will descend, that you will have that confrontation [with Darkness] sooner or later. And every twenty-four hours is a period to increase the momentum [of Light].

Blessed ones, if you do not walk about with the sensation of fire in your heart, you ought to be concerned! And you ought to stop a moment and pray to the Sacred Heart of Jesus and take sixty seconds to close your eyes and intensify your love of Jesus Christ and to call to Jesus to come into your heart until you are filled with the fire once again.

The fire of your heart is your only passport to heaven. It is true, beloved, I tell you. Become masters. Do credit to me, your Guru, and show the world that this path can be walked and that people of any sort or nature or background or sin or shortcoming can conquer and can win. Do not accept yesterday's memory of you by anyone. You are not your yesterday, but everyone else will believe it. Do not believe it. . . .

Blessed ones, all of you have gotten smarter this year. But some of you have learned the hard way. I come to introduce a decade of great severity, a decade of great challenge. You can roll through it the hard way and receive every knock and blow and negative astrological portent that comes your way or you can come to this altar and pray your heart out and then live your life as a noble son and daughter of God. You can do it, beloved! And I have come to tell you you can do it.

I have also come to tell you that the only way to get through the decade of the nineties [and other difficulties] is as a living conqueror in the Spirit. Be not hopeless with or without the body. By this sign you conquer. It is the sign of the Sacred Heart. It is the sign of the will of God. It is the sign, beloved. And there shall no other sign be given save the sign of the prophet Jonas.[13] Enter, then, into the belly of the mother whale for three days and three nights and emerge unscathed and clothed in your Christhood.

Yes. Yes. Celebrate the passion of Easter and walk with Jesus every step of the way. Pull out your Bibles and read! Read the story from Palm Sunday to the finish and say, "Yea, Lord, I am with you there! And I shall be resurrected with you on Easter morn." Each and every one shall pass through pain and trial and tribulation until he is purged through and through by the Refiner's fire[14] and does awake in the likeness of his God.

I AM here. Remember that I AM here. I do not leave you. Do not leave me in vibration. Let us see, then, how we will defeat the latest plot. Many pass through to the judgment.

I tell you, beloved, my communications to the messenger are day by day. I will not prognosticate the future this night but only to say, be alert, expect the unexpected and you will win.

To the heart of my beloved messenger and to all of you I say, a happy birthday. [28-second standing ovation]

April 8, 1990
Palm Sunday
Royal Teton Ranch
Park County, Montana
ECP

EPILOGUE

Morya's heart. His students call it Morya's Diamond Heart, just as they speak about his mind as a vehicle for the diamond-shining mind of God. His heart and mind are crystal clear. Nothing escapes him. Nothing gets by him. No problem so muddy or convoluted that it can't be solved by the brilliance of his being.

But, from these pages we understand that Morya's heart is not just a dazzling diamond; it's a dazzling *pink* diamond! This master's love for his students—and for those who *could* be his students—is so tender it makes your own heart melt like wax before the noonday sun.

How to respond to such a love? There are really only two ways. Either you move away—it's too much, too intense, you feel not ready yet for this intense master. Or you move closer, drawn into the fire of his being by the force of your own love that wants to become more like him. For that's the process. If you can handle his intensity and don't let the fire scare you away, there's a wondrous process of rapprochement and assimilation waiting for you.

El Morya himself speaks about it in the last chapter of this book. He calls it the bonding process—bonding to his heart.

Think of superglue. First you sand down the surfaces that need to be bonded. In chelaship terms, this means that as the student approaches closer to the master, there's the refining of the student's vibration. Under the watchful eye of the master, you are given inner guidance and direction. You're being tested to see if you can uphold a higher, purer frequency that is more like that of the master. We're not expected to become superhuman overnight—this chelaship thing is an ongoing process that can take many years and much effort. But we need to show the master we're determined to rise above the mundane pulls of life. That even when we slide back, we will have enough willpower and love in our hearts to try, try, try again—and succeed!

When we prove we can live consistently in this higher way and are willing to work for the welfare of our fellowman rather than just for our own, we enter the next step of the bonding process. The two surfaces are placed against each other to see if there's a tight fit. And if there is, we're ready for the glue. It's spread over both pieces that are to be bonded, nice and evenly. The glue is the love between master and student. It's like a liquid magnet. Once the glue is spread we push hard and we hold, firmly, until the glue solidifies. The magnet becomes strong and unbreakable and the bonding is complete.

It's an incomplete analogy, for sure, but it gives you a basic idea of how the ascended masters see and evaluate the process of taking on embodied students. Morya himself is looking for those students who have the desire, the will and the love to bond to his heart.

Once you engage in this process, you must know that you won't be the same. He'll take you by the hand and lead you step by step into the inner recesses of that pink diamond heart. It *will* change you—he won't leave you where he finds you—but it's a change for the better, one that will gradually lift you out of the old self to the new Self he wants to reveal to you. For the goal of life is not just to connect deeply to an ascended master as his student. This is but a means to an end—the end of becoming one with your glorious divine source, your mighty I AM Presence. Like his fellow chohans, Morya can take you there. He *wants* you to ask him to take you there. In a dictation he once said the following about this very process:

> I desire you to have—and I shall so train any student who knocks on my door—to have conscious and continuous contact with your mighty I AM Presence and to have it, whether conscious or unconscious, in the physical body and at the change called death. When you can reach that point, there is safety in your life and lifestream. There is safety for come what may.[1]

This safety and more is what Morya offers you. It's the greatest adventure you could possibly want to embrace—the sacred adventure that leads you to the self-realized being that you really are. From the moment you were conceived as a spark of the Divine, this was your destiny. Striving for this goal has been your future since you entered your current embodiment. Take Morya's hand and embrace that future right here and now!

Next Steps

Where to go from here?

The Summit Lighthouse offers you a number of different avenues for growing closer to El Morya and pursuing the spiritual path he advocates. Below is a brief overview.

Home Study Courses

One of the best ways to take in the scope of the Path explained by the ascended masters is our Sacred Adventure Series, developed by Summit University. It consists of three volumes that explain the spiritual path from beginning to end and introduce you to the Lords of the Seven Rays, including El Morya and the first ray. Each book contains numerous interactive exercises that will help you assimilate what you are learning.

Volume 1: *The Spiritual Quest*
Volume 2: *Meeting the Masters*
Volume 3: *Working with the Masters*

https://www.SummitLighthouse.org/SacredAdventureSeries

Books

The Summit Lighthouse has published more than 100 books on the teachings of the ascended masters released through Mark L. Prophet and Elizabeth Clare Prophet. They range from introductory level teachings to profound, detailed spiritual source texts released by the masters themselves.

To get started, we recommend the following:

- *Access the Power of Your Higher Self*
- *Keys to the Kingdom*
- *Karma and Reincarnation*
- El Morya: *The Chela and the Path*

https://www.SummitLighthouse.org/FurtherReading

Summit University

Summit University, the educational arm of The Summit Lighthouse, offers spiritual-themed courses varying from introductory material to advanced, academic-level curriculum. Try a mini-course or explore the free units of our extension courses to see if these are what you are looking for.

https://www.SummitLighthouse.org/SU-Courses

Online options

Explore the wealth of teachings, resources and events available on our website: **www.SummitLighthouse.org**.

Keepers of the Flame Fraternity

This fraternity, sponsored by the ascended master Saint Germain, consists of those who feel the calling to keep the flame of life on behalf of humanity. For a small monthly fee, Keepers of the Flame receive illustrated lessons and are invited to group activities such as scientific prayer sessions aimed at directing spiritual energy and light into pressing world situations.

https://www.SummitLighthouse.org/KOF-Fraternity

These are some of the options available to you at The Summit Lighthouse. Say a prayer to El Morya and he will infallibly lead you to the next best step on your spiritual path!

APPENDIX

EMBODIMENTS OF EL MORYA

The purpose of this appendix is to offer you, the reader, more detail about the soul of El Morya. This purpose may be discerned first by studying El Morya's known embodiments in different cultures, religions and ages. These known embodiments are described here in chronological order.

Come with us on a journey through the lives of Morya as we learn of his experiences, tests, trials and his victories. The master himself explains the way:

> How many aeons ago did I become a chela [disciple] of the will of God before I even knew the meaning of the word chela or of the concept of the Guru? But God to me was the golden light of the dawn. And I sensed in the first rays of the dawn the will of a cosmic purpose—the will of a Life and of a Creator beyond myself.
>
> And for a number of incarnations the focal point of my observation of the Deity was the morning light of the sun. And by and by through that contact, unbeknownst

to me, with Helios and Vesta, there was established an arc—an arc of flow over the arc of my own attention. And I began to feel the response of my own God flame within to the God of very gods in that Sun behind the sun.

The observation of this attunement with Life continued for several more embodiments until I was not able to even begin the day of my life without this contact and this flow of energy—a literal infusion of my consciousness with ideas, with the understanding of the work that I should do. Almost, as it were, at subconscious levels I would move into and out of the sun as my point of contact.

And so it came to pass as my devotions increased and the concentration of energies increased within my chakras, that after succeeding embodiments I contacted a teacher—a teacher of the ancient science of astrology. It was the science of the study of heavenly bodies and their influences upon the evolutions in time and space. And that teacher gave me insight into the energy and the contact that I had made with the very core of creation.

And so it was by will, not my own yet which I made my own, that the contact with Life was established, that it grew and expanded. And the light of Helios and Vesta that glowed within my heart became a magnet—a magnet of the pursuit of God through the application of science.

I have always, then, followed the path of science, whether on Mercury or on Earth or other planetary homes of this system and other systems of worlds. The LORD God has permitted me to understand the law of the heavenly bodies and the earthly bodies and of the flow of energies in time and space.

And I have found myself becoming one with the cycles of Matter for the mastery of those cycles, almost, as it were, going within—within the heart of Matter before going to the outside of Matter. Growing from within—from within the sun within the earth and the Sun behind the sun—I learned the way of God and God's laws by the inner geometry of the molecule, the atom, the cosmos.

And my appreciation of that which I did not at first call God came through the humble awareness, the awesome awareness of this thing—this thing that is Life, this thing that is energy, this thing which is the harmony, this thing that I now behold as the will of God.

Through countless incarnations and services rendered to the Hierarchy, learning the ways of the world and the ways of the cosmos, I came to the place where I could follow the ray of my own God Presence back to the heart of the flaming One. And so at the conclusion of the last century [the nineteenth], I followed that ray to the white-fire core, and I did not return with the dawn of the morning light to Mater. But I accepted the ritual of the ascension for one purpose—to serve the will of God in a greater capacity than I was able while in embodiment.[1]

Master Mason of the Great Pyramid

This is the earliest embodiment of El Morya we know of. The Great Pyramid is not a tomb. It is the construction in stone of the record of the path of initiation, whereby the soul, beginning in matter, designs and builds the base of the pyramid on four sides. By striving and mastery the soul rises incrementally from the center of the pyramid to the apex of the ascension.

The architect of the Great Pyramid was the master we know today as Serapis Bey. The master mason was Morya. We do not have specific dates for this embodiment, but according to various esoteric sources, including Theosophy, the Great Pyramid could have been built anywhere between 75,000 B.C. and 10,500 B.C.

In *The Sacred Adventure,* Morya states, "I AM the Master

Mason, directing the pyramid of lives to the summit of attainment." This statement encapsulates the purpose for building the Great Pyramid, both physically and spiritually.[2]

Name Unknown, Son of Enoch

Enoch (circa 10,000 B.C.) lived before the time of the great flood which sank the island continent of Atlantis. When Enoch was 65 he had a son, Methuselah; later, Enoch had many other sons and daughters. Master Morya was one of his sons. In an early dictation (1958 or 1959) El Morya explained that his earthly father was Enoch: "This is he of whom it was said, 'He walked with God and was not, for God took him.'"[3]

El Morya shared the advice his father gave him:

> "I as your father want you to have everything which is good that the world contains and I want you to lack nothing. But many of my gifts and endowments to you are held in trust by your Higher Self and will come to you naturally and automatically like magic if not interfered with by you or any other part of life.
>
> "This I pray, that your strength will flow forth to claim that which is your own and that you will do your part to expand the talents life and nature hold in trust for you by reverencing what may seem the most simple of gifts; and those which you may deem commonplace may in reality be both the glory and power of the kingdom without end." These were the simple words of my once earthly father, who long since took his own ascension—the ascended master Enoch.[4]

Abraham, the Patriarch

Abraham (circa 2100 B.C.) was born of a priestly family of royal blood in Nippur, an ancient city of Sumer, now in Iraq. Abraham's father had a large household and a private army.

His family moved to Ur, the political and economic center of Sumer and later traveled to Haran, in what is now Turkey.

The Book of Genesis portrays Abraham as a "mighty prince," a powerful chieftain who dealt with kings, made military alliances and negotiated land purchases. He loved peace, was skilled in war and magnanimous in victory. He embodied the qualities of justice, righteousness, integrity and hospitality. He is also described as a prophet and an intercessor before the LORD. But, most important, Abraham is the prototype of the man who holds strong to his faith in the LORD's repeated promises—that he would be a "father to many nations," even when outer circumstances indicate just the opposite.

Genesis records that after his father's death, Abraham was called by the LORD to settle in Canaan. Abraham left Haran with his wife, Sarai (later Sarah), and his nephew, Lot, along with all of their possessions and the people they had acquired in Haran and eventually arrived in Canaan. Here he set up an altar and called on the name of the LORD.

Abraham received a promise from the LORD: "unto thy seed I will give this land." After sojourning in Egypt due to a plague in Canaan, Abraham parted company with Lot (who eventually settled in the city of Sodom) and again received the LORD's promise that his seed would be innumerable and would cover all the land that he could see. Abraham and Sarah, however, were childless.

Genesis next depicts Abraham as a military leader. When a powerful coalition of kings captured Lot and all his possessions, Abraham armed 318 of his own "trained servants" and joined other chieftains to defeat the kings and rescue Lot. Returning from this victory, Abraham was blessed by Melchizedek, King of Salem (Jerusalem) and priest of the Most High God (El Elyon), who "brought forth bread and wine" and to whom Abraham gave a tithe (tenth) of the spoils. Abraham returned all the captives and plundered goods to the King of Sodom and refused the king's offer to partake of the goods himself.

Genesis also depicts Abraham in the role of intercessor. The LORD confided to Abraham his intention to destroy the wicked in the cities of Sodom and Gomorrah. Abraham secured God's assurance that Sodom would be spared if ten righteous men could be found in Sodom. Although the city was ultimately destroyed, two angels warned Lot of the impending calamity and he escaped.

Despite the LORD's repeated promises that Abraham's seed would become innumerable, Sarah was still childless after ten years in Canaan. She proposed, after the custom of the day, that Abraham sire a child by her maid Hagar, who then bore Abraham a son, Ishmael. Thirteen years later, when Abraham was 99 and Sarah 90, the LORD revealed himself to the patriarch as El Shaddai, "the Almighty God," and established an everlasting covenant with Abraham, to be God to him and his seed. He revealed that Sarah would bear a son, Isaac, "at this set time in the next year" and that Isaac, not Ishmael, was to be Abraham's heir. As the LORD had prophesied, Sarah finally "conceived and bare Abraham a son in his old age."

Yet the supreme test of the patriarch's faith was still to come. God commanded him to sacrifice Isaac, his long-awaited heir, on a mountain in Moriah. At the end of a three-day journey Abraham built an altar, laid Isaac on the wood and raised his knife to slay the youth when the angel of the LORD called out, "Lay not thine hand upon the lad, neither do thou any thing unto him: for now I know that thou fearest God, seeing thou hast not withheld thy son, thine only son from me." Abraham sacrificed a ram instead and for the final time the LORD confirmed his covenant with Abraham. After Sarah passed on, Abraham married Keturah, who bore him six children. Although the patriarch provided for his other children, he "gave all that he had unto Isaac."

Abraham died at the age of 175 and was buried beside Sarah in the cave of Machpelah, which is hallowed today by Jews, Christians and Muslims—who all trace their lineage back to Abraham.[5]

Name Unknown, Embodiment in Ancient Greece

Both El Morya and Saint Germain have mentioned an important embodiment of El Morya's soul in ancient Greece. Although they did not offer a name, place or other details they did feel it important to state the divine qualities he exemplified in that life:

"In ancient Greece . . . I sponsored early forms of democracy and the right of the individual to be freeborn, to rule in the consciousness of the Christ."[6] Saint Germain indicates this embodiment was exemplary to civilization at that time but hints that El Morya's soul also faced opposition or inertia. "In ancient Greece, the beloved El Morya tried to shed his light that they [the Greeks] might have a very wonderful civilization to externalize perfection and beauty."[7]

Melchior, Magi of Persia

Melchior (first century B.C.) was one of the magi, a member of the priestly class of ancient Persia who visited Jesus at his birth. The magi were followers of Zoroaster and were astrologers and astronomers who knew how to navigate by the stars. They are remembered today through the Christmas songs and symbols of the Three Wise Men.

The other two magi who visited the infant Jesus were Caspar (now the ascended master Djwal Kul) and Balthazar (the ascended master Kuthumi). Although the magi visited King Herod, they knew his murderous intent and avoided any cooperation with him. Melchior was also known as Melchon, which means "king of light."[8] Melchior paid homage to the Christ in the child Jesus with a gift of gold.

Name Unknown, Gnostic Leader

We know from El Morya himself that following his life as Melchior he had another Middle Eastern embodiment as a key figure in the "Gnostic revolution" (second or third century A.D.). Again, the master chose not to provide a name or place, only the statement that he was instrumental in the codifying and distribution of Jesus' teachings on knowing (gnosis) God within.

"I welcome the community to the study of these Gnostic gospels. Know that I and many of thee were there at the inception of the Gnostic revolution."[9]

King Arthur of Britain

King Arthur (fifth and sixth centuries A.D.) was a British king who reigned in the period after the departure of Roman power from Britain (410 A.D.). At that time Italy and Rome itself was under siege by Visigoths, and Emperor Honorius directed Roman cities in distant Britain to defend themselves. Without the Roman legions it was a time of lawlessness within Britain and invasion from without, as Saxon warlords occupied and held the south and east.

Whether the call for help originated with King Arthur or another British leader, we know a message dated about 446 A.D., recorded by the historian Gildas, was sent to Aetius, the leading Roman general of the western Roman Empire in Gaul, to persuade him to return the withdrawn legions to defend Britain from invading Jutes, Angles and Saxons. But Aetius was focused on maintaining alliances with the Franks and others to defend Gaul against Attila the Hun. It was left to King Arthur and his knights to defend Britain against enemies, within and without.

During his reign King Arthur led and won twelve battles against the invading Saxons and adversarial warlords in various parts of Britain. His superior military power was derived from his own leadership skills and the unity of his heavy cavalry, known as the Order of the Knights of the Round Table. This highly effective order of knights was unified by a code of chivalry that bound them by a common oath to defend the helpless and to uphold ideals of purity, truth, mercy, faithfulness and generosity.

The folklore that developed around King Arthur, Queen Guinevere and the knights of this order was both historical and symbolic. The metaphor of the young Arthur pulling the sword from the stone represented the power of the soul that is free from attachment to human limitations. Arthur, the youth, was unmoved by the conventional wisdom that he could not act above and beyond peer expectations.

King Arthur is credited with establishing a "mystery school" at Camelot, in the area now known as Glastonbury, in southeast England. Arthur's teacher and guide was Merlin, an adept of the Druidic-Christian mysteries. The mysteries of divine law were the cohesive force behind the knights' code of chivalry and can be traced to the first century when Joseph of Arimathea, Mary (Jesus' mother) and other disciples established a spiritual community in Glastonbury, at that time in Roman Britain.

Nearly five hundred years later, the quest for the Holy Grail at Arthur's Camelot was also a metaphor for the quest for the inner, mystical teaching of Jesus, namely the quest for the Higher Self, demonstrated through selflessness and service to life in defense of the kingdom. The continuity of the spiritual standards of community, established by Jesus' disciples in the first century, was echoed in King Arthur's leadership of the community of Camelot, the code of chivalry and the knight-initiates' quest for the Holy Grail in themselves.

The cohesive unity which held the Order of the Knights of the Round Table and the court at Camelot together was the same love as that of the disciples. However, that unifying love was subject to disruption by the profane. Among the knights of the Round Table, Sir Modred (possibly Arthur's son, sired prior to his marriage) harbored jealousy, even hatred for the king. The motivation behind Modred's enmity is unknown but may have been related to non-recognition as heir to the throne. As it was widely known at the time that the military strength of Arthur was unsurpassed, Modred allied himself with the sorceress Morgana le Fay to disrupt court unity by subtlety.

Together Modred and Morgana employed the unseen entrapments of witchcraft, gossip, treachery, and court intrigue to destroy the sacred trust of king, queen, and knights of the Round Table by spreading false reports that Guinevere and Lancelot were lovers. Arthur's betrayer was not Lancelot but the court intriguer, Modred.

King Arthur was in Gaul when he received notice that Modred had usurped the throne, imprisoned Queen Guinevere and divided the court into factions. Returning to Britain, Arthur gathered the knights still loyal to him and faced off against Modred's knights in the Battle of Camlann. The prolonged battle wasted the military might and spiritual promise of Camelot. Arthur killed Modred but was himself mortally wounded.

As Arthur lay dying on the battlefield, literary legend indicates he sighted a young boy in whom he perceived the hope of the future. The king knighted the lad and bequeathed to him the precious vision of Camelot come again. This aspect of legend as metaphor suggests Arthur's realization that his spiritual experiment at Camelot had failed to defend itself against the inner enemy. It would need renewed opportunity—another chance in the future, protected by greater vigilance.[10]

Thomas Becket, Lord Chancellor of England and Archbishop of Canterbury

Thomas Becket (1118–1170) was born in London. His father was, for a period, sheriff of London. As a young man, Becket was educated in London schools, served in the household of a wealthy family friend, Theobald, the Archbishop of Canterbury, and later studied in Paris, Bologna and Auxerre. Under Theobald's patronage, Becket became an effective administrator, holding a series of ecclesiastical offices before being recommended by Theobald for the vacant post of Lord Chancellor, responsible for King Henry II's revenue collection from landowners, churches and bishops.

During Becket's tenure as Lord Chancellor he became friends with King Henry. The king trusted Becket enough to send his heir, the next Henry, to live in Becket's household, a custom among nobility at the time. The younger Henry reportedly said that Becket showed him more fatherly love in a day than his father did in his entire life.

Archbishop Theobald died in 1161 and King Henry called Becket to take up the now vacant office of Archbishop of Canterbury. Becket declined, however, warning the king that holding such an office would separate them on moral principles. Sir Thomas told the king: "There are several things you do now in prejudice of the rights of the Church which make me fear you would require of me what I could not agree to." The king ignored the warning and had Becket consecrated as archbishop in 1162. Obedient to the king and in loving submission to the will of God, Becket left his household and his finery and began the life of an ascetic. As archbishop, Becket distributed alms to the poor, studied scripture, visited infirmaries, and supervised monks in their work.

Growing into his role as Archbishop of Canterbury, Thomas Becket became as strong a supporter of the papacy as he had once been of the king and freely excommunicated courtiers and nobles for unlawful uses of church property and other breaches. King Henry had expected continuity from Becket as a loyal enforcer of the royal will in all Church matters, not an effective defender of the Church. Displeased, Henry intended to imprison him, but Becket exiled himself to France for six years.

King Louis (VII) of France was able to effect a partial reconciliation between Thomas and Henry, but when Becket returned to London on December 1, 1170, he was met with ecclesiastical hostility. Three bishops who had been excommunicated by Thomas for direct disobedience to the Pope appealed to Henry while he was traveling in France.

In a fit of anger, Henry shouted, "Are there none who will rid me of this troublesome priest?" Four of Henry's knights took this outburst as cause to set out for England, to arrest the archbishop while he was in the sanctuary of Canterbury Cathedral. They demanded he accompany them and when Becket refused they murdered him by sword-stroke. The sacrilege of murdering an archbishop in his own cathedral produced a reaction of horror throughout Christendom. When the news was brought to the king, he realized his impatient outburst had been the cause of Becket's murder. Henry secluded himself, fasted for forty days and later did public penance in Canterbury Cathedral.

The body of Thomas Becket was placed in a tomb in the cathedral, which became a shrine for hundreds of thousands of pilgrims. Many healing miracles were reported after Becket's death and were attributed to his intercession as a saint in heaven. Within three years, Thomas Becket was officially canonized as a saint and martyr.

Saint Sergius, Patron Saint of Russia

The main source of information about Saint Sergius of Russia (1314–1392) was written in 1417–1418 by Sergius' disciple Epiphanius the Wise, who spent twenty years collecting stories of the saint's life.[11]

Sergius' parents, Cyril and Maria, were very devout. Maria gave birth to three boys, of whom Sergius was the middle child. The boy was baptized with the name, Bartholomew. A priest, Father Michael, who officiated at his baptism told his parents, "Be filled with happiness and joy; your son will be a servant of the Holy Trinity."

Bartholomew did not learn as easily as his brothers and often prayed for enlightenment, as he was saddened that he could not read the scriptures. Bartholomew was only seven when his father sent him out looking for lost horses. He saw a holy man in the forest, praying in tears under an oak tree. To Bartholomew the man looked like an angel.

The boy asked the holy man to pray for him so that God could help him to read and learn. The holy man prayed for Bartholomew to be able to read and understand the scriptures and instructed him, "Don't feel sad. From this day our Lord gives you a good knowledge of writing."

Later, the holy man prophesied to the boy's parents: "This boy will be great before God and man and will direct others, thanks to his virtuous life. He will be a dwelling of the Holy Trinity and will lead many to an understanding of the divine commandments." The holy man then disappeared, leaving the parents also to wonder if they had heard and seen an angel.

After this visit the boy could understand any book, was submissive to his parents, attended church, studied holy writings, disciplined his body and preserved himself in purity of body and soul.

The family then moved to the town of Radonezh. Bartholomew's two brothers married. Although Bartholomew wanted to become a monk he had to take care of his sick parents, who eventually passed on. Bartholomew then gave away his inheritance, and together with his brother Stefan (who lost his wife), built a small chapel in a dense forest. At this time Bartholomew was 23 years of age.

Bartholomew's brother, Stefan, eventually left him to go to Moscow, but Bartholomew remained living like a monk. An abbott came to visit him, consecrated him a monk, and bestowed upon Bartholomew the name of Sergius. From that time, he was filled with the Holy Spirit.

Sergius continued to live a monastic life in the forest. Wild animals were unafraid of him, including a bear who visited Sergius every day to be fed. Two years later twelve monks came to live with him and each built his own hut. Sergius' life was one of prayer, fasting, and work. He built huts, ground flour, made bread, sewed clothing, made shoes and carried water from a spring.

As the years passed, the abbott who had consecrated Sergius as a monk came to live at the small monastic community. The other monks asked Sergius to become their abbott but he refused, preferring humility and not desiring power or attention. Finally, a bishop convinced him to be obedient to the will of God and ordained Sergius to the priesthood. Sergius then became pastor, abbott and physician to his brother monks.

During the Christmas fast of 1379, Mother Mary appeared to Sergius (as she had done before) and promised that his disciples would multiply and not diminish, and that the monastery would prosper after he passed. These words are similar to the prophecy given to Abraham, that his seed would be as the sands of the seashore, innumerable. As prophesied, his disciples grew in number.

Thus, Sergius became the founder of an entire spiritual school. His disciples and followers founded more than 30 monasteries in central and northern Russia. Sergius was also a miracle-worker, finding a pool of rainwater and turning it into a flowing spring for the monks with a prayer and the sign of the cross. He healed the sick and possessed and even raised a boy from the dead.

Sergius' fame spread throughout Russia. He received envoys from Constantinople and other countries. He founded a major monastery, now named the Trinity Lavra of Saint Sergius. It is said he had the gift of bilocation, appearing to Cossacks on the Don River and simultaneously in the city of Kazan.

But Sergius' concerns extended beyond the Cossacks to a unifying vision for all Russians. In 1380 Sergius blessed Prince Dimitry Donskoy of Moscow before a famous battle against the Tatars, or the Golden Horde of the Mongols. Dimitry withheld tribute from the empire of the Mongols, knowing they could besiege and burn Moscow. With Sergius' blessing, Dimitry drew together an army of 60,000 Russians against 130,000 Tatars at Kulikovo on the Don River. By careful planning and battlefield decisions, the Russians were victorious, as Sergius had prophesied.

Even though the Russians won overwhelmingly at Kulikovo, it took another 100 years for full Russian freedom from the Mongols and for Russian sovereignty to take effect in 1480. But it was Sergius' blessing (and possibly his advice) as well as Dimitry's courage and leadership that set the stage for the founding of the nation of Russia. This is one of the reasons Sergius is known as the patron saint of Russia.

Less than twelve years after the victory at Kulikovo, Sergius foresaw his own passing. Six months before his death Sergius called the monks together and gave authority to his favorite disciple, Nikon. From that day on he kept a holy silence.

In September 1392 Sergius became ill and seeing he was going to die he summoned the monks again, received the eucharist and spoke to them: "Be one in your thoughts, stay pure in heart and body, love honestly, stay away from unclean passions, live in humbleness, continue in love for wanderers, refrain from contradiction."

After passing, his face was snowy white. The monks sang and placed him in his coffin. He had wanted to be buried in the cemetery among the ordinary people, but this was not to be. He did not desire fame in life or death, but God's will and power made him famous.

Sir Thomas More, Lord Chancellor of England

Thomas More (1478–1535) was born in London, England. His father, a prominent lawyer and judge, provided him with an excellent education at one of London's finest private schools. At age twelve, More served as a household page for John Morton, who was both the Archbishop of Canterbury and Lord Chancellor of England. At age 14, after studying classics for two years at

Oxford University, More was directed by his father to study law in London and was admitted to the bar in 1502, age 24.

More became a close friend of the eminent Dutch theologian and writer Erasmus, who witnessed his deep interest in and admiration for the Carthusian monks at the monastery near his home. He would frequently join their spiritual disciplines, and according to Erasmus considered leaving his law career for a religious life. More practiced extraordinary austerities for the rest of his life, as a way to test his own self-discipline.

But in 1504 More chose to combine his law career with his spiritual disciplines and was elected to Parliament. He married the next year. More's public career expanded in 1510, as both representative for London and an Undersheriff for the City of London. He became Master of Requests and Privy Counsellor in 1514, took on diplomatic missions to Rome, was Under-Treasurer of the Exchequer and knighted in 1521.

At this time More became a personal advisor and secretary to King Henry VIII, then liaison between the king and the Lord Chancellor, as well as Speaker of the House of Commons.

As prominent as Thomas More may have been in public, his family life was his greatest joy. He was considered an affectionate father and provided equal education in music, literature and classics for his wife, three daughters, one son and three adopted girls. His first wife, Jane, died in 1511. More's estate at Chelsea eventually housed Thomas' entire family, including his second wife, her daughter and eleven grandchildren.

More often called his home in Chelsea "little Utopia," a center of learning and culture, a home of goodwill for both family and the most learned men of the day, even the king himself, who would visit for counsel and for comfort. At Chelsea, More wrote *Utopia,* a witty exposé of the superficiality of English life and the flagrant vices of English law.

In 1529, Sir Thomas More was appointed Lord Chancellor of

England and Keeper of the Great Seal. He devoted himself to his duties with efficiency until King Henry, lacking a male heir to the throne, declared his marriage to Catherine of Aragon null and announced his intent to marry Ann Boleyn. Since the divorce was without papal approval and directly opposed to the laws of the Church, More refused to support the king's decision.

In 1532 at the height of his career, More resigned his office on principle. He retired to Chelsea, where he continued his writings in defense of the Catholic faith and against the Protestant revolt. Without friends and without office, his living standards declined into poverty. Nevertheless, Henry had been insulted at the Lord Chancellor's public disapproval of him. The king, therefore, sought to defame More in order to restore his royal image and publicly secure himself as head of the Church.

More refused to take the Oath of Supremacy, which was required of all the king's subjects. Taking the Oath implied the rejection of papal authority, effectively making King Henry VIII the self-appointed ruler of the Church in England. The king, insulted again by the refusal, had More imprisoned in the Tower of London. Fifteen months later, Sir Thomas More was convicted of treason on perjured evidence. He was beheaded on Tower Hill July 6, 1535, affirming himself, "the king's good servant, but God's first." He was made a Catholic saint four-hundred years later, in 1935.

Lawyer, judge, statesman, man of letters, author, poet, farmer, lover of pastoral life, ascetic, husband and father, champion of women's education, humanist and saint, Thomas More was an outstanding contributor to the avant-garde of the English Renaissance.

Akbar the Great, Emperor of India

In the sixteenth century the once great Mogul Empire of India had been effectively reduced by foreign conquest until, in 1556, only the capital city, Delhi, remained. At that time, the youth, Akbar Jalal Ud-din Mohammed (1542–1605) inherited the throne.

Not yet fourteen at his accession, the brilliant young Emperor Akbar set out to reconquer his realm. He became known throughout the world as Akbar the Great, the most powerful of the Mogul emperors.

Tremendous physical stamina characterized Emperor Akbar and contributed to his extraordinary military success. Akbar could ride 240 miles in twenty-four hours to surprise and defeat an enemy. Nevertheless, it took the major part of his long reign (1556–1605) to subject the rebellious princes of northern India and to secure peace by establishing sound provincial governments.

Akbar was also endowed with a genius for administration. He increased trade efficiency by constructing roads, developing advanced marketing systems and instituting postal services. Concerned for all peoples under his jurisdiction, Akbar abolished the hated *jizya,* the poll tax levied on non-Muslims, and gave Hindus prominent positions in government. The new capital city, Fatehpur Sikri, soon became a flourishing cultural center, larger than the city of London at that time.

As an observer of the competing religious faiths in India, Emperor Akbar assembled scholars of the major Muslim and Hindu sects, Jains, Zoroastrians and Jesuits at his palace. After an in-depth study of the world's religions, Akbar called a council of the learned of all faiths to establish a universal religion. He had noted the factionalism and wanted to unify them by identifying and supporting common themes. The members of the council could not agree among themselves and remained supportive only of their own religions.

Akbar then founded his own religion, Din-i-Ilahi, "Divine Faith," or Tauhid-i-Ilahi, "Divine Monotheism." As Abul Fazl comments, Akbar, in establishing the tenets of the new religion, "seized upon whatever was good in any religion. . . . He is truly a man who makes Justice his leader in the path of inquiry, and who culls from every sect whatever Reason approves of."

Akbar strongly supported the art of India, and under his direction more than 100 state workshops were established for various crafts. The emperor was fond of music and encouraged composition and performances as a means of communication between Hindus and Muslims. Although illiterate, Akbar's library of illustrated manuscripts was as celebrated as the finest collections in Europe.

Toward the end of his life and reign, the peace and prosperity which Akbar had brought to India was disturbed by the court intrigues and subversive activities of his son, Jahangir. When Jahangir inherited the throne he rejected his father's reforms, especially those of religious tolerance, and the empire rapidly crumbled.

Jahangir's son, Shah Jahan, inherited only a small and unruly kingdom but retained a great love for the cultural heritage of his grandfather. As the greatest of the Mogul builders, Shah Jahan gave to India its most cherished architectural romance: the Taj Mahal.

Thomas Moore, Poet Laureate of Ireland

Thomas Moore (1779–1852) was a prolific writer of both prose and poetry and also a singer, songwriter and entertainer. He graduated from Dublin's Trinity College in 1799 and moved to London. As an impressionable young man with a "quick Irish temper," the execution of a close college friend during the United Irishmen's Rebellion in 1798 aroused in Moore a patriotic fervor which provided his greatest literary inspiration. His direct style and youthful attitude made him useful to the British liberalist cause as a witty satirist, and his poems served as controversial political cartoons of the day.

Thomas Moore's greatest works included a brilliant biographical masterpiece taken from the confidential memoirs of Lord Byron. His own *Memoirs, Journal,* and *Correspondence* are an invaluable social record of life in England and Ireland during the first half of the nineteenth century. Although he spent most of his life in England, Moore became known and loved as the national lyricist of Ireland through his *Irish Melodies*—a collection of verses written to the tunes of old Irish folk songs. The best remembered of these romantic ballads is "Believe Me, If All Those Endearing Young Charms," which to the present day draws the power of his intense love for the will of God:

Believe me, if all those endearing young charms,
Which I gaze on so fondly to-day,
Were to change by to-morrow, and fleet in my arms,
Like fairy-gifts fading away,
Thou wouldst still be adored, as this moment thou art,
Let thy loveliness fade as it will,
And around the dear ruin each wish of my heart
Would entwine itself verdantly still.

It is not while beauty and youth are thine own,
And thy cheeks unprofan'd by a tear,
That the fervour and faith of a soul can be known,
To which time will but make thee more dear;
No, the heart that has truly lov'd never forgets,
But as truly loves on to the close,
As the sun-flower turns on her god, when he sets,
The same look which she turn'd when he rose.

Lord John Russell wrote of Thomas Moore as follows: "Of two things all who knew him must have been persuaded: the one, his strong feelings of devotion, his aspirations, his longing for life and immortality, and his submission to the will of God; the other, his love of his neighbor, his charity, his Samaritan kindness for the distressed, his goodwill to all men. In the last days of his life he frequently repeated to his wife: 'Lean upon God, Bessy; lean upon God.' That God is love was the summary of his belief; that a man should love his neighbor as himself, seems to have been the rule of his life."[12]

Mahatma Morya, Rajput Prince

In this, his last incarnation (?–1898), Morya was born a Rajput prince in India, concurrent, in part, with his embodiment as Thomas Moore. Concurrency is rare and permitted only for advanced souls. A Rajput (Sanskrit: *raja-putra,* "son of a king") was a member of one of the patrilineal clans of western, central and northern India and some parts of Pakistan. Rajput are descendants of the ruling Hindu warrior class (Kshatriya caste) of north India, esteemed for their courage and honor. The name "Morya" is the same as that of the Maurya clan, which ruled India from 322–185 B.C. According to Mark Prophet, the Mahatma's actual name was prince Mori Wong of Koko Nor.

During this final physical incarnation Morya, building on aeons of attainment, became an adept known as the Mahatma Morya, dedicated to the unification of science and religion rather than worldly administration.

In 1875, Mahatma Morya founded the Theosophical Society with his friend and spiritual brother the Mahatma Kuthumi, through Helena P. Blavatsky and Henry Steel Olcott. Their purpose in that endeavor was to reveal the basic truths underlying and unifying the world's religions.

The masters dictated *The Secret Doctrine* to Helena Blavatsky, which contained extensive teaching on the origin of man and the universe. The Mahatmas' voluminous correspondence with Alfred P. Sinnett, a would-be disciple, is preserved in *The Mahatma Letters,* containing detailed teachings on spiritual and physical evolution, the law of cycles and discipleship. The original letters in the masters' handwriting are on file in the British Museum.

In *The Masters and the Path,* C. W. Leadbeater, another Theosophist, describes the Mahatma Morya as having "a dark beard divided into two parts, dark, almost black, hair falling to his shoulders, and dark and piercing eyes, full of power. He is six feet six inches in height, and bears himself like a soldier, speaking in short terse sentences as if he were accustomed to being instantly obeyed. In his presence there is a sense of overwhelming power and strength, and he has an imperial dignity that compels the deepest reverence."[13]

In about 1898, Master Morya took his final initiation, the ritual of the ascension, no more to return to earth in a physical body. Master Morya holds the office of Chief of the Darjeeling Council of the Great White Brotherhood. His retreat is the Temple of Good Will over Darjeeling, India.

Sources

1. El Morya, "To Awaken America to a Vital Purpose," in Mark L. Prophet and Elizabeth Clare Prophet, *Lords of the Seven Rays: Mirror of Consciousness* (Gardiner, Mont.: Summit University Press, 1986), Book 2, chap. 1, pp. 293–95.
2. El Morya, *The Sacred Adventure* (Los Angeles: Summit University Press, 1981), p. 51; Elizabeth Clare Prophet, August 11, 1979; August 8, 1993; Mark L. Prophet, November 4, 1969.
3. Gen. 5:21–24.
4. El Morya dictation, circa 1958, 1959.
5. The account of Abraham's life is found in Gen. 12–18, 21–23, 25.
6. El Morya, November 4, 1973.
7. Saint Germain, August 7, 1958.
8. Elizabeth Clare Prophet, July 2, 1984.
9. Elizabeth Clare Prophet, August 13, 1991.
10. *The Chela and the Path,* pp. 130–33; lectures by Elizabeth Clare Prophet; "Following the Grail," inset in *Mysteries of the Holy Grail.*
11. El Morya's embodiment as Saint Sergius was told to Russian Keepers of the Flame by Elizabeth Clare Prophet.
12. Quote from Lord John Russell at www.libraryireland.com/biography/ThomasMoore.php.
13. C. W. Leadbeater, *The Masters and the Path* (Adyar, India, and Wheaton, Ill., Theosophical Publishing House), pp. 28–29.

NOTES

PROLOGUE

1. *The Mahatma Letters to A. P. Sinnett,* various editions.
2. *chela:* a Sanskrit word meaning student or disciple of a spiritual master.
3. The other rays and their chohans:
   Second ray: yellow / wisdom / Lord Lanto
   Third ray: pink / love / Paul the Venetian
   Fourth ray: white / purity / Serapis Bey
   Fifth ray: green / wholeness / Hilarion
   Sixth ray: purple and gold / peace / Nada
   Seventh ray: violet / transmutation / Saint Germain
4. El Morya, *The Chela and the Path,* chap. 1.
5. Ibid., chap. 2.
6. *The Mahatma Letters to A. P. Sinnett,* trans. and comp. A. Trevor Barker (Pasadena, Calif.: Theosophical University Press, 1975), Letter XXX.

CHAPTER 1: With a Smile of Hope

1. See the Maha Chohan, August 7, 1958, "The Heart Center of a New Activity," 2008 *Pearls of Wisdom,* vol. 51, no. 12.
2. Theosophy, the I AM Activity, and the Bridge to Freedom.
3. Refers to the Walt Disney production of *Snow White and the Seven Dwarfs,* which was adapted from the Grimms' fairy tale.
4. Matt. 5:14.
5. Matt. 25:24–30.
6. Matt. 26:41; Mark 14:38.

N.B. Books listed here are published by Summit University Press unless otherwise noted. Audio products are available at www.AscendedMasterLibrary.org.
For information about ascended masters mentioned in this book, see *The Masters and Their Retreats,* by Mark L. Prophet and Elizabeth Clare Prophet.

7. Refers to Frances Ekey, who had worked with the Ballards in the I AM Activity and subsequently with the Bridge to Freedom. She joined her group in Philadelphia with Mark Prophet's group in Washington, D.C., in the early days of The Summit Lighthouse.
8. Refers to Chrystel Anderson, first secretary of The Summit Lighthouse.

CHAPTER 2: **Chelas Mine!**

1. Guy W. Ballard, the messenger of Saint Germain in the I AM Activity, was affectionately known by his students as Daddy Ballard. He is now the ascended master Godfre.
2. I AM Activity. The organization founded in the 1930s by the ascended master Saint Germain through Guy and Edna Ballard. They brought forth the Great White Brotherhood's teaching on the I AM Presence and the violet flame.
3. The Bridge to Freedom was founded by El Morya in the early 1950s. In 1958 El Morya founded The Summit Lighthouse.
4. Frances Ekey. See p. 326, note 7.
5. The name Lighthouse of Freedom was changed to The Summit Lighthouse.
6. I Sam. 15:22.
7. Phil. 4:7.
8. The I AM Activity and the Bridge to Freedom.
9. The universal Christ consciousness of divine love.

CHAPTER 3: **To Work and To Win**

1. John 5:17.
2. Portcullis. A heavy iron grating that hung over the gateway of a fortified castle or fort. It was lowered into position to prevent passage.
3. Hos. 11:1; Matt. 2:15.
4. Phil. 4:7.

CHAPTER 4: **"As the Sunflower Turns on Her God"**

1. Thomas Moore, "Believe Me, If All Those Endearing Young Charms," stanza 2. El Morya was embodied as the Irish poet Thomas Moore (1779–1852).

2. Mary Myneta Boos was a student of the I AM Activity and the Bridge to Freedom. She was, for a time, a co-worker with Mark Prophet in the early days of The Summit Lighthouse. A number of dictations of the ascended masters through Mark were given from a sanctuary in her home in New York.
3. See C. W. Leadbeater, *The Masters and the Path* (Adyar, Madras: Theosophical Publishing House, 1925, 1979), pp. 69–71.
4. Ps. 82:6.
5. John 10:34–36.
6. Prov. 4:7.
7. Thomas Moore, "Believe Me, If All Those Endearing Young Charms," stanza 2.
8. Mark 6:35–44.
9. John 8:11.
10. Matt. 5:6.
11. Acts 9:18.
12. In his dictation on October 13, 1960, Saint Germain said: "I call for a new Christ renaissance. I call for a new golden age. I call it into manifestation in God's name here in New York City. That which has been so long promised, which we have told you you are entering in, even at the threshold of, must by cosmic law come into manifestation. It is unthinkable that human consciousness should further delay the manifestation of that for which all heaven waits and for which all earth hungers."

CHAPTER 5: **Unity through The Summit Lighthouse**

1. "The Harp That Once through Tara's Halls" was published in Thomas Moore's *Irish Melodies,* a collection of verses written to tunes of old folk songs, for which Moore became known and loved as the national lyricist of Ireland.
2. Masters Morya and Kuthumi founded the Theosophical Society through Helena P. Blavatsky and Henry Steel Olcott in 1875 in New York City. Their purpose in this endeavor was to reveal the ancient truths that underlie both Eastern and Western religions. They also sought to acquaint mankind with the spiritual Brotherhood that works behind the scenes to help mankind grow spiritually. The teachings of theosophy can be found in *The Secret Doctrine,* by

H. P. Blavatsky, *The Mahatma Letters to A. P. Sinnett* (by Morya and Kuthumi), and *The Masters and the Path,* by C. W. Leadbeater, among other works.

3. Godfré Ray King, pen name of Guy W. Ballard, through whom Saint Germain founded the I AM Activity in the 1930s.
4. Mark 14:22; I Cor. 11:24.
5. Matt. 10:16.
6. "Believe me, if all those endearing young charms, / Which I gaze on so fondly to-day, / Were to change by to-morrow, and fleet in my arms, / Like fairy-gifts fading away, / Thou wouldst still be adored. . . ," Thomas Moore, "Believe Me, If All Those Endearing Young Charms," stanza 1.
7. John 13:4–17.

CHAPTER 6: The Law of the Circle and the Great Solar Quiet

1. II Tim. 2:15.
2. Acts 9:1–18.
3. John 14:27; 16:33.
4. Phil. 4:7.
5. Gal. 6:7.

CHAPTER 7: The Will of God: A Precious Treasure Mined from the Heart

1. Gen. 1:26, 27.
2. Rev. 3:4, 5; 7:9, 13, 14.
3. II Cor. 3:17.
4. Acts 2:2.
5. Gen. 1:3.
6. John 1:3.
7. John 14:2.

CHAPTER 9: Minarets of Our Abode

1. Luke 2:49.
2. Matt. 11:29, 30.
3. Matt. 21:42, 44.
4. Rev. 6:15, 16.
5. Matt. 25:21, 23.

CHAPTER 10: Holy Purpose

1. Rev. 12:5.
2. Phil. 3:14.

CHAPTER 11: BENEDICTION: A Pulsing Fire Surges through Thee!

1. Refers to the dictation given by the Great Divine Director through the messenger Mark L. Prophet prior to El Morya's dictation. In this dictation (lasting 56 minutes), the Great Divine Director gave admonitions, warnings and teachings "to bring to mankind an awareness, a breathing, pulsating, vibrant expression that is the fullness of the Godhead at any given time made manifest in their own life expression. . . . You become co-creators of the destiny of planets, stars, suns and moons. You become the creator of the destiny of worlds yet unborn. And you fulfill the intent of God to give you dominion not only over the earth but over all life everywhere and share it with the joy of the angels and the speed of light as cosmic majesty is unfolded before your vision everywhere. You understand that the scion of God's love is yourself. When you understand that, you no longer can permit lesser forces to use your consciousness, and the reign of evil in man's consciousness is ended."

CHAPTER 13: The Will of God: A Manifestation of Purity

1. Rev. 22:17.
2. John 14:1.

CHAPTER 14: "Thy Law Is Love, O God!"

1. Gen. 6:3.

CHAPTER 15: The Feast of the Epiphany

1. Rev. 14.
2. Jer. 23:6; 33:16.

CHAPTER 16: A Glow on the Mountain

1. Refers to the messenger's teaching on *A Report,* the October 26, 1962, *Pearl of Wisdom* which El Morya requested be reprinted in pamphlet form.

2. See Elizabeth Clare Prophet, *Imperil: A Commanding Danger!* Lecture, available from Ascended Master Library.
3. In his October 11, 1981, *Pearl of Wisdom,* "This Land, This Land, This Focus of the Flaming Yod" (read by the messenger prior to this dictation), El Morya expressed his gratitude to all who supported the signing, the sealing, and the delivery of the Inner Retreat. See 1981 *Pearls of Wisdom,* vol. 24, no. 41, pp. 431–34.
4. The Inner Retreat. On April 18, 1981, Gautama Buddha came to establish the Inner Retreat. "In this hour I contemplate—note it well—the arcing of the flame of Shamballa to the Inner Retreat as the Western abode of the Buddhas and the Bodhisattvas and the Bodhisattvas-to-Be who are the devotees of the Mother light. . . . Our longing is to lower into physical dimensions all that is prepared; for in the physical octave the light shineth, the light is come. In the physical octave we would celebrate the light of the Central Sun." (*Pearls of Wisdom,* vol. 24, no. 20, pp. 226, 227) On July 4, 1981, Saint Germain dedicated the Inner Retreat "as the Place of Great Encounters where each one might come to encounter the LORD God Almighty, his own I AM Presence, Sanat Kumara, Gautama Buddha, Lord Maitreya, and the Lord Jesus Christ." He said: "Blessed hearts, souls encountering truth, souls uniting one with the other, forging a union, forging a nucleus, forging a magnet for transition into the New Age—when have we ever seen re-created again the original seed of Sanat Kumara gathered together in one place? . . . When have we ever seen gathered together, in the numberless numbers of thousands, the body of light of planet Earth? . . . Let us, therefore, confirm that freedom upon this soil and in this heart and in this Inner Retreat. Let us confirm it by drawing a mighty circle of sacred fire around this place—and this place that is dedicated to God-mastery, the place of the secret chamber of the heart, the place of community, and the land that is chosen to be that Inner Retreat for ye all and for all who will come after you." (*Pearls of Wisdom,* vol. 24, no. 34, pp. 359, 360)
5. Matt. 25:14–30.
6. Refers to Elizabeth Clare Prophet's Columbus Day Address, October 12, 1981, *The State of the World: "The Harvest";* Lecture, available from Ascended Master Library.

7. "Undifferentiated suchness." *Ratnagotravibhāga* I. See *Buddhist Texts through the Ages,* eds. Edward Conze, I. B. Horner, David Snellgrove, Arthur Waley (New York: Harper & Row, 1964), p. 181.
8. "Angels' Ascent" is the new name for the landmark rock formation known as "Devils Slide" on Cinnabar Mountain near the "East Gate" of the Inner Retreat.
9. For Cyclopea's teaching on "The Mystery of the Capstone" (March 23, 1980) and "The Components of the Capstone" (March 30, 1980), see 1980 *Pearls of Wisdom,* vol. 23, no. 13, pp. 71, 73–74.
10. Rev. 19:7.
11. See Wesak celebration and dictation by Gautama Buddha, May 20, 1981, "The Path of Perfect Love," 1981 *Pearls of Wisdom,* vol. 24, no. 28, pp. 299–306; Jesus' Ascension Day Service and dictation, May 28, 1981, "The Marriage of Your Soul unto the Lamb of God," 1981 *Pearls of Wisdom,* vol. 24, no. 29, pp. 307–26.
12. Matt. 25:1–13.
13. See Alpha, April 17, 1981, "The Time Is Short," and September 6, 1981, "The Anchoring Light for the Divine Plan of the New Dispensation." 1981 *Pearls of Wisdom,* vol. 24, no. 19, p. 223; no. 40, p. 428.
14. At the *Feast of the Resurrection Flame,* on April 17, 1981, Mother Mary brought her message on "The Hour of the Mother's Crucifixion with Maitreya Attended by the Avatars Lord Jesus and Lord Gautama," followed by Jesus' Easter Address, April 19, 1981, on "The Woman Crucified within the Chamber of Thy Heart . . . and Her Resurrection." See 1981 *Pearls of Wisdom,* vol. 24, no. 17, p. 210; no. 24, pp. 256–57.
15. Refers to the Summit University seminar *The Incarnations of the Magnanimous Heart of Lanello* (the messenger Mark L. Prophet), June 12–14, and subsequent lectures given June 15, 17, 21, August 15, 16, 30, October 11, November 1, 1981.
16. Rev. 15:2.

CHAPTER 17: **Rejoice, O People of God!**

1. The LORD shall have them in derision. Pss. 2:4; 59:8.
2. "Dearly beloved, avenge not yourselves, but rather give place unto wrath: for it is written, Vengeance is mine; I will repay, saith the Lord. Therefore, if thine enemy hunger, feed him; if he thirst, give

him drink: for in so doing thou shalt heap coals of fire on his head. Be not overcome of evil, but overcome evil with good." Rom. 12:19–21. See also Deut. 32:35; Heb. 10:30.

3. On April 5, 1981, the messenger announced the release of the third issue of *The Coming Revolution: A Magazine for Higher Consciousness* (spring 1981).
4. El Morya was embodied as the Hebrew patriarch Abraham, who placed his son, Isaac, upon the altar and prepared to sacrifice him in obedience to the command of the LORD. Gen. 22:1–18.

CHAPTER 18: **Message of the Chohan of the First Ray**

This dictation by El Morya is published in its entirety in 1982 *Pearls of Wisdom,* vol. 25, no. 56, August 25, 1982.

1. "And it came to pass, that, when the sun went down, and it was dark, behold a smoking furnace, and a burning lamp that passed between those pieces." Gen. 15:17.
2. Plains of Mamre. *Mamray,* symbolizing the Motherhood of God which endows the planes of Matter, Mater, as the launching platform of the soul's ascension. See Gen. 13:14–18; 18:1.
3. Refers to *Utopia,* the principal literary work of Sir Thomas More (1478–1535), published in 1516. In his masterpiece, More considers what is the best form of government. The ideas expressed in his discussion of the imaginary commonwealth Utopia (meaning "no place") have made More one of the great, original political scientists of all time.
4. In *The New Atlantis,* a treatise on political philosophy written as a fable, Francis Bacon (1561–1626, an embodiment of Saint Germain) explores the components of an ideal society. The unfinished work was published posthumously in 1626.
5. "And there was given me a reed like unto a rod: and the angel stood, saying, Rise, and measure the temple of God, and the altar, and them that worship therein." Rev. 11:1.
6. See El Morya, July 4, 1981, "A Mighty Hip, Hip, Hooray for Saint Germain!" 1981 *Pearls of Wisdom,* vol. 24, no. 35, pp. 376–77, hardbound.
7. Acts 9:1–22.
8. *The Chela and the Path,* paperback, or 1975 *Pearls of Wisdom,* vol. 18, nos. 1–16, pp. 1–88, hardbound.

9. Matt. 21:44; Hos. 10:8; Luke 23:30; Rev. 6:15–17.
10. July 4, 1965.

CHAPTER 19: Between Two Worlds

This dictation by El Morya is published in its entirety in 1983 *Pearls of Wisdom,* vol. 26, no. 53, December 21, 1983.

1. *The Chart of Your Divine Self* represents the I AM Presence (upper figure), the Christ Self (middle figure), and the soul evolving in matter (lower figure). See Mark L. Prophet and Elizabeth Clare Prophet, *The Path of the Higher Self* (volume 1 of the Climb the Highest Mountain series), pp. 229–38, paperback.
2. Luke 19:13.
3. Isa. 5:26; 11:10–12; Zech. 9:16.
4. Matt. 24:28; Luke 17:37. See *Where the Eagles Gather* (1981 *Pearls of Wisdom,* vol. 24, nos. 20, 30–37 and 40–42), pp. 225–28, 327–406, 427–38.
5. See "Shamballa," 1983 *Pearls of Wisdom,* vol. 26, no. 14, April 3, 1983, p. 110.
6. The cosmic clock is a systematic approach to charting the cycles of the soul's development, karma and initiations, taught by Mother Mary to Mark L. Prophet and Elizabeth Clare Prophet. For more information, see *Predict Your Future: Understand the Cycles of the Cosmic Clock,* by Elizabeth Clare Prophet.
7. Exod. 3:14.
8. Exod. 4:1–12, 17.

CHAPTER 20: The Mission of Twin Flames Today

1. "Decree to Beloved Mighty Astrea," 10.14 in *Prayers, Meditations, and Dynamic Decrees for Personal and World Transformation.*
2. See Kuthumi and Djwal Kul, *The Human Aura: How to Activate and Energize Your Aura and Chakras,* new deluxe edition, "Muddied Aura" illustrations 2 and 4, pp. 274–75, 278–80; also published in Djwal Kul, *Intermediate Studies of the Human Aura,* "Muddied Aura" illustrations, color plates 11 and 14. The heart is depicted dripping with a red-orange human sympathy, which falls to the solar plexus, colors the soul and soul awareness, and eventually results in misuse of the base-of-the-spine chakra.

3. False gurus. The false guru replaces not only the twin flame but also the individual I AM Presence and the personal Mediator and teacher, the Holy Christ Self, and aborts the search for the beloved by attaching the chela to himself by means of various devices such as: (1) Tantric initiations or forced raising of the Kundalini prior to the attainment of a certain self-mastery and equilibrium gained through the balancing of karma; (2) by engaging both male and female neophytes in sexual rites, secret mantras for the supposed transfer of supernatural powers or so-called initiation, thereby engendering emotional attachment or mindless enslavement to himself; (3) by the lure of ancient traditions, languages and lineage whereby the false guru lays claim to legitimacy by association with or descendancy from the ascended masters, Gautama Buddha, Maitreya and Sanat Kumara; (4) plus physical adeptship through developed *siddhis* (powers); (5) the mischievous misuse of the mantra (black magic) to manipulate nature spirits into capricious control of elemental forces, heaping disaster against enemies or those in disfavor; (6) influencing the sincere, trusting student to do the bidding of the false guru; (7) encouraging the practice of meditating on the guru's picture together with the recitation of the guru's "secret" mantra—this practice, instead of giving light to the chela, is the means whereby the false guru, having no light of his own, in fact takes the light from his chelas. The entrapments of dress, diet, airs of holiness and meditation for private peace, powers, and personal gain (including financial) without application to the goal of world service all lead to a path of selfish introspection—a counterfeit of the path of Jesus Christ and his disciples taught by the ascended masters—divorcing aspirants from the mighty Work of the ages: the saving of souls and a planet in distress through full participation in the economic and political challenges of self-government and individual economic and spiritual self-determination in God's grand experiment in free will.
4. Death rider. In his New Year's Eve address, December 31, 1984, Gautama Buddha warned that "it is the year of the Four Horsemen and of the fourth," signifying that the karma of the death cult and death consciousness would ride this year, with famine, terminal disease, war, terrorist raids, storm, flood, and fire in its wake, bringing sudden death to many. See Rev. 6:1–8 and 1985 *Pearls of Wisdom*, vol. 28, no. 6, p. 64.

5. Lion, Calf, Man, Flying Eagle. See *The Opening of the Seventh Seal: Sanat Kumara on the Path of the Ruby Ray*, softbound, pp. 21–77, 159–69; diagrams, pp. 77, 84, 140, 247–49 (also published in 1979 *Pearls of Wisdom*, vol. 22, pp. 1–128, 201–8; diagrams, pp. 136, 142, 186, 274–75, hardbound). See also Rev. 4:6–8; Ezek. 1:5–10.

CHAPTER 21: The Universal Religion

1. In the first century B.C., El Morya was embodied as Melchior, one of the three wise men who paid homage to the Christ Child. He was accompanied by Balthazar (an embodiment of Kuthumi) and Caspar (an embodiment of Djwal Kul).
2. John 1:5, 14.
3. Matt. 2:1–12.
4. Akbar the Great. Abu-ul-Fath Jalal-ud-Din Muhammad Akbar (1542–1605), greatest of Mogul emperors, an embodiment of El Morya. See appendix, pp. 319–21.
5. King Arthur. El Morya was embodied as Arthur, fifth- or sixth-century king of the Britons. He drove the Saxon invaders from Britain, united the kingdom, and established the order of the Knights of the Round Table, whose code of chivalry bound them to defend the helpless from the wicked and evildoers and to uphold the ideals of purity, truth, mercy, faithfulness and generosity. See appendix, pp. 310–12.
6. Christianity as a Roman religion. From 303 to 311, Christians suffered their most severe persecution under the Roman emperors Diocletian and Galerius. Diocletian's edicts and those of Galerius brought the destruction of churches and sacred books, the enslavement of Christian household servants, torture, and death to some 1,500 believers. The obstinance of the Christians, who refused to sacrifice to the gods or pay homage to the Roman emperor, as well as the astounding growth of their religion, was a threat to the established order. But the persecutions failed to suppress the spread of Christianity, and the hopelessly ill Galerius issued an edict of toleration in 311 shortly before his death, asking for the prayers of the Christians in return for "our most gentle clemency." In what is considered a turning point for Christianity, Constantine, competing for control of the Roman empire, won a decisive battle in

312 after seeing a vision of a cross in the sky bearing the words "in this sign conquer" and then ordering his soldiers to paint the cross on their shields as he was directed to do in a dream. Constantine became sole emperor in 324, and while declaring himself a Christian he continued to support both paganism and Christianity. Writing of the growing synthesis of Christian and pagan thinking, author Ian Wilson notes, "That Constantine himself mixed Christianity and the Sol Invictus [pagan sun god] cult is clear from a second commemorative medallion issued by him within two years of the first, on which he represented himself with a Chi-Rho monogram [Christian symbol formed from the first two letters, X and P, of the Greek word for Christ] on his helmet, and with a leaping Sol chariot horse below. How far Jesus had become divorced in western Christians' minds from the Jew of history is forcefully illustrated by a portrait of him as a beardless Apollo-like youth in a mosaic that once decorated the floor of the Romano-Christian villa at Hinton St. Mary in Dorset. Only the Chi-Rho monogram identifies it as Jesus." Although Constantine became an ever-stronger defender of the Christian cause and was baptized on his deathbed, some historians claim that he shrewdly used religion as a means to further his own political ends. In 325, when the bitter Arian controversy threatened schism in the Church, Constantine himself called the first ecumenical council of more than 300 bishops in Nicaea, presided over the opening session, and took part in its debates; for "in the Arian controversy lay a great obstacle to the realization of Constantine's idea of a universal empire which was to be attained by aid of uniformity of divine worship" (*The New Schaff-Herzog Encyclopedia of Religious Knowledge,* s.v. "Nicaea [Nice], Councils of"). Arius taught that Christ was not equal or eternal with the Creator but as the [archetypal Son] was the first and highest of created beings, whereas his opponents said the Son was "of one substance with the Father." As historian Will Durant observes, "If Christ was not God, the whole structure of Christian doctrine would begin to crack; and if division were permitted on this question, chaos of belief might destroy the unity and authority of the Church, and therefore its value as an aide to the state." The council rejected Arius' position and adopted the

Nicene Creed, which read in part: "We believe in one God, the Father Almighty, . . . and in one Lord Jesus Christ, the Son of God, the only-begotten of his Father, . . . God of God, Light of Light, very God of very God." Athanasius, who became the chief proponent of Nicene orthodoxy, explained that the intent of the creed was to show that "the resemblance of the Son to the Father, and his immutability, are different from ours: for in us they are something acquired, and arise from our fulfilling the divine commands" (*A Select Library of Nicene and Post-Nicene Fathers of the Christian Church* [Grand Rapids, Mich.: Wm. B. Eerdmans Publishing Company, 1979], 2d. ser., 14:34). Arius, anathematized by the council, was exiled by edict of Constantine, who also ordered all his books to be burned upon penalty of death. Some of the bishops who assented in the presence of Constantine to the wording of the creed later expressed their remorse. "Only on returning home," says Wilson, "did Eusebius of Nicomedia, Maris of Chalcedon and Theognis of Nicaea summon the courage to express to Constantine in writing how much they regretted having put their signatures to the Nicene formula: 'We committed an impious act, O Prince,' wrote Eusebius of Nicomedia, 'by subscribing to a blasphemy from fear of you.'. . . Although no gospel regarded Jesus as God, and not even Paul had done so, the Jewish teacher had been declared Very God through all eternity, and a whole new theology would flow from this. . . . Even in the John gospel, the one most inclined to make Jesus divine, he is reported as stating quite categorically, 'the Father is greater than I' (John 14:28)." Furthermore, the emperor's involvement in Church affairs created a precedent for civil leadership in Church councils. Nicaea "marked the replacement of paganism with Christianity as the religious expression and support of the Roman Empire," says Durant. "By [Constantine's] aid Christianity became a state as well as a church, and the mold, for fourteen centuries, of European life and thought." See Ian Wilson, *Jesus: The Evidence* (San Francisco: Harper and Row, 1984), pp. 162, 168, 176; and Will Durant, *Caesar and Christ,* vol. 3 of *The Story of Civilization* (New York: Simon and Schuster, 1944), pp. 652, 659, 661, 664.

7. Pillars of eternity. See El Morya, May 9, 1971, "The Pillars of

Eternity," in *Masters of the Far East on the Pillars of Eternity* (1971 *Pearls of Wisdom,* vol. 14, no. 19), pp. 75–77.

8. Heb. 10:7, 9.
9. John 9:39.
10. The joyous yogi. In his autobiography, Paramahansa Yogananda tells the story of his guru Sri Yukteswar's joyous confrontation with a deadly four-foot cobra. As it raced toward him, ready to strike, the master simply chuckled and rhythmically clapped his hands. A cobra will normally strike at any moving object within its range, yet this serpent became motionless before Sri Yukteswar, then slithered between his feet and disappeared into the bushes. See Paramahansa Yogananda, *Autobiography of a Yogi* (Los Angeles: Self-Realization Fellowship, 1975), pp. 131–32.

CHAPTER 22: **Take a Stand for Principle!**

1. Prior to the dictation, El Morya and the messenger conducted a meeting on "The Path of Personal Christhood" called for by Mighty Victory in his dictation of July 20, 1986. In light of the community approaching the 28th anniversary of The Summit Lighthouse (4 o'clock line of the cosmic clock) on August 7, 1986, the responsibility of each chela to bear his own dharma as well as karma and to recognize and slay the dweller-on-the-threshold opposing his Christhood was made clear. Drawing from examples of initiations recently faced by chelas, the master and Mother explained various points of vulnerability on the Path resulting from being out of alignment with the Guru and from nonfulfillment of one's dharma. Scriptural readings included: Isa. 14:1–3 on the LORD's mercy upon the house of Israel; Matt. 18:11, 12, 14–35; I Cor. 6:1–11; Rom. 13 on the inadvisability of litigation between Church members, recourse to divine justice through the mantle of the messenger, and the law of forgiveness.

CHAPTER 23: **A Sapphire Chalice**

1. Dispensations confined to the lightbearers. See 1988 *Pearls of Wisdom,* vol. 31, no. 3, p. 33, n. 2.
2. The cult of the Divine Mother on Lemuria and the fall of Mu. See Mark L. Prophet and Elizabeth Clare Prophet, *The Path of the*

Higher Self (volume 1 of the Climb the Highest Mountain series), pp. 411–13; *The Lost Teachings of Jesus II,* softbound, pp. 260–61.

3. Hercules and Amazonia's stitch in time. In a dictation given July 1, 1987, during *FREEDOM 1987* in the Heart of the Inner Retreat, the Elohim Hercules said: "By your presence I send through your body chalices—which I do qualify with sapphire diamond light—a current of the first ray to summon all earth to divine purpose. [10-second intonation] The sound I have sounded in that instant, beloved, reached the Central Sun and did return as a cosmic stitch in time through this heart. So, make thy heart a chalice of God's will and be those who sewed up the garment of earth with a stitch in time. I, Hercules, the cosmic tailor, will sew it through your heart." 1987 *Pearls of Wisdom,* vol. 30, no. 34, p. 317.
4. Exod. 19:3–25; 33:9–11; Deut. 5:2, 4, 5.
5. On May 28, 1987, Jesus called for ten thousand Keepers of the Flame: "I am sent by the Father for the quickening now of ten thousand saints in the City Foursquare that I mark as North America. . . . Blessed hearts, I have come, then, to make a plea to you and to send my messenger abroad across this continent for the gathering of ten thousand who will call themselves Keepers of the Flame of life and who will understand that I, Jesus, have called them. . . . Blessed ones, this North America, a place consecrated by love to the reunion of souls with God, is a place where if the lightbearers would respond and *make the Call,* even as I call you this night, there should be established even the white light over a continent to protect it from those calamities of the Four Horsemen, which could indeed appear for want of mediators in the earth. Understand, beloved, that the mediators who must stand between a people and a planet and their karma must be in physical embodiment." On October 2, 1987, El Morya said: "I come in the power that God has given unto me as the Lord of the First Ray to summon the troops and to say to you, the Lord Christ has called for ten thousand Keepers of the Flame. Can he save the city and North America with ten thousand? He has said so, beloved, and I believe him. . . . To be a Keeper of the Flame and to give that daily support in decrees as well as an activism that does display one's heart and thought and mind for a cause—this is the calling of the hour." 1987 *Pearls of Wisdom,* vol. 30, nos. 27, 54, pp. 269, 273, 274–75, 475.

6. El Morya's retreat, the Temple of Good Will, is located on the etheric plane over Darjeeling, India. See El Morya, *The Chela and the Path,* pp. 36–42, 56, 140–41.

CHAPTER 24: The Universal Ashram of Devotees of the Will of God

1. The *Ashram Notes* were dictated between 1952 and 1958 by the ascended master El Morya to his amanuensis Mark L. Prophet. The published volume includes 39 letters to chelas who participated in the "Ashram" and six rituals to be given simultaneously around the world. In chapter 2 of *Ashram Notes,* El Morya explains, "Our principal reason for founding this Ashram is for the linking of hearts worldwide in a ritual of scheduled group meditations. Even though we are separated by time and space, we shall all meet in a union of consciousness, laboring and travailing together to give birth to our Ashram for God." The six rituals are: The Unison Ritual; Great Central Sun Ritual: O Cosmic Christ, Thou Light of the World; Sacred Ritual for Attunement with God's Holy Will; Sacred Ritual for Soul Purification; Sacred Ritual for Transport and Holy Work; and Sacred Ritual for Oneness. Rituals also published in *Ashram Rituals,* 64-page booklet. For audio recordings, see Ascended Master Library.
2. See *Ashram Notes,* pp. 1, 6, 35, 144, 146.
3. John 10:30.
4. Isa. 40:31.
5. See Jesus Christ, August 26, 1990, "The Gift of Resurrection's Flame." 1990 *Pearls of Wisdom,* vol. 33, no. 33, pp. 423–27.
6. The Five Dhyani Buddhas are celestial Buddhas visualized during meditation. Each embodies one of the five wisdoms that antidotes one of the five poisons that are a danger to spiritual progress. The Buddhas, their wisdom and the poison antidoted: *Vairochana,* the All-Pervading Wisdom of the Dharmakaya, ignorance. *Akshobhya,* Mirrorlike Wisdom, hatred and anger. *Ratnasambhava,* Wisdom of Equality, spiritual, intellectual and human pride. *Amitabha,* Discriminating Wisdom, the passions—all cravings, covetousness, greed and lust. *Amoghasiddhi,* All-Accomplishing Wisdom/Wisdom of Perfected Action, envy and jealousy. For more information, see *The Masters and Their Retreats,* by Mark L. Prophet and

Elizabeth Clare Prophet. See also p. 342, n. 13.

7. Refers to Cyclopea, Elohim of the fifth ray (green ray) of truth, vision, healing and abundance, who holds the focus of the All-Seeing Eye of God. See decree 50.05, "Beloved Cyclopea, Beholder of Perfection," in *Prayers, Meditations and Dynamic Decrees for Personal and World Transformation.*
8. "Panis Angelicus," by composer César Franck.
9. John 6:26–59.
10. John 9:4, 5; 12:35.
11. "Lest they should be converted." Isa. 6:9, 10; Matt. 13:13–15; Mark 4:11, 12; Luke 8:10; John 12:37–40; Acts 28:25–28.

CHAPTER 25: The Greater Cause of Divine Love

1. Master Morya gave this dictation on August 8, 1993, at a service commemorating the thirty-fifth anniversary of the founding of The Summit Lighthouse on August 7, 1958. El Morya requested that this dictation be published as his Christmas letter for 1994. The letter was prepared for publication by the messenger Elizabeth Clare Prophet under El Morya's direction. The letter was lovingly dedicated "in honor of our master's incarnation as Melchior, one of the three wise men."
2. Prior to El Morya's dictation, the messenger delivered her lecture "Akbar the Great: The Shadow of God on Earth." Akbar was an incarnation of El Morya. Lecture is available at Ascended Master Library.
3. Akbar the Great (1542–1605) is honored as the greatest of the Mogul emperors of India and as a father of religious tolerance. For more information, see note 2 above and the appendix in this volume, pp. 319–21. See also Mark L. Prophet and Elizabeth Clare Prophet, *Lords of the Seven Rays,* chapter 1, pp. 21–27, 57–59 (reprint, pp. 23–30).
4. The doctrine of divine love. On August 7, 1993, in an interview with Philippe Coste, a reporter for the French magazine *L'Express,* the messenger said: "The one divine doctrine that is going to get you to heaven is love. If you are loving to your fellowman, if you are Christlike, if you are kind, if you walk in that path, . . . you're going to get to heaven. And when you get to heaven, you will not be a Jew, Muslim or Christian. You will be a citizen of heaven,

and nobody is going to care what you did on earth as long as you walked the path of love. Without love, you can't get to heaven. . . . Doctrine, what you believe, is immaterial. It's what you do that creates union with God."

5. "Ye are the salt of the earth." Matt. 5:13; Mark 9:50; Luke 14:34.
6. John 21:22.
7. Long-forgotten records may be cast into the violet flame. In her lecture before El Morya's dictation, the messenger gave the following teaching: "You never have to feel bad about yourself again. You can go to confession, to the heart of hearts and the Holy of holies of the altar of your being and confess to those things that you did in past lives but that you no longer remember. You can confess to everything you have done in *all* past lives since the moment you first left Maitreya's Mystery School. And you can ask that God give you a penance, or you can take on your own penances, giving the violet flame daily for the transmutation of the records. This is the key to joy, . . . the key to freedom. It is the key whereby you can continually love."
8. Phil. 4:8.
9. See *The Secret Teachings of Jesus: Four Gnostic Gospels,* trans. Marvin Meyer.
10. Warring in your members. Rom. 7:15–25; Gal. 5:16–26; James 4:1–8; I Pet. 2:11.
11. *FREEDOM 1993: "Healing the Earth"* was held from June 25 through July 4, 1993, in the Heart of the Inner Retreat.
12. On August 7, 1993, Philippe Coste of *L'Express* asked the messenger: "What is your greatest fear?" She responded: "What I 'fear' is that the world will remain in ignorance and that in the next two thousand years we could repeat the cycle of going into a dark age of ignorance—ignorance of God, ignorance of oneself, ignorance of the path of love. That is my greatest concern—that the people will not receive the divine flame."
13. See 1994 *Pearls of Wisdom,* vol. 37, nos. 2, 29, "Introduction to the Five Dhyani Buddhas and Their Mandala," pp. 13–26, and "The five poisons," p. 347, n. 4.
14. "A sower went forth to sow." Matt. 13:3–8, 18–23; Mark 4:3–8, 13–20; Luke 8:4–8, 11–15.
15. I Cor. 3:5, 6.

16. Ashram rituals. See p. 340, n. 1.
17. Matt. 7:14.
18. John 14:30.

CHAPTER 26: Bonded to the Lord of the First Ray

This dictation by El Morya is published in its entirety in 1990 *Pearls of Wisdom,* vol. 33, no. 13, April 8, 1990.

1. The Elohim Cyclopea announced at the conclusion of the November 26, 1989 service that he was placing the capstone on the pyramid of the United States of America at the level of the etheric octave. See 1989 *Pearls of Wisdom,* vol. 32, no. 62, pp. 789–94. For the astrological chart of this event see 1988 *Pearls of Wisdom,* Book II, Introduction, pp. 58–61.
2. "Great Central Sun Ritual: O Cosmic Christ, Thou Light of the World!" in El Morya, *Ashram Notes,* pp. 16–18.
3. Vajrasattva. See 1989 *Pearls of Wisdom,* vol. 32, nos. 38, 59, pp. 537, n. 4; 764, n. 20.
4. "Sacred Ritual for Attunement with God's Holy Will," in El Morya, *Ashram Notes,* pp. 19–23.
5. Matt. 26:39; Mark 14:36; Luke 22:42.
6. Rom. 12:9.
7. See Lady Master Venus, November 17, 1985, 1986 *Pearls of Wisdom,* vol. 29, no. 8, Book I, pp. 48–49.
8. See El Morya, August 8, 1988, 1988 *Pearls of Wisdom,* vol. 31, no. 77, Book II, pp. 593–94.
9. *Ashram Notes.* See p. 340, n. 1.
10. II Cor. 6:14–18.
11. Exod. 20:17; Deut. 5:21.
12. I Cor. 9:27.
13. See Jesus Christ, April 14, 1974, 2014 *Pearls of Wisdom,* vol. 57, no. 7, pp. 55–56. Matt. 12:38–40; 16:4; Luke 11:29, 30; Jon. 1:17.
14. Zech. 13:9; Mal. 3:1–3; Matt. 3:11, 12; Luke 3:16, 17; I Cor. 3:13–15; I Pet. 1:7; 4:12.

EPILOGUE

1. El Morya, "Purity of Heart," *Pearls of Wisdom,* vol. 29, no. 80, December 28, 1986. (https://www.SummitLighthouse.org/pearls/1986pows/861228EM.html)

The Summit Lighthouse®
63 Summit Way
Gardiner, Montana 59030 USA

1-800-245-5445 / 406-848-9500

Se habla español.

TSLinfo@TSL.org
SummitLighthouse.org

www.SummitLighthouse.org/El-Morya/
www.ElMorya.org

Mark L. Prophet (1918–1973) and Elizabeth Clare Prophet (1939–2009), were visionary pioneers of modern spirituality and internationally renowned authors. Their books are published in more than 30 languages, and millions of copies have been sold online and in bookstores worldwide.

Together, they built a worldwide spiritual organization that is helping thousands to find their way out of human problems and reconnect to their inner divinity. They walked the path of spiritual adeptship, advancing through the universal initiations common to mystics of both East and West. They taught about this path and described their own experiences for the benefit of all who desire to make spiritual progress.

Mark and Elizabeth left an extensive library of spiritual teachings from the ascended masters and a thriving, worldwide community of people who study and practice these teachings.

CPSIA information can be obtained
at www.ICGtesting.com
Printed in the USA
FFOW03n1903110618
47061537-49445FF

9 781609 882921